ETHIOPIAN
AMHARIC
PHRASEBOOK

Tilahun Kebede

Ethiopian Amharic phrasebook
2nd edition – August 2002
First published – April 1996

Published by
Lonely Planet Publications Pty Ltd ABN 36 005 607 983
90 Maribyrnong St, Footscray, Victoria 3011, Australia

Lonely Planet Offices
Australia Locked Bag 1, Footscray, Victoria 3011
USA 150 Linden St, Oakland CA 94607
UK 10a Spring Place, London NW5 3BH
France 1 rue du Dahomey, 75011 Paris

Cover illustration
Spot the Blue Donkey by Patrick Marris

ISBN 1 74059 133 X

text © Lonely Planet Publications Pty Ltd 2002
cover illustration © Lonely Planet Publications Pty Ltd 2002

10 9 8 7 6 5 4 3 2 1

Printed by The Bookmaker International Ltd
Printed in China

About the Authors

Tilahun Kebede was inspired to write an Amharic phrasebook after working as a guide/translator for travellers to Ethiopia. He's now based in Sydney where he balances a career in finance and freelance translating. Catherine Snow is an Australian researcher/writer who has spent some of her finest moments in Ethiopia and East Africa.

From the Author

Thanks to Ethiopian diaspora everywhere for keeping community life and the Internet alive with Ethiopian music and culture. Special thanks to Tilahun's parents, Roman for medical expertise and Kebede for general assistance. Thanks to Kefyalew Mekonnen for insightful advice, and other friends, colleagues and family who gave support and assistance.

From the Publisher

Publishing Manager Jim Jenkin was a blur through the smoke from the starting pistol's retort – the Amharic marathon had begun. Taking the lead, he ran with ease through the opening stages to set his team up for a pain-free race. Senior Editors Karina Coates and Karin Vidstrup Monk moved smoothly through the pack, made molehills from mountains with their effortless grace and ensured that every foot landed in the right place. Ben Handicott kept hurting his, but set the pace and edited out the pain. Adrienne Costanzo weeded out the weaklings with her proofer's eye. Sophie Putman showed late dictatorial form, so launching the weary competitors towards the end. Patrick Marris found it such a breeze, he had time to stop and draw the pretty pictures. He then helped fellow designers Yukiyoshi Kamimura and Belinda Campbell (in a swan-song performance) get it all on to the printed page. Natasha Velleley, with a sweat-free brow, kept everyone on track with her fantastic map. Senior Designer Fabrice Rocher kept the team neat and tidy throughout, while cheering it past the wall and over the finish line with encouraging cries of əg·zer yi·ma·rəh, just before lighting up.

CONTENTS

6 Contents

ETHIOPIAN AMHARIC

LANGUAGE REGIONS

- Predominant Amharic
- Amharic second language in towns and cities

While local languages abound in Ethiopia, Amharic speakers can be found in most towns and cities throughout the country.

YEMEN

Gulf of Aden

Red Sea

Indian Ocean

DJIBOUTI

SOMALIA

Domo •
Ogaden Desert

Harar •
Dire Dawa •

Wabi Shebele River

Asaite •
Mek'ele •
Aksum •

Awash River

Nazret •
Shashamane •

E T H I O P I A

Dessie •
Gonder •
Mt Ras Dashen (4620m) ▲

Lake Tana

Bahar Dar •

ADDIS ABABA ☆

Lake Abaya

Moyale •

KENYA

Blue Nile River

Gambela •
Jimma •

Omo River

Lake Turkana

ERITREA

SUDAN

ELEMI TRIANGLE (Under Kenyan Administration)

0   150   300 km
0   100   180 mi

Approximate boundaries only

LP

INTRODUCTION

Amharic is indigenous to Ethiopia and is the most widely used and understood language in the country. Just a few basic phrases will guide you through stunning landscapes to mystical churches, ancient sites and the bustling backstreets of Ethiopian towns. Here, bold Ethiopic script adorns shop fronts, murals and drink bottles, stamping everything with a distinct regional flavour.

Amharic is the official language of the media and government, and widely used in cross-cultural communications. It's the mother tongue of the Amhara people, who originate from the central and north-western highlands. There are over 80 other indigenous languages spoken in Ethiopia, including Tigrinya, Oromo and Gurage. English is also spoken, but mainly by educated urban people.

Like Arabic, Hebrew and Assyrian, Amharic is a Semitic language, belonging to the Afro-Asiatic family. There are three main subgroups of this family in Ethiopia: the Ethiopic subgroup, including Amharic and Tigrinya; the Cushitic subgroup, including Somali and Oromo languages; and Omotic, including the Wolayitta language. In Ethiopia's south-west, you'll also come across Nilo-Saharan languages, including Nuer and Mursi dialects. For many Ethiopians, Amharic remains a second language; learning a few words in local languages will be a boon to your travels.

Historical Origins

Ethiopia's rich and ancient culture is reflected in the history of its languages. Around the first millennium BC, the people of northern Ethiopia and present-day Eritrea began to establish solid contacts with the people of south-west Arabia, just over the Red Sea. New languages began to emerge from this interaction, including Ge'ez.

Ge'ez is the current liturgical language of the Ethiopian Orthodox Church – used in church chants, and sacred manuscripts even to this day. The current Ethiopic alphabet, used to write Amharic and Tigrinya, is adapted from Ge'ez.

INTRODUCTION

Ge'ez began as the language of the Aksum Empire that dominated northern Ethiopia from the 1st to the 6th centuries AD. As the empire went into decline, the power base shifted to the Amhara region. From the 10th to the 12th centuries, the use of Amharic became more widespread.

Over following centuries, ruling regimes tended to be Amhara-led. This, combined with the region's mountainous terrain and geographic isolation, ensured the spread and development of the language continued. Apart from the Italian occupation from 1936 to 1941, Ethiopia escaped long periods of European colonial domination. Extensive bodies of Amharic literature and sophisticated grammar and vocabulary were able to evolve unhindered. Although the written language was initially the domain of the church and the elite, modernisation in the 19th and 20th centuries encouraged its use among Ethiopians from all backgrounds. The last decade has seen a greater emphasis on regional languages for literacy, learning and the bureaucracy, so more people in Oromo regions are using Oromo, more people in Tigre are using Tigrinya, and so on.

As a visitor to the country, you'll invite both hospitality and curiosity. By speaking Amharic and throwing in some local words and phrases, your finest moments will be encounters with local people – the chat with a farmer after he ushers you into his hut to escape the rain, the jokes with kids at streetside markets, and the camaraderie with local bus passengers as you travel across the country.

ABBREVIATIONS USED IN THIS BOOK

adj	adjective	n	noun
f	feminine	pl	plural
inf	informal	pol	polite
lit	literal translation	sg	singular
m	masculine	v	verb

PRONUNCIATION

Tune into the sounds of Ethiopia's streets for tips on pronunciation: a mini-bus worker trilling his r as he calls the destination, a·rat ḳi·lo!; a vendor clicking her ḳ's as she advertises her spicy snacks, ḳo·lo, ḳo·lo!; a man waving down a friend from a street-side café, weun·dəm!, 'Hey brother!'. Though some Amharic sounds have no English equivalents, with a bit of practice, you'll be told you're gob·beuz, 'brilliant', by native Amharic speakers.

VOWEL SOUNDS

Listen for eu and ə, the most common Amharic vowels. They can sound quite similar to non-native speakers, but they are different. Be on the 'look out' and you'll soon discover the subtleties for yourself.

a	as the 'a' in 'father'
ai	as the 'ai' in aisle
ay	similar to the 'ay' in 'day'
e	as the 'e' in 'bed'
eu	as the 'e' in 'her' (without the 'r' sound); similar to the 'eu' in the French *neuf*
ə	as the 'e' in 'garden'
i	as the 'i' in 'bit'
o	similar to the 'o' in 'hot'
ow	similar to the 'ow' in 'cow'
ō	as the 'o' in 'both'
u	as the 'u' in 'flute'

CONSONANT SOUNDS

The following consonants are used throughout the book and pronounced pretty much as you'd expect in English:

b, d, f, m, n, v, w

The consonants below are pronounced as specified:

ch   as the 'ch' in 'chew'
g   as the 'g' in 'get'
h   as the 'h' in 'horse'
k   as the 'k' in 'kin'
j   as the 'j' in 'jaw'
l   as the 'l' in 'light'
ny   similar to 'ny' in 'canyon' (never as the 'ny' in 'pony')
p   as the 'p' in 'pot'
r   trilled, like the Spanish 'r'
s   as the 's' in 'plus'
sh   as the 'sh' in 'ship'
t   as the 't' in 'time', but the tongue touches the teeth
y   as the 'y' in 'yes'
z   as the 'z' in 'zoo'
zh   as the 's' in 'pleasure'

PRONUNCIATION

DOUBLE TALK

Double consonants indicate a longer, clearer sound than a single consonant – however don't divide them completely, as they're not two separate sounds.

| Double consonant: | al·leu | 'there is' |
| Single consonant: | a·leu | 'he said' |

Glottalic Consonants

Glottalic consonant sounds are made by tightening and releasing the glottis (the space between the vocal chords) when pronouncing a consonant, and may require some practice.

They're similar to the vocal movements made in 'uh-oh' or the cockney 'tt' in 'butter'. Try the following with basic vowels (eg, k̲a, k̲eu, k̲i, k̲o, k̲u, etc) before rolling them into words like t̲euj, 'honey wine', k̲euz·k̲az-za, 'cold', and s̲eu·hai, 'sun'. Pronouncing these sounds as if the under-dot wasn't there is often OK, but beware of exceptions. For example, 'he hit' is meut·ta, while 'he came' is meut̲·t̲a.

c̲h	like an emphasised 'tch' in 'witch'
k̲	like an emphasised 'ck' in 'yuck'
p̲	a short, popping 'p', as the first 'p' in 'pop'
s̲	a hissing 's' sound like an emphasised 's' in 'its'
t̲	a spitting 't' sound like an emphasised 't' in 'hot'
'	as the 'tt' in the·cockney 'butter'

PRONUNCIATION

STRESS

In general, stress falls equally on each syllable in Amharic. Pace things slowly and evenly to start with – for example, bun·na meug·zat ə·feul·lə·gal·lō, 'I want to buy coffee'. You'll loosen up as you develop a feel for the rhythms used.

INTONATION

In Amharic, a rising tone at the end of a sentence signifies a question – and there is no re-ordering of words as there often is in English sentences. For example, the English 'Is he going?' would simply be yi·he·dal? (lit: he is going?). 'Does it work?' in Amharic is simply yi·seu·ral? (lit: it works?).

PRONUNCIATION

TRANSLITERATION

There's not always a clear relationship between the spelling of Amharic script and its pronunciation. The spelling of words transliterated into Roman script in this book has therefore been modified to enable you to pronounce words more easily and accurately. Be aware that there is a range of transliteration schemes used in Amharic language courses, dictionaries and software – always look at the transliteration/pronunciation guides to avoid confusion.

SCRIPT

As well as helping you to read public signs and notices, the Amharic alphabet will help you to communicate – if you have trouble pronouncing a phrase, just point to the script!

Alphabet – *Fidel*

The unique Ethiopic alphabet (commonly referred to as a syllabary) was adapted from Ge'ez and is used to write Amharic and several other regional languages, including Tigrinya and Tigre. Oromo is now mainly written in roman script.

In a syllabary, characters usually represent consonant-vowel clusters. The Amharic version (known as *fi·deul*) consists of 33 basic characters. Each character combines with an additional stroke or symbol to produce one of seven possible consonant-vowel combinations or single vowels. As with roman script, the characters run from left to right across the page.

Note that some sounds have more than one character – this reflects historical changes to the writing system and, like English spelling, Amharic spelling is not always regular.

PRONUNCIATION

AMHARIC SYLLABARY

	eu	u	i	a	e	ə	o
h	ሀ	ሁ	ሂ	ሃ	ሄ	ህ	ሆ
l	ለ	ሉ	ሊ	ላ	ሌ	ል	ሎ
h	ሐ	ሑ	ሒ	ሓ	ሔ	ሕ	ሖ
m	መ	ሙ	ሚ	ማ	ሜ	ም	ሞ
s	ሠ	ሡ	ሢ	ሣ	ሤ	ሥ	ሦ
r	ረ	ሩ	ሪ	ራ	ሬ	ር	ሮ
s	ሰ	ሱ	ሲ	ሳ	ሴ	ስ	ሶ
sh	ሸ	ሹ	ሺ	ሻ	ሼ	ሽ	ሾ
ḳ	ቀ	ቁ	ቂ	ቃ	ቄ	ቅ	ቆ
b	በ	ቡ	ቢ	ባ	ቤ	ብ	ቦ
t	ተ	ቱ	ቲ	ታ	ቴ	ት	ቶ
ch	ቸ	ቹ	ቺ	ቻ	ቼ	ች	ቾ
h	ኀ	ኁ	ኂ	ኃ	ኄ	ኅ	ኆ
n	ነ	ኑ	ኒ	ና	ኔ	ን	ኖ
ny	ኘ	ኙ	ኚ	ኛ	ኜ	ኝ	ኞ
vowel	አ	ኡ	ኢ	ኣ	ኤ	እ	ኦ
k	ከ	ኩ	ኪ	ካ	ኬ	ክ	ኮ
h	ኸ	ኹ	ኺ	ኻ	ኼ	ኽ	ኾ
w	ወ	ዉ	ዊ	ዋ	ዌ	ው	ዎ
vowel	ዐ	ዑ	ዒ	ዓ	ዔ	ዕ	ዖ
z	ዘ	ዙ	ዚ	ዛ	ዜ	ዝ	ዞ
zh	ዠ	ዡ	ዢ	ዣ	ዤ	ዥ	ዦ
y	የ	ዩ	ዪ	ያ	ዬ	ይ	ዮ
d	ደ	ዱ	ዲ	ዳ	ዴ	ድ	ዶ
j	ጀ	ጁ	ጂ	ጃ	ጄ	ጅ	ጆ
g	ገ	ጉ	ጊ	ጋ	ጌ	ግ	ጎ
ṭ	ጠ	ጡ	ጢ	ጣ	ጤ	ጥ	ጦ
çh	ጨ	ጩ	ጪ	ጫ	ጬ	ጭ	ጮ
p	ጰ	ጱ	ጲ	ጳ	ጴ	ጵ	ጶ
ṣ	ጸ	ጹ	ጺ	ጻ	ጼ	ጽ	ጾ
ṣ	ፀ	ፁ	ፂ	ፃ	ፄ	ፅ	ፆ
f	ፈ	ፉ	ፊ	ፋ	ፌ	ፍ	ፎ
p	ፐ	ፑ	ፒ	ፓ	ፔ	ፕ	ፖ

PRONUNCIATION

LOST IN THE TRANSLATION

Colonial powers were shameless in their efforts to conquer Ethiopia, even resorting to a tactic of mistranslating state documents.

In 1889, Ethiopia's Emperor Menelik II signed the Treaty of Wechale with the Italian government. The treaty allowed for an Italian protectorate to be established over Ethiopia. At least, that's what the Italian version said – the Amharic version mentioned no such thing! Menelik only discovered the deception when Britain and Germany refused invitations to his coronation on the grounds that he was meant to communicate with them 'via the Italian government'. Menelik stopped the Italian expansion into the country by famously defeating them at the Battle of Adwa (northern Ethiopia) in 1896.

A few points on grammar will help you construct your own basic sentences in Amharic. Before you dive in, it's wise to take heed of an old Amharic saying: ƙeus beu ƙeus ən·ƙu·lal beug·ru yi·he·dal, 'Slowly, slowly an egg learns to walk'. Take things bit by bit and, slowly but surely, it'll start to come together.

Note that the system used to represent Amharic in this chapter differs to that described in the Pronunciation chapter and used in the rest of the book. This is to help illustrate the grammatical structure of words and phrases.

SENTENCE STRUCTURE

The word order of Amharic sentences is generally subject-object-verb:

Lydia wants coffee.	lidiya bunna təfeulləgalleuch
	(lit: Lydia coffee she-wants)
David bought a shirt.	david sheumiz geuzza
	(lit: David shirt he-bought)

However, the subject and object is often built into the verb:

They bought it.	geuzzut
	(lit: they-bought-it)

DON'T GET IN AF-FIX

One Amharic word often carries the same meaning as two or three English words, for example, abbate (lit: father-my) or yihedal (lit: he-is-going).

This is because Amharic uses many affixes (letters attached to words) instead of separate words to indicate things like tense, subject, object and gender. These include suffixes (letters attached to the end of words) and prefixes (letters attached to the beginning of words). Recognising the sound and meaning of these affixes will benefit you in your efforts to learn Amharic.

ARTICLES

The indefinite articles 'a' and 'an' aren't used in Amharic:

I want a taxi.   taksi əfeulləgallō
                                  (lit: taxi I-want)

The definite article 'the' is used in Amharic.

When nouns are the subject of a sentence, the definite article appears as a suffix attached to the end of the noun, as follows:

• When nouns are the subject of a verb ('what' or 'who' is performing the action) you generally use -u after a consonant or -w after a vowel:

The bus is going.   owtobəs-u yihedal
                                 (lit: bus-the it-is-going)

Note that when the definite article -w follows a vowel, it often changes the sound of that vowel. Following an 'a', for example, the sound will be ow, as in 'cow'. In contrast, after an 'o', the sound is ō as in 'toe'.

• If the subject is female, small, or the object of affection, use -wa, -itu or -itwa:

The child sings.   ləj-itwa təzeufeunalleuch
                                 (lit: girl-the she-sings)

• When sō, 'man', or set, 'woman', is the subject of a sentence, use the following endings:

sō-yō   (lit: man-the)
setə-yowa   (lit: woman-the)

Nouns that are the object of a sentence (what or whom the verb is referring to, or acting on) also take the definite article. Add -n to the appropriate subject suffixes for the definite article listed above:

I see the bus.   owtobəs-u-n aiyō
                                 (lit: bus-the I-see)

Call the man.   sō-yō-n təra (m)
                                 (lit: man-the you-call)

NOUNS
Plurals

There's no need to mark a noun plural in Amharic if the number is clear from the context. Take, for example, the phrase bəzu kərchat (lit: many basket) – bəzu implies more than one, so the notion of 'plural' is clear. Or if you point to a bunch of flowers, and say, konjo abeuba (lit: beautiful flower), it's obvious you mean the whole bunch.

If the quantity is not obvious from the context, nouns are made plural by attaching the suffix -och to words ending in a consonant or -woch to words ending in a vowel:

I want to see a lion.	anbeussa mayeut əfeulləgallō
	(lit: lion to-see I-want)
I want to see lions.	anbeussa-woch mayeut əfeulləgallō
	(lit: lion-s to-see I-want)

The plural suffix comes before the definite article suffix (in this example, the object definite article, -un):

Look at the lions.	anbeussa-woch-un teumeulkeut (m)
	(lit: lion-s-the you-look-at)

YOU TALKIN' TO ME?

You'll notice the use of (m), 'masculine', and (f), 'feminine', after a number of the phrases throughout this book. These refer to the gender of the person you're speaking to, not your own gender. So, if you're speaking to a woman, use the (f) form, whether you're a man or a woman.

You'll also see (pol), 'polite', and (pl), 'plural' – if you're speaking to elders or authority figures, use the (pol) form, and if you're speaking to a group of people, use the (pl) form.

ADJECTIVES

Adjectives generally precede the noun:

> I want a cheap umbrella.   rəkash janṭəlla əfeulləgallō
> (lit: cheap umbrella I-want)

Attach definite articles to the adjective, not the noun:

> The big bus is going.   təlləḳ-u owtobəs yihedal
> (lit: big-the bus it's-going)
> Look at the small bird.   tənnish-wan weuf teumeulkeut
> (lit: small-the bird look-at)

Adjectives often change form if the noun is plural:

> təlləḳ meukina   (lit: big car)
> təlälləḳ meukinawoch   (lit: big cars)

Using the singular form of an adjective with a plural noun will still get the message across though.

Forming Adjectives

Some adjectives are formed by attaching the prefix yeu (meaning 'of' or 'pertaining to') to the noun:

> cultural performance   yeu bahəl cheuwata
> (lit: of culture performance)

yeu- is also often used to indicate possession (see page 24).

Descriptive Verbs

Often the subject and descriptive word is itself a verb in Amharic, for example:

> I'm hot.   moḳeuny
> (lit: hot-I'm)
> I'm cold.   beureudeuny
> (lit: cold-I'm)

Comparatives

There are a number of ways to form comparatives in Amharic. One way is to place keu, 'from', between the subjects:

He's taller than me. əssu keu əne reujim nō
(lit: he from I tall he-is)

You can do the same thing using descriptive verbs instead of adjectives. A few descriptive verbs even have comparative meanings:

Trousers are better suri keu ḳeumiss yishalal
than a dress. (lit: trousers from dress it's-better)

Sometimes the words for 'more', yiləḳ or yibeulṭ, are used between the items being compared, for emphasis:

Wine's better than beer. keu bira yiləḳ wain ṭəru nō
(lit: from beer more wine good it-is)

Superlatives

There are no specific superlative adjectives in Amharic. However, you can form something close to a superlative by using beuṭam, 'very', before the adjective and attaching the definite article (-u or -wa) to the adjective:

the cheapest hotel beuṭam rəkash-u hotel
(lit: very cheap-the hotel)
the nearest monastery beuṭam ḳərb-wa deubər
(lit: very near-the monastery)

ADVERBS

Adverbs generally come before the verb in Amharic. It's not necessary to make them agree in number, gender, etc:

Please go slowly.	əbakəh ḵeuss beul (m)
	(lit: please slow you-be)
Please come quickly.	əbakəsh tolo nay (f)
	(lit: please quick you-come)

The prefix beu- is sometimes attached to abstract nouns to form adverbs:

| He drives fast. | beu-fəṭneut yineudal |
| | (lit: by-speed he-drives) |

PRONOUNS
Personal Pronouns

Amharic subject pronouns in the 2nd and 3rd person singular, 'you' and 'he/she/it', have a polite form, a masculine form and a feminine form. Use the polite form when addressing people older than you or people in positions of authority. The feminine form is also used for people or things that are small or the object of affection (the diminutive form).

You'll find that subject and object pronouns are often omitted in Amharic sentences, as they're built onto the verb stem (see Verbs, page 24).

Personal Pronouns			
I/me	əne	she/it	əsswa, ərswa
you	anteu/anchi (m/f)	you (pl)	ənnanteu
	ərswo/əsswo (pl/pol)	we	ənya
he/it	əssu, ərsu	they	ənneussu

Possessive Pronouns

Possessive pronouns are indicated by attaching a suffix to the noun.
They can also be formed with the use of yeu.

	nouns ending in consonants	noun ending in vowels
my	-e	-ye
your (m)	-əh	-h
your (f)	-əsh	-sh
your (pol)	-wo	-wo
his/its	-u	-w
her/its	-wa	-wa
your (pl)	-achu	-chu
our	-achən	-chən
their	-achō	-chō

my bag	shanṭa-ye
	(lit: bag-my)
your name	səm-əh (m)
	səm-əsh (f)
	(lit: name-your)
our dinner	ərat-achən
	(lit: dinner-our)

If the noun is the object of a sentence, attach the definite article
-n after the possessive pronoun:

Give me my ticket.	tiket-e-n səṭeuny (m)
	(lit: ticket-my-the you-give-me)

GRAMMAR

POSSESSION

The prefix yeu is commonly used to indicate that something belongs to or pertains to something else:

the man's hat	yeu sōyō ḳob
	(lit: of man-the hat)

Similarly, yeu is rolled into pronouns to form possessive pronouns:

It's your towel.	yanchi foṭa nō (f)
	(yeu + anchi = yanchi)
	(lit: of-you towel it-is)
She's my friend.	yeune gwadeunya nat
	(yeu + əne = yeune)
	(lit: of-me friend she-is)

VERBS

Verbs in Amharic change form to agree in tense, number and gender with the subjects and objects they refer to. This is achieved by attaching suffixes and prefixes to the verb stem. The meu- or ma- form is generally the infinitive. Some examples of verb stems you can use are:

hed	from	meuhed (to go)
geuz	from	meugzat (to buy)
beul	from	meublat (to eat)

These verb stems act as a kind of bare branch onto which leaves (affixes) are added to make the word whole. This will become clearer as you read through the examples below.

Present & Future

In Amharic, the present and future tenses are not distinguished by changes to the verb – exactly the same words (the same stems and affixes) are used for both:

I	ə...allō	she/it	tə...alleuch
you	tə...alleuh (m)	he/she/it	yi...allu (pol)
	tə...alleush (f)	we	ən...alleun
you	yi...allu (pol)	you (pl)	tə...allachu
he/it	yi...al	they	yi...allu

Take, for example, the verb stem hed from meuhed, 'to go':

She goes/is going/will go.	tə-hed-alleuch
They go/are going/will go.	yi-hed-allu
You go/are going/will go.	tə-hej-alleush (f)

Note that spelling is often adjusted with 2nd person feminine.

As a rule, the above forms used alone indicate present tense – the future tense is usually indicated by context or time words:

She'll go tomorrow.	neugeu tə-hed-alleuch
	(lit: tomorrow she-goes)

Simple Past

For simple past tense (actions that have already been completed), add the following suffixes to the verb stem. Note that suffixes can vary depending on the type of infinitive verb.

I	...ow/ku
you	...h/kh (m)
you	...sh/sh (f)
you	...u (pol)
he/it	...a/eu
she/it	...ch/euch
you (pl)	...chu/achu
we	...n/ən
they	...u

For example:

She went.	hed-euch
We drank.	ṭeuṭa-n
I arrived.	deurreus-ku

Continuous

To form a continuous past tense, attach the prefix əyeu- to the simple past tense, outlined above, and then add neubbeur, 'was'.

She was going.   əyeu-hedeuch neubbeur

For present continuous tense, use nō, 'is', instead of neubbeur.

Objects in Verbs

Amharic verbs often contain objects as well as subjects. This is done by attaching special object pronoun affixes, such as -aw- or -euw-, 'him/it' or -at-, 'her/it':

he'll bring	yameuṭal
He'll bring it.	yameuṭawal
I want	əfeulləgallō
I want it.	əfeulləgeuwallō
Let's ask.	ənṭeuyik
Let's ask her.	ənṭeuyikat

Negatives

There isn't a word for 'no' in Amharic. Instead, affixes are attached to verbs to form negative verbs. The most common are:

yeulleum	'there isn't/it's not there'
aideulleum	'it's not/it isn't'

Others include:

alfeulləgəm	(lit: I don't want)
alchəlləm	(lit: I can't)
yeuɬeunem	(lit: we don't have)

GRAMMAR

To make present/future tense verbs negative, you generally attach the following suffixes and prefixes to the verb stem. Suffixes may alter their vowel sounds depending on which verb stem is used:

I	al...m (əm)
you	at...m (əm)/at...m (im) (m/f)
you	ai...um (pol)
he/it	ai...m (əm)
she/it	at...m (əm)
you (pl)	at...um
we	an...m (əm)
they	ai...um

You can't.	atchəlləm
We don't like ...	... anweuddəm
They're not going.	aihedum

Note that in contrast to English, the answer to a negative question in Amharic is, in part, a positive response:

You're not eating?	atbeuyim? (f)
Yes, I'm not eating.	ow, albeulam

TO HAVE

The verb of existence – 'there exists', alleu, and 'there doesn't exist', yeulleum – is sometimes used on its own in place of 'have' and 'don't have', particularly when asking if something is available.

Do you have a candle?	shama alleu?
	(lit: candle there-exists)

In other situations, use the following words as you would in English:

I have	alleuny
you have	alleuh/alleush (m/f)
you have	allot (pol)
he/it has	allō
she/it has	allat
you (pl) have	allachu
we have	alleun
they have	allachō

GRAMMAR

TO BE

Note that in Amharic, the verb of existence – 'there exists' (alleu) and 'there doesn't exist' (yeulleum) – is often used where in English, the verb 'to be' would be used:

I am	neuny
you are	neuh/neush (m/f)
you are	not (pol)
he/it is	nō
she/it is	neuch
you (pl) are	nachu
we are	neun
they are	nachō

I'm a tourist.	gobəny neuny
	(lit: tourist I-am)
You're kind.	deugg neuh (m)
	(lit: kind you-are)

GRAMMAR

ESSENTIAL VERBS

Remember that verbs change their form according to tense, subject and gender. You can try extracting verb stems derived from the infinitives below and using them with the affixes outlined in Present & Future tense, page 24. There may be some adjustments you need to make to the verb stem (eg, eu may be needed for consonants without a vowel between them) – the following table is intended as a general guide only.

Essential Verbs

to arrive	meudreus
it arrived	deurswal
to ask	meuṭeuyeuḳ
ask him	ṭeuyəḳō
to buy	meugzat
I bought	geuzow
to come	meumṭat
we came	meuṭan
to do	madreug
she's doing	tadeurgalleuch
to drink	meuṭeuṭat
they're drinking	yiṭeuṭallu
to give	meusṭeut
give me	səṭeuny
to go	meuhed
it isn't going	anhedəm
to know	maweuḳ
I don't know	alawəḳəm
to learn	meumaŕ
he's learning	yimaral
to like	meuwdeud
do you like?	yiweudallu? (pol)
to live (somewhere)	meunor
you live ...	... tənoralleuh (m)
to love	mafḳeur
he loves her	yafeuḳratal
to make	meusrat
you (pl) are making	təseurallachu
to meet	meugeunanyeut
let's meet	ənəgeunany
to pay	meukfeul
he paid	keufəlwal
to read	manbeub
you read (past)	anəbeushal (f)
to return	meumeulleus
she'll return	təmeulleusalleuch

Essential Verbs (cont)	
to stay	meuḳoyeut
I'm staying	əḳoyallō
to see	mayeut
you see	aiyeuh (m)
to speak	meunageur
I speak	teunageurku
to write	meuṣaf
you write	yiṣafu (pol)

MODALS

To indicate 'must', 'can' or 'want' in Amharic, use the Amharic equivalent of an infinitive – eg, meuhed, 'to go', mayeut, 'to see' – then add the modal ('must', 'can' or 'want'). The modal must agree with the subject in number and gender:

I want to go.   meuhed əfeulləgallō
                       (lit: to-go I-want)

Must

I must	alleubəny
you must	alleubəh/alleubəsh (m/f)
you must	alleubəwot (pol)
he/it must	alleubeut
she/it must	alleubat
you (pl) must	alleubachu
we must	alleubən
they must	alleubachō

We must go today.   zare meuhed alleubən
                       (lit: today to-go we-must)

Can

I can	əchəlallō
you can	təchəlalleuh/təchəyalleush (m/f)
you can	yichəlallu (pol)
he/it can	yichəlal
she/it can	təchəlalleuch
you (pl) can	təchəlallachu
we can	ənchəlalleun
they can	yichəlallu

We can go.   meuhed ənchəlalleun
(lit: to-go we-can)

Want

I want	əfeulləgallō
you want	təfeulləgalleuh/ təfeulləgiyalleush (m/f)
you want	yifeulləgallu (pol)
he/it wants	yifeulləgal
she/it wants	təfeulləgalleuch
you (pl) want	təfeulləgallachu
we want	ənfeulləgalleun
they want	yifeulləgallu

We want to go by bus.   beu owtobəs meuhed
ənfeulləgalleun
(lit: by bus to-go we-want)

QUESTIONS

In Amharic, a raised tone at the end of a sentence signifies a question and there's no reordering of words as there often is in English (see Intonation, page 13).

Amharic question words include:

What?	mən/məndən?
When?	meuche?
Who?	man?
Where?	yeut?
Why?	leumən/leuməndən?
How much/many?	sənt?

ከየት አገር ነህ?

ከ አየርላንድ ነኝ

You'll most often see these with ... nō?, '... is it?', eg, sənt nō?, 'how much is it?', məndən nō?, 'what is it?' – but they can be used in many different contexts:

What are you doing?	mən tareugalleuh? (m)
	(lit: what you're-doing)
When does it leave?	meuche yineusal?
	(lit: when it-leaves)
Who is it?	man nō?
	(lit: who it-is?)
Where can I find	jeubeuna yeut yigeunyal?
a coffee pot?	(lit: coffee-pot where
	it's-found)
Why didn't you come?	leumən almeutashəm?
	(lit: why you-didn't-
	come?)
How much time will it take?	sənt gize yiweusdal?
	(lit: how-much time it-takes)

GRAMMAR

CONJUNCTIONS

The conjunctions əna, 'and', and waym, 'or', appear between the two words they connect, as in English (note that if əna follows a word ending in a vowel, it becomes the suffix -na):

> I see a donkey and a horse.   ahəya-na feureus aiyō
> (lit: donkey-and horse I-see)

Some conjunctions like gən/neugeur gən, 'but', are used to join clauses (much as they are in English):

> It's good but it's very   ṭəru nō gən beuṭam wədd nō
> expensive.   (lit: good it-is but very
>   expensive it-is)

COW IN THE SKY

You'll find an Amharic saying to suit any situation – here are a few:

I have a cow in the sky and I haven't seen the milk.	lam a·leuny beu seu·mai weu·teut·wa·nəm a·lai *(Nothing has come of it.)*
A person who has too much will start chewing porridge.	yeu·deu·low muk yan·yə·ḳal *(A person who has too much will do useless things.)*
Spider webs joined together can catch a lion.	dər bi·ya·bər an·beus·sa yas·sər *(Much can be accomplished by joining together.)*

PREPOSITIONS & POSTPOSITIONS

Prepositions (like 'in', 'at', 'on' or 'before') are attached to nouns as prefixes. In this book they appear separated from the noun to make them easier to read:

of	yeu
at/from	ə, keu
in/at/by	beu
for/to	leu
to	weudeu

Some common Amharic postpositions (those that go after the noun) include lai, 'up/on/over', wəch, 'out', and wəsṭ, 'in'. They're often used in conjunction with prepositions like keu and beu:

It's outside the car.   keu meukinow wəch nō
                               (lit: from car-the out it-is)

But this is not always necessary:

It's in the bus.   owtobəs wəsṭ nō
                              (lit: bus-the in it-is)

One of the first things you'll notice when meeting people in Ethiopia is the əj meun·sat (bow or head nod) used in greetings, goodbyes, acknowledgment or thanks.

YOU SHOULD KNOW   ማወቅ ያለብዎት

Many Amharic words and phrases, including greetings, change form, depending on whether a male (m), female (f), elder person/authority figure (pol) or group (pl) is being addressed. In most cases, only (m) and (f) have been provided here, except in some of the most common phrases where you'll also see (pl) or (pol) forms used.

Yes.	ow	አዎ
OK/Yes.	ə·shi	እሺ
There is.	al·leu	አለ
There isn't.	yeul·leum	የለም
Excuse me.	yi·kər·ta	ይቅርታ
Please.	ə·ba·kəh (m)	እባክህ
	ə·ba·kəsh (f)	እባክሽ
	ə·ba·kon (pol)	እባክዎን
	ə·ba·ka·chu (pl)	እባካችሁ
Thank you.	a·meu·seu·gə·nal·lō	አመሰግናለሁ
Sorry.	az·nal·lō	አዝናለሁ ·

ሰላም ደህና ነህ?

ደህና ነኝ

Amharic uses negative verb forms in place of 'no'. The main forms are: yeul·leum, 'there isn't, it's not there/available' and ai·deul·leum, 'it isn't'. See Grammar, page 26, for more details.

GREETINGS & GOODBYES ሰላምታ መለዋወጥ

Ethiopian greetings range from a passing bow or 'hello', to several minutes of polite inquiries about how you and your family or loved ones are. When you meet, bow and offer your right hand – or wrist if you can't offer your hand – for a handshake. Once you know someone, you're likely to shake hands, embrace lightly and touch cheeks – right, left, then right again. The following greetings can be used any time of the day:

Hello./Greetings./Goodbye.
   țe·na yis·țəl·ləny   ጤና ይስጥልኝ
                                        (lit: may health be given
                                           to you)

Hello.
  seu·lam   ሰላም
How are you?
  deu·na neuh? (m)   ደህና ነህ?
  deu·na neush? (f)   ደህና ነሽ?
  deu·na not? (pl)   ደህና ነዎት?

You'll also hear ən·deu·mən, a polite way of asking 'how', instead of deu·na 'fine':

How are you?
  ən·deu·mən neuh? (m)   እንደምን ነህ?
  ən·deu·mən neush? (f)   እንደምን ነሽ?
I'm fine.
  deu·na neuny   ደህና ነኝ

On a more informal level, you might hear:

Hello/Hi.
  ta·di·yass   ታዲያስ
How are things?
  ən·det nō?   እንዴት ነው?
So, what's new?
  mən ad·dis neu·geur al·leu?   ምን አዲስ ነገር አለ?

There are also different greetings for different times of the day:

How is your morning?
   deu·na ad·deurk? (m)   ደህና አደርክ?
   deu·na ad·deursh? (f)   ደህና አደርሽ?
   deu·na ad·deu·ru? (pol)   ደህና አደሩ?
How's your day going?
   deu·na walk? (m)   ደህና ዋልክ?
   deu·na walsh? (f)   ደህና ዋልሽ?
   deu·na wa·lu? (pol)   ደህና ዋሉ?
How are you this evening?
   deu·na a·meu·sheuh? (m)   ደህና አመሼህ?
   deu·na a·meu·sheush? (f)   ደህና አመሼሽ?
   deu·na a·meu·shu? (pol)   ደህና አመሹ?
Good night.
   deu·na deur (m)   ደህና ደር
   deu·na deu·ri (f)   ደህና ደሪ
   deu·na yi·deu·ru (pol)   ደህና ይደሩ

Goodbyes   መሰያየት

A useful lead-up to goodbye is ə·shi meu·he·de nō, 'OK, I'm about to go'. Bow or shake hands as you say goodbye.

Bye/See you!
   chow!   ቻው!
Have a nice day.
   deu·na wal (m)   ደህና ዋል
   deu·na wai (f)   ደህና ዋይ
Goodbye.
   deu·na hun (m)   ደህና ሁን
   deu·na hu·nyi (f)   ደህና ሁኚ
   deu·na hu·nu (pl)   ደህና ሁኑ
Goodbye. (when leaving
for some time)
   deu·na seun·bət (m)   ደህና ሰንብት
   deu·na seun·bach (f)   ደህና ሰንብች
   deu·na seun·bə·tu (pl) ደህና ሰንብቱ

MEETING PEOPLE

Come back safely!
beu·cheur yi·meul·lə·səh! (m)	በፍቻ ይመልስህ!
beu·cheur yi·meul·lə·səsh! (f)	በፍቻ ይመልስሽ!

People may say teu·cha·weut geu·na nō (m), 'Keep us company, it's still early'. If you need to go, some polite responses are:

Sorry, I have to go now.
yi·kər·ta a·hun meu·hed al·leu·bəny	ይቅርታ አሁን መሄድ አለብኝ

Sorry, I have an appointment.
yi·kər·ta keu·teu·ro al·leu·bəny	ይቅርታ ቀጠሮ አለብኝ

We'll meet again.
le·la gi·ze ə·nə·geu·na·nyal·leun	ሌላ ጊዜ እንገናኛለን

CIVILITIES   ሰዎችን ማስተናገድ

Hospitality is a major part of Ethiopian social life, and you'll often be invited for a coffee, drink or meal. If you're invited to someone's house, leave your shoes at the entrance if your host does the same. Bow as you receive tea, coffee and snacks, or say əg·zer yis·ṭəl·ləny (lit: may God give to you).

Welcome.
ən·kwan deu·na meu·ṭah (m)	እንኳን ደህና መጣህ
ən·kwan deu·na meu·ṭash (f)	እንኳ ደህና መጣሽ
ən·kwan deu·na meu·ṭu (pol)	እንኳን ደህና መጡ

Come in.
gə·ba/gə·bi/yig·bu (m/f/pol)	ግባ/ግቢ/ይግቡ

Please sit down.
ə·ba·kəh kuch beul (m)	እባክህ ቀጭ በል
ə·ba·kəsh kuch bay (f)	እባክሽ ቀጭ በይ

Thank you for your hospitality.
sə·leu meus·teun·gə·dō a·meu·seu·gə·nal·lō	ስለ መስተንጋዶ· አመሰግናለሁ

You're very kind.
beu·ṭam deugg not	በጣም ደግ ነዎት

Don't mention it.
ˈmə·nəm ai·deul·leum	ምንም አይደለም

FORMS OF ADDRESS ስም

When addressing someone in Ethiopia, always use their first name. In more formal situations, use the first name preceded by a title. For example, Dawit Sissay is a·to da·wit, 'Mr Dawit'. Ethiopians often use their father's first name where Westerners use surnames. After marriage, women retain their maiden names, and only change their title.

Ethiopians also use friendly terms to address people: weun·dəm, 'brother', for a man around your own age; ə·hət, 'sister', for a woman around your own age; ab·bab·ba, 'papa', for old men; ə·mam·ma, 'mama', for old women; and ga·she, 'my shield', for a man slightly older than you. There are also yeu·kə·ṣəl səm, 'nicknames'.

Mr	a·to	አቶ
Mrs	way·zeu·ro	ወይዘሮ
Miss	way·zeu·rit	ወይዘሪት

Asking Names ስም መለዋወጥ

Asking names·is a friendly ice-breaker in Ethiopia. Sometimes people will explain the meaning of their name in English. For example, tə·la·hun (Tilahun) means 'be my shade', ṣeu·hai (Sehay) means 'sun' and a·beub·ba (Abeba) means 'flower'.

What's your name?
  sə·meh man nō? (m)   ስምህ ማነው?
  sə·mesh man nō? (f)   ስምሽ ማነው?
  sə·mə·wot man nō? (pol)   ስምዎት ማነው?
My name's ...
  sə·me ... nō   ስሜ ... ነው
This is ...
  yi·he ... nō (m)   ይህ ... ነው
  yi·chi ... nat (f)   ይቺ ... ናት

MEETING PEOPLE

FIRST ENCOUNTERS   ለመጀመሪያ ጊዜ መገናኘት

A simple smile, nod or yi·ḳər·ta, 'excuse me', followed by a greeting
is a common way to initiate conversation.

Do you like ...?	... tə·weud·dal·leuh? (m)	... ትወዳለህ?
	... tə·weu·jal·leush? (f)	... ትወጃለሽ?
our country	a·geu·ra·chən	አገራ·ችን
this place	yi·hen bo·ta	ይሀን ቦታ

I like it (a lot).
(beu·tam) ə·weud·dal·lō   (በጣም) እወዳለሁ·

When did you arrive?
meu·che meu·taḥ? (m)   መቼ መጣህ?
meu·che meu·tash? (f)   መቼ መጣሽ?

I arrived (yesterday/last week).
(tə·nan·tə·na; ya·leu·fō   (ትናንትና/ያለፈ·ወ·
sam·mənt) meu·tow   ሳምንት) መጣሁ·

Why did you come here?
leu·mən meu·taḥ? (m)   ለምን መጣህ?
leu·mən meu·tash? (f)   ለምን መጣሽ?

For tourism/a holiday.
leu gub·bə·nyit; leu ə·reuft   ለጉብኝት/ለእረፍት

For work/study.
leu sə·ra; leu təm·hərt   ለስራ/ለትምህርት

Which places have you been to?
mən mən bo·ta·wo·chən   ምን ምን ቦታዎችን
a·yeuh/a·yeush? (m/f)   አየህ/አየሽ?

I've been to (Lalibela) and (Harar).
(la·li·beu·lan) ə·na (ha·ra·rən)   (ላሊበላን) እና (ሃረርን)
ai·chal·lō   አይቻለሁ·

Did you like (Gonder)?
(gon·deur) teus·ḥma·mah/   (ጎንደር) ተስማማህ/
teus·ma·mash? (m/f)   ተስማማሽ?

Where are you staying?
   yeut nō ya·reuf·kō? (m)   የት ነው· ያረፍከው·?
   yeut nō ya·reuf·shyu? (f)   የት ነው· ያረፍሽው·?
Where are you going?
   yeut tə·he·dal·leuh? (m)   የት ትሄዳለህ?
   yeut tə·he·jal·leush? (f)   የት ትሄጃለሽ?
   yeut yi·he·dal·lu? (pol)   የት ይሄዳሉ·?
I'm/We're going to ...
   weu·deu ... ə·he·dal·lō/   ወደ ... እሄዳለሁ·/
   ən·he·dal·leun   እንሄዳለን
Who are you with?
   keu man gar neuh? (m)   ከማን ጋር ነህ?
   keu man gar neush? (f)   ከማን ጋር ነሽ?

I'm with ...	keu ... gar neuny	ከ ... ጋር ነኝ
a tour group	go·bə·nyi·woch	ጉብኝዎች
my friend/	gwa·deu·nya·ye/	ጓደኛዬ/
friends	gwa·deu·nyo·che	ጓደኞቼ
my wife/	ba·leu·be·te	ባለቤቴ
husband		

BEAUTIFUL!

One of the great Ethiopian phrases is ḳon·jo nō, 'It's beautiful', which can be used to describe anything, from a delicious meal to a panoramic view of the Simien Mountains.

It's beautiful!
   ḳon·jo nō!   ቆንጆ ነው·!
This place is beautiful!
   yi·he bo·ta ḳon·jo nō!   ይሄ ቦታ ቆንጆ ነው·!
Isn't it beautiful?
   ḳon·jo nō ai·deul·leum?   ቆንጆ ነው· አይደለም?
What a beautiful baby/child!
   ḳon·jo ləj!   ቆንጆ ልጅ!

MEETING PEOPLE

Is there a problem?	chig·gər al·leu?	ችግር አለ?
No problem.	chig·gər yeul·leum	ችግር የለም
Just a minute.	and gi·ze	አንድ ጊዜ
🔊 It's possible.	yi·cha·lal	ይቻላል
It's not possible.	ai·chal·ləm	አይቻልም
Good luck!	meul·kam ə·dəl!	መልካም እድል!
I'm joking.	ķeul·den nō	ቀልዴን ነው·
That's amusing!	ya·sə·ķal!	ያስቃል!

KEEP TALKING

Ethiopians love chatting and there are lots of friendly interjections in Amharic conversation. One you may hear sounds like a small gasp or hiccup. This means 'Please continue/I'm listening'. The word teu·cha·weut!/ teu·cha·weu·chi!/teu·cha·weu·tu! (m/f/pl) means 'Play!' and is a friendly way of saying, 'Let's have a chat!' or 'Keep chatting!'. The word ən·teu·wa·weuķ, 'Let's get to know each other', is an offer of friendship.

How was it?	ən·det neub·beur?	እንዴት ነበር?
OK./Yes./Go on.	ə·shi	እሺ
Really?	əw·neut?	እውነት?
Maybe.	mə·nal·bat	ምናልባት
That's surprising!	yi·geur·mal!	ይገርማል!
It's true!	əw·neūt nō!	እውነት ነው·
It's a lie!	wu·sheut nō!	ውሸት ነው·
Brilliant!	gob·beuz!	ጎበዝ!
Oh!	a·ra!	እራ!

Be strong/Chin up! ai·zoh/ai·zosh! (m/f)		አይዞህ/አይዞሽ!
What did you say? mən alk/alsh? (m/f)		ምን አልክ/አልሽ?

It's important.
    as·feul·la·gi nō   አስፈላጊ ነው።

It's not important.
    as·feul·la·gi ai·deul·leum   አስፈላጊ አይደለም

What's this/that?
    yi·he/ya mən·dən nō?   ይሄ/ያ ምንድን ነው?

Look!
    teu·meul·keut! (m)   ተመልከት!
    teu·meul·keuch! (f)   ተመልከች!
    teu·meul·keu·tu! (pl)   ተመልከቱ!

Listen!
    sə·ma!/sə·mi!/sə·mu! (m/f/pl)   ስማ!/ስሚ!/ስሙ!

Can you please help me?
    ə·ba·kəh ər·dany? (m)   እባክህ እርዳኝ?
    ə·ba·kəsh ər·jiny? (f)   እባክሽ እርጂኝ?

What are you doing?
    mən ta·reu·gal·leuh? (m)   ምን ታረጋለህ?
    mən ta·reu·gi·yal·leush? (f) ምን ታረጊያለሽ?
    mən ta·reu·gal·la·chu? (pl) ምን ታረጋላችሁ?

NATIONALITIES   ዜግነት

Ethiopians will be keen to hear which country you're from.
The following question can also be used to ask which region
Ethiopian people come from.

Where are you from?
keu yeut a·geur neuh? (m)	ከየት አገር ነህ?
keu yeut a·geur neush? (f)	ከየት አገር ነሽ?

I'm from ...	keu ... neuny	ከ ... ነኝ
(South) Africa	(deu·bub) af·ri·ka	(ደቡብ) አፍሪካ
Asia	əs·ya	እስያ
Australia	ow·stra·li·ya	አውስትራሊያ
Canada	ka·na·da	ካናዳ
Egypt	gəbs	ግብጽ
England	ən·gliz	እንግሊዝ
Ethiopia	i·tə·yo·pi·ya	ኢትዮጵያ
Europe	i·rop	ኤሮፕ
France	feu·reun·sai	ፈረንሳይ
Germany	jeur·meun	ጀርመን
Greece	grik	ግሪክ
India	hənd	ሕንድ
Ireland	aiyr·land	አየርላንድ
Israel	əs·ra·el	እስራኤል
Italy	ṭal·yan	ጣሊያን
Japan	ja·pan	ጃፓን
the USA	a·me·ri·ka	አሜሪካ

I live in the ...	... ə·no·ral·lō	... እኖራለሁ
city	keu·teu·ma wəsṭ	ከተማ ውስጥ
countryside	geu·ṭeur	ገጠር

Which region/city are you from?
keu yeu·tə·nyow kəl·ləl/	ከየትኛው ክልል/
keu·teu·ma neuh? (m)	ከተማ ነህ?
keu yeu·tə·nyow kəl·ləl/	ከየትኛው ክልል
keu·teu·ma neush? (f)	ከተማ ነሽ?

STAYING IN TOUCH   መጠየየቅ

People won't be shy about asking if you can meet again or exchange addresses. When someone hasn't seen you for a while, they'll probably say ṭeu·fah!/ṭeu·fash! (m/f), 'You've been lost!'.

Can we meet again?
  ən·deu·geu·na
  ə·nə·geu·na·nyal·leun?   እንደገና እንገናኛለን?

When/Where will we meet?
  meu·che/yeut   መቼ/የት
  ə·nə·geu·na·nyal·leun?   እንገናኛለን?

Let's meet at Piazza at (six o'clock).
  (sə·dəst seu'at) lai pi·yas·sa   (ስድስት ሰዓት) ላይ
  ə·nə·geu·nany   ፒያሳ እንገናኝ

We'll meet tomorrow/tonight.
  (neu·geu; za·re ma·ta)   (ነገ/ዛሬ ማታ)
  ə·nə·geu·na·nyal·leun   እንገናኛለን

I'll visit you (on my way back).
  (sə·meul·leuss) ə·meu·ṭal·lō   (ስመለስ) እመጣለሁ

I'll be back in (two weeks).
  beu (hu·leutt sam·mənt)   በ (ሁለት ሳምንት)
  wəsṭ ə·meul·leu·sal·lō   ውስጥ እመለሳለሁ

I'll send you a letter.
  deub·dab·be ə·lə·kal·lō   ደብዳቤ እልካለሁ

I'll call you.
  səlk ə·deu·wə·lal·lō   ስልክ እደውሳለሁ

Please give me your address/
phone number.
  ə·ba·kəh (ad·ra·sha·hən;   እባክህ (አድራሻህን/
  yeu səlk kuṭ·rə·hən) sə·ṭeuny (m)   የስልክ ቁጥርህን) ስጠኝ
  ə·ba·keush (ad·ra·sha·shən;   እባክሽ (አድራሻሽን/
  yeu səlk kuṭ·rə·shən) sə·chiny (f)   የስልክ ቁጥርሽን) ስጭኝ

BODY LANGUAGE & ETIQUETTE   ሥነ ምግባር

Ethiopia tolerates a range of different customs and beliefs. The general rule of thumb is to observe what the locals do. For tips on eating, see page 144, and for religion, see page 191. In general, social etiquette carries enormous weight in Ethiopia. The idea of yə·luny·ta, concern about the opinions of others, is common, as is the phrase neu·wər nō!, 'It's impolite!'.

Displays of affection between men and women are unacceptable in public, but moderate displays of affection between members of the same sex is fine.

Dress fairly conservatively. Women should avoid wearing shorts, miniskirts or crop tops, particularly in rural and Muslim areas. Men should always wear a shirt and avoid torn clothing and short shorts.

If you're staying with a family or at the receiving end of hospitality, fruit or raw coffee beans are appropriate gifts.

It's usual to give informal guides or porters 'tea money' to thank them for their services, but use discretion. Some people will be offended by an offer of money, so instead you might like to invite them for coffee or a meal.

Respect for authority figures and older people is highly valued.

Be discreet about smoking and drinking in public, particularly in rural and Muslim areas. Women should be especially discreet.

Belching and breaking wind are considered totally unacceptable. Say yi·kər·ta!, 'Excuse me!', if you slip up.

Most Ethiopian body language, like nodding, shaking the head, and waving goodbye, carries the same meaning as it does in English. You'll notice Ethiopians use very expressive hand gestures in day-to-day conversation – a great benefit to non-Amharic speakers!

CULTURAL DIFFERENCES የባህል ልዩነት

Is this a local custom?
yi·he yeu a·ka·ba·bi·yu ይኸ የ አካባቢው·
ba·həl nō? ባህል ነው-?

I don't want to offend you.
las·keu·ya·məh al·feul·lə·gəm (m) ላስቀይምህ አልፈልግም
las·keu·ya·məsh al·feul·lə·gəm (f) ላስቀይምሽ አልፈልግም

I'm sorry, it's not the custom
in my country.
yi·kər·ta ya·geu·re ይቅርታ ያገሬ
ba·həl ai·deul·leum ባህል አይደለም

Thank you, but I'd rather just watch.
a·meu·seu·gə·nal·lō ma·yeut አመሰግናለሁ ማየት
bə·cha ə·feul·lə·gal·lō ብቻ እፈልጋለሁ

I'll give it a go!
ə·mo·kə·reu·wal·lō! እሞክረዋለሁ!

I'm sorry, it's against my ...	yi·kər·ta yeu·ne ... ai·feuk·deu·wəm	ይቅርታ የኔ ... አይፈቅደውም
beliefs	əm·neut	እምነት
culture	ba·həl	ባህል
religion	hai·ma·not	ሃይማኖት

AGE ዕድሜ

It's impolite for men to ask women their age, but fine for a woman to inquire about another woman's age. See Numbers & Amounts, page 223, for your age.

How old are you?
əd·meh sənt nō? (m) ዕድሜህ ስንት ነው-?
əd·mesh sənt nō? (f) ዕድሜሽ ስንት ነው-?

I'm (20) years old.
(ha·ya) a·meu·te nō (ሃያ) አመቴ ነው-

MEETING PEOPLE

OCCUPATIONS

ሥራ

What's your job?

sə·rah mən·dən nō? (m)		ሥራህ ምንድን ነው?
sə·rash mən·dən nō? (f)		ሥራሽ ምንድን ነው?

I'm (a/an) ...	... neuny	... ነኝ
accountant	yeu hi·sab seu·ra·teu·nya	የሂሳብ ሠራተኛ
artist	seu'al·li	ሰዓሊ
businessperson	neug·ga·de	ነጋዴ
cook	mə·gəb seu·ri	ምግብ ሰሪ
doctor	ha·kim	ሐኪም
engineer	meu·han·dis	መሃንዲስ
farmer	geu·beu·re	ገበሬ
homemaker	yeu bet ə·meu·bet	የቤት እመቤት
journalist	ga·ze·ţeu·nya	ጋዜጠኛ
lawyer	ţeu·beu·ķa	ጠበቃ
nurse	neurs	ነርስ
office worker	yeu bi·ro seu·ra·teu·nya	የቢሮ ሠራተኛ
scientist	teu·meu·ra·ma·ri	ተመራማሪ
student	teu·ma·ri	ተማሪ
teacher	as·teu·ma·ri	አስተማሪ
tour guide	as·gob·nyi	አስጎብኚ
tradesperson	yeu əj ba·leu·mu·ya	የእጅ ባለሙያ
unemployed	sə·ra feut	ሥራ ፈት

I'm retired.

ţu·reu·ta weu·ţə·chal·lō	ጡረታ ወጥቻለሁ

What are you studying?

mən tə·ma·ral·leuh? (m)		ምን ትማራለህ?
mən tə·ma·ri·yal·leush? (f)		ምን ትማሪያለሽ?

I'm studying ...	... ə·ma·ral·lō	... እማራለሁ·
business	nəgd	ንግድ
computer science	kom·pyu·teur	ኮምፒዉተር
engineering	in·jə·neu·riny	ኢንጅኔሪንግ
fine arts	ki·neu ṭə·beub	ኪነ ጥበብ
languages	ḳwan·ḳwa	ቋንቋ
law	həg	ሕግ
medicine	hə·kə·mə·na	ሕክምና
science	sai·yəns	ሳይንስ
social studies	həb·reu təm·hərt	ሕብረ ትምህርት

FEELINGS

ስሜቶች

In Amharic, feelings are often expressed as verbs with the subject attached, so you only need to use one word.

I'm ...		
angry	teu·na·də·jal·lō	ተናድጃለሁ·
cold	beu·reu·deuny	በረደኝ
depressed	deu·bro·nyal	ደብሮኛል
happy	deus blo·nyal	ደስ ብሎኛል
hot	mo·ḳeuny	ሞቀኝ
hungry	ra·beuny	ራበኝ
sad	a·zə·nyal·lō	አዝኛለሁ·
thirsty	wu·ha ṭeu·many	ዉሃ ጠማኝ
tired	deu·keu·meuny	ደከመኝ

BREAKING THE LANGUAGE BARRIER

የቋንቋ አለመግባባትን ማስወገድ

To form a language name in Amharic, add the suffix -ə·nya to the language or region. Local languages include o·ro·mə·nya (Oromo) and ti·grə·nya (Tigrinya) while common foreign languages include feu·reun·sai·ə·nya (French) and a·ra·bə·nya (Arabic).

Do you speak (English/Amharic)?

ən·gli·zə·nya/a·ma·rə·nya	እንግሊዝኛ/አማርኛ
tə·chə·lal·leuh? (m)	ትችላለሁ?
tə·chi·yal·leush? (f)	ትችያለሽ?

᛭ᎾᎬᏘ

Does anyone here speak (English)?
   (ən·gli·zə·nya) yeu·mi·chəl al·leu?   (እንግሊዝኛ) የሚችል አለ?

Yes, I speak (a little).
   ow (tən·nish tən·nish)   አዎ (ትንሽ ትንሽ)
   ə·chə·lal·lā   እችላለሁ

I don't speak (Amharic).
   (a·ma·rə·nya) al·chəl·ləm   (አማርኛ) አልችልም

Do you understand?
   geub·bah? (m)   ገባህ?
   geub·bash? (f)   ገባሽ?

I understand/don't understand.
   geub·to·nyal/al·geu·ba·nyəm   ገብቶኛል/አልገባኝም

Please speak slowly.
   ə·ba·kəh ḳeuss bə·leuh   እባክህ ቀስ ብለህ
   teu·na·geur (m)   ተናገር
   ə·ba·kəsh ḳeuss bə·leush   እባክሽ ቀስ ብለሽ
   teu·na·geu·ri (f)   ተናገሪ

What does it mean in
Amharic/English?
   beu a·ma·rə·nya/   በ አማርኛ/እንግሊዝኛ
   ən·gli·zə·nya mən ma·leut nō?   ምን ማለት ነው?

Please write it down in
roman/Amharic script.
   ə·ba·kon beu (ən·gli·zə·nya/   እባክዎን በ (እንግሊዝኛ/
   a·ma·rə·nya) yi·ṣa·fu·liny   አማርኛ) ይፃፉልኝ

Is there a translator?
   as·teur·gwa·mi al·leu?   አስተርጓሚ አለ?

I want someone who speaks
(Oromo) and (English).
   (o·ro·mə·nya) na (ən·gli·zə·nya)   (አሮምኛ) ና (እንግሊዝኛ)
   yeu·mi·chəl sō ə·feul·lə·gal·lō   የሚችል ሰው እፈልጋለሁ

አገር
ማየት

እስከ+ዓ6ጭም

GETTI
AROU

52

ING AROUND

Whether making friends on the bus, enjoying breathtaking views from the comfort of a plane, or rolling along in a horse and cart, half the fun is in the gu·zo, 'journey'. However you travel, meul·kam gu·zo!, 'Enjoy your trip!'.

FINDING YOUR WAY የሚሄዱበትን ማወቅ

Start with a greeting or yi·ḵər·ta, 'Excuse me'. An optional extra is meun·geud ṭeuf·to·bə·nyal, 'I've lost my way'.

Where's the (nearest) ...?	(yeu·mi·ḵeur·bō) ... yeut nō?	(የሚቀርበው·) ... የት ነው·?
airport	ai·ro·plan ma·reu·fi·ya	አይሮፕላን ማረፊያ
bus stop	ow·to·bəs ma·ḵo·mi·ya	አውቶብስ ማቆሚያ
(city) bus station	(yeu keu·teu·ma) ow·to·bəs ṭa·bi·ya	(የ ከተማ አውቶብስ) ጣቢያ
city centre	meu·hal keu·teu·ma	መሃል ከተማ
highway	ow·ra go·da·na	አውራ ጎዳና
intercity bus station	yeu kəf·leu ha·geur ow·to·bəs ṭa·bi·ya	የ ክፍለ ሃገር አውቶብስ ጣቢያ
main road	wan·na meun·geud	ዋና መንገድ
road to (Goba)	weu·deu (go·ba) yeu·mi·weus·dō meun·geud	ወደ (ጎባ) የሚወስደው· መንገድ
... street/road	... meun·geud	... መንገድ
taxi stand	tak·si ma·ḵo·mi·ya	ታክሲ ማቆሚያ
ticket office	ti·ket meu·sheu·cha	ትኬት መሸጫ
train station	ba·bur ṭa·bi·ya	ባቡር ጣቢያ

Finding Your Way

Is this the way to (Entoto)?
  (ən·to·to) beuz·zi beu·kul nō? (እንጦጦ) በዚህ በኩል ነው?

Is it (very) near/far?
  (beu·ṭam) ḳərb/ruḳ nō? (በጣም) ቅርብ/ሩቅ ነው?

Can I walk there?
  beu·gər yas·ke·dal? በግር ያስኬዳል?

Please show me the way.
  ə·ba·kəh meun·geud
  a·sa·yeuny (m) እባክህ መንገድ አሳየኝ

  ə·ba·kəsh meun·geud
  a·sa·yiny (f) እባክሽ መንገድ አሳይኝ

Can you show me on the map?
  kar·tow lai
  ta·sa·yeu·nyal·leuh? (m) ካርታው ላይ ታሳየኛለህ?

  kar·tow lai
  ta·sa·yi·nyal·leush? (f) ካርታው ላይ ታሳይኛለሽ?

What town/road is this?
  yi·he keu·teu·ma/meun·geud
  mən yi·ba·lal? ይህ ከተማ/መንገድ
  ምን ይባላል?

Can I pass this way?
  beuz·zi beu·kul ma·leuf yi·cha·lal? በዚህ በኩል ማለፍ ይቻላል?

Is there another way?
  le·la meun·geud al·leu? ሌላ መንገድ አለ?

NO, I HAVEN'T FORGOTTEN THIS ...

If you want to answer 'no' to a question, remember to use the appropriate negative verb form:

There isn't./It's not there.	yeul·leum
It's not.	ai·deul·leum
I can't.	al·chel·ləm
I don't want	al·feul·lə·gəm
I don't have	yeu·leu·nyəm
OK! I haven't forgotten!	ə·shi! a·reu·sa·hum!

DIRECTIONS   አቅጣጫ

When describing locations, Ethiopians often use nearby landmarks such as hotels instead of street addresses. See The Sights, page 83, for additional words.

Go (straight ahead).
  (beu·ḳeu·ṭə·ta) hid/hij (m/f)   (በቀጥታ) ሂድ/ሂጅ

When you reach (the kiosk),
turn to the left/right.
  (ki·yosk) sə·tə·deurs weu·deu   (ኪዖስክ) ስትደርስ
  gra/ḳeuny ta·ṭeuf (m)   ወደ ግራ/ቀኝ ታጠፍ
  (ki·yosk) sə·tə·deursh weu·deu   (ኪዖስክ) ስትደርሽ
  gra/ḳeuny ta·ṭeu·fi (f)   ወደ ግራ/ቀኝ ታጠፊ

It's ...	... nō	... ነው‑
at the next (corner)	yeu·mi·ḳeu·ṭəl·lō (meu·ta·ṭeu·fi·ya)	የሚቀጥለው‑ (መታጠፊያ)
here/there	əz·zi/əz·zi·ya	እዚህ/እዚያ
in front/behind	fit leu fit/ beus·teu·jeur·ba	ፊት ለፊት/ በስተጀርባ
in this area	əz·zi a·ka·ba·bi	እዚ አካባቢ
inside/outside	wəsṭ/wəch	ውስጥ/ውጭ
near to ...	... a·ka·ba·bi	... አካባቢ
next to ...	... a·ṭeu·geub	... አጠገብ
on the left/right	beu gra/ḳeuny beu·kul	በ ግራ/ቀኝ በኩል
to the north	weu·deu seu·men	ወደ ሰሜን
to the south	weu·deu deu·bub	ወደ ደቡብ
to the east	weu·deu məs·raḳ	ወደ ምስራቅ
to the west	weu·deu mə'ə·rab	ወደ ምዕራብ

GETTING AROUND

GETTING THERE   የሚፈልጉበት ቦታ መድረስ

Is there a/an ...	weu·deu (jim·ma)	ወደ (ጅማ)
to (Jimma)?	... al·leu?	... አለ?
aeroplane	ai·ro·plan	አይሮፕላን
boat	jeul·ba	ጀልባ
bus	ow·to·bəs	አውቶብስ
car	meu·ki·na	መኪና
minibus	wə·yə·yət/mi·ni·bas	ውይይት/ ሚኒባስ
pick-up vehicle	pik·ap	ፒክ አፕ
train	ba·bur	ባቡር
truck	yeu chə·neut meu·ki·na	የጭነት መኪና

Let's go!	ən·hid!	እንሂድ!
Wait!	ḳoy/ḳo·yi! (m/f)	ቆይ/ቆዪ!

What time does the (next) ...
leave/arrive?
    (yeu·mi·ḳeu·ṭəl·lō) ... beu sənt   (የሚቀጥለው·) ... በስንት
    seu'at yi·neu·sal/yi·deur·sal?   ሰዓት ይነሳል/ይደርሳል?
Does it go to (Aksum)?
    weu·deu (ak·sum) yi·he·dal?   ወደ (አክሱም) ይሄዳል?
How do I get to (Harar)?
    weu·deu (ha·rar) beu·mən   ወደ (ሐረር)
    ə·he·dal·lō?   በምን እሄዳለሁ·?
How much to ...?
    weu·deu ... sənt nō?   ወደ ... ስንት ነው?
How long does it take?
    sənt gi·ze yi·weus·dal?   ስንት ጊዜ ይወስዳል?
I'll return.
    ə·meul·leu·sal·lō   እመለሳለሁ·
I'm in a hurry.
    cheu·ku·yal·lō   ቸኩያለሁ·
Are you ready?
    teu·zeu·gaj·teu·hal? (m)   ተዘጋጅተሃል?
    teu·zeu·gaj·teu·shal? (f)   ተዘጋጅተሻል?

TAXIS & GARIS

ታክሲ ና ጋሪ

In many towns, you can choose between a ga·ri (horse and cart)
or tak·si. Taxis often take up to five passengers. If the taxi isn't
going to your destination, the driver will tell you ai·he·dəm, 'I'm
not going there'. If you want a cab to yourself, ask for it 'on
contract'. Negotiate a price before leaving.

To ... please.
   ə·ba·kəh/ə·ba·kəsh   እባክህ/እባክሽ ወደ ...
   weu·deu ... (m/f)
I want it on contract.
   kon·trat meu·yaz ə·feul·lə·gal·lō ኮንትራት መያዝ እፈልጋለሁ
How much to ...?
   weu·deu ... sənt nō?   ወደ ... ስንት ነው?
I'll pay (two) birr.
   (hu·leutt) bərr ə·keuf·lal·lō   (ሁለት) ብር እከፍላለሁ
This is my stop. *(for shared taxi)*
   wo·raj al·leu   ወራጅ አለ
Please stop here.
   əz·zi a·kum   እዚህ አቁም

Special Instructions

ልዩ መመሪያዎች

Please wait for me.
   ə·ba·kəh ţeu·bə·ķeuny (m)   እባክህ ጠብቀኝ
This is not (Hawi) hotel.
   yi·he (ha·wi) ho·tel   ይህ (ሃዊ) ሆቴል
   ai·deul·leum   አይደለም
(Please) Slow down.
   (ə·ba·kəh) ķeuss bə·leuh   (እባክህ)
   nə·da (m)   ቀስ ብለህ ንዳ
(Please) Hurry.
   (ə·ba·kəh) to·lo beul (m)   (እባክህ) ቶሎ በል
Please don't hit the horse so much.
   ə·ba·kəh feu·reu·sun bə·zu   እባክህ ፈረሱን ብዙ
   a·təm·tow (m)   አትምታው

GETTING AROUND

BUYING TICKETS ትኬት መግዛት

Student discounts aren't normally given to foreigners, but children's tickets are available.

Where can I get tickets to ...?
weu·deu ... ti·ket yeut ወደ ... ትኬት የት ይገኛል?
yi·geu·nyal?

You buy it on the bus.
ow·to·bəs wəsṭ yig·zu አውቶብስ ውስጥ ይግዙ

There are no seats left.
ti·ket al·kwal ትኬት አልቋል

For (tomorrow morning).
leu (neu·geu ṭeu·wat) ለ (ነገ ጠዋት)

How much is a ticket to ...?
weu·deu ... ti·ket sənt nō? ወደ ... ትኬት ስንት ነው?

(Three) tickets to ...
weu·deu ... (sost) ti·ket ወደ ... (ሶስት) ትኬት

I want to reserve a ticket to ...
weu·deu ... ti·ket beu·kəd·mi·ya ወደ ... ትኬት በቅድሚያ
meug·zat ə·feul·lə·gal·lō መግዛት እፈልጋለሁ

I'd like to return my ticket.
ti·ke·ten meu·meu·leus ትኬቴን መመለስ
ə·feul·lə·gal·lō እፈልጋለሁ

IT'S A SEARCH!

It could happen on buses, trains, or as you enter buildings ... it's a fə·teu·sha, 'search'. Officials go through luggage to check for dangerous or contraband goods. If you're worried about having your dirty socks exposed to the world, rest assured the searches are usually short, painless and routine.

Please open your bag.
ə·ba·kon shan·ṭa·won እባክዎን ሻንጣዎን
yik·feu·tu·liny ይክፈቱልኝ

one-way ticket	meu·he·ja bə·cha ti·ket	መሄጃ ብቻ ትኬት
return ticket	deur·so meuls ti·ket	ደርሶ መልስ ትኬት
child's ticket	leu lə·joch ti·ket	ለልጆች ትኬት

AIR
የአየር መንገድ

It's a domestic/international flight.

   yeu (a·geur wəst; wəch)   የ (አገር ውስጥ/
   beu·reu·ra nō   ውጭ) በረራ ነው

My luggage hasn't arrived.

   shan·ṭa·ye al·deu·reu·seum   ሻንጣዬ አልደረሰም

bag/luggage	shan·ṭa/gwaz	ሻንጣ/ጓዝ
pass/permit	yeu yi·leuf feu·ḳad	የይለፍ ፈቃድ
luggage weight	yeu shan·ṭa kəb·deut	የሻንጣ ክብደት

Customs & Immigration
ግምሩክ ና ኢምግሬሽን

Customs and immigration staff generally speak English, and words like pas·port and vi·za are similar to English. More words and phrases can be found in Paperwork, page 88, and Specific Needs, page 213.

I have something/nothing to declare.

   yeu·mas·meu·zeu·gə·bō ə·ḳa   የማስመዝገበው ዕቃ
   al·leu/yeul·leum   አለ/የለም

Do I have to declare this?

   yi·hen mas·meuz·geub   ይሄን ማስመዝገብ
   al·leu·bəny?   አለብኝ?

This is all my luggage.

   shan·ṭa·ye yi·he hul·lu nō   ሻንጣዬ ይህ ሁሉ ነው

That's not mine.

   ya yeu·ne ai·deul·leum   ይ የኔ አይደለም

I didn't know I had to declare it.

   mas·meuz·geub ən·da·leu·bəny   ማስመዝገብ እንዳለብኝ
   a·la·weu·kum   አላወኩም

border	dən·beur	ድንበር
customs	gəm·ruk	ግምሩክ
customs form	yeu gəm·ruk ḳəṣ	የግምሩክ ቅፅ
export permit	wəč meu·la·ki·ya	ወጭ መላኪያ
	feu·ḳad	ፈቃድ
immigration office	i·mi·gre·shən bi·ro	ኢሚግሬሽን ቢሮ
receipt	deu·reu·seuny	ደረሰኝ

BUS, MINIVAN & PICK-UP TRUCK

አውቶብስ፤ ውይይት ና ፒክአፕ

Often packed with an interesting array of chickens, pots and household goods, Ethiopian inter-town buses are cheap, quite comfortable and a great way to meet people.

The word wə·yə·yət, 'conversation', is another name for mini-buses or pick-up vehicles that service urban and inter-town routes. Listen for the destination to be called, eg, *'Merkato, Merkato, Merkatooo!'*. The phrase and sō! means 'Only room for one more'. See Car, page 61, for hiring and Hitchhiking, page 65, for other pick-up truck terms.

Which (bus) goes to ...?
  yeu·tə·nyow (ow·to·bəs)   የትኛው (አውቶብስ)
  weu·deu ... yi·hed·al?   ወደ ... ይሄዳል?
Does it stop overnight?
  ma·ta yi·ḳo·mal?   ማታ ይቆማል?
Where does it stop?
  yeut yi·ḳo·mal?   የት ይቆማል?
Can you please tell me when we get to ...?
  ə·ba·kəh ... sə·nə·deurs
  nə·geu·reuny? (m)   እባክህ ... ስንደርስ ንገረኝ?
  ə·ba·kəsh ... sə·nə·deurs
  nə·geu·riny? (f)   እባክሽ ... ስንደርስ ንገሪኝ?

Do I have to catch another (minibus)?
   le·la (mi·ni·bas) meu·yaz
   al·leu·bəny?

ሌላ (ሚኒባስ)
መያዝ አለበኝ?

Where should I get off?
   yeut lu·reud?

የት ልወረድ?

This is my stop!
   wo·raj al·leu!

ወራጅ አለ!

Is someone sitting here?
   sō al·leu?   ሰው አለ?

(Please) Put my luggage on top
of the bus.
   (ə·ba·kəh) shan·ṭa·yen   (እባክህ) ሻንጣዬን
   sə·keul·ləl·ləny (m)   ስቀልልኝ

(Please) Get my luggage down.
   (ə·ba·kəh) shan·ṭa·yen   (እባክህ) ሻንጣዬን
   owr·dəl·ləny (m)   አውርድልኝ

TRAIN   ባቡር

Where's my seat?
   bo·ta·ye yeut nō?   በታየ የት ነው-?

Excuse me, this is my seat.
   yi·kər·ta bo·ta·ye nō   ይቅርታ በታየ ነው-

What station is this?
   yi·he ba·bur ṭa·bi·ya mən   ይህ ባቡር ጣቢያ ምን
   yi·ba·lal?   ይባላል?

TRAVEL HITCHES

The bus is leaving now!
   ow·to·bə·su teu·neus·twal!   አውቶብሱ ተነስቷል!

(My friend) isn't back!
   (gwa·deu·nya·ye) al·geu·bam/   (ጓደኛዬ) አልገባም!/
   al·geu·ba·chəm! (m/f)   አልገባችም!

(The train) is delayed.
   (ba·bu·ru) zeu·gi·twal   (ባቡሩ) ዘግይቷል

I feel sick.
   a·meu·meuny   አመመኝ

Please open the window.
   meus·ko·tun   መስኮቱን ይክፈቱልኝኛ
   yi·kə·feu·tu·liny

BOAT & CANOE   ጀልባ ና ታንኳ

Can you take me to ...?
    weu·deu ...
    tə·weus·deu·nyal·leuh? (m)   ወደ ... ትወስደኛለህ?

Which (monasteries) do you go to?
    weu·deu yeu·tə·nyow (deu·bər)   ወደ የትኛው· (ደብር)
    tə·he·dal·leuh? (m)   ትሄዳለህ?

What time does it return?
    beu sənt seu'at yi·meul·leu·sal?   በስንት ሰዓት ይመለሳል?

boat	jeul·ba	ጀልባ
canoe	tan·kwa	ታንኳ

See also Outdoor Sports on page 184.

CAR   መኪና

Research your route before leaving. Road and safety conditions vary, as does the availability of mechanical assistance, petrol and spare parts.

Where can   ... yeut meu·keu·ra·yeut   ... የት መከራየት
I rent a ...?   ə·cha·lal·lō?   እችላለሁ?
    4WD   for·wil draiv   ፎር ዊል ድራይቭ
    car   meu·ki·na   መኪና
    minivan   mi·ni·van   ሚኒቫን

I'd like a translator/driver.
    as·teur·gwa·mi/shu·fer   አስተርጓሚ/
    ə·feul·lə·gal·lō   ሹፌር እፈልጋለሁ·

How much is it for (a day/a week)?
    leu (and ḳeun/sam·mənt)   ለ አንድ (ቀን/ሳምንት)
    sənt nō?   ስንት ነው?

Does that include insurance?
    in·shu·rans·nəm   ኢንሹራንስንም
    yi·cheu·mə·ral?   ይጨምራል?

GETTING AROUND

How far is	yeu·mi·keu·teul·lō	የሚቀጥለው ...
the next ...?	... men ya·hel yi·re·kal?	ምን ያህል ይርቃል?
petrol station	neu·daj ma·deu·ya	ነዳጅ ማደያ
police station	po·lis ta·bi·ya	ፖሊስ ጣቢያ
town	keu·teu·ma	ከተማ

Can I park here?
    əz·zi ma·kom yi·cha·lal?   እዚህ ማቆም ይቻላል?
Please fill it up.
    ə·ba·keh ben·zin mul·la·liny   እባክህ ቤንዚን ሙላልኝ
(Six) litres of petrol please.
    ə·ba·keh (sə·dəst)   እባክህ (ስድስት)
    li·tər ben·zin   ሊትር ቤንዚን
Is it a dirt/asphalt road?
    meun·geu·du dən·ga·yam·ma/   መንገዱ ድንጋያማ/
    as·falt nō?   አስፋልት ነው·

TRAFFIC SIGNS

መንገድ ልቀቅ	**GIVE WAY**
መግባት ክልክል ነው·	**NO ENTRY**
ማቆም ክልክል ነው·	**NO PARKING**
ዝግታ	**SLOW**
ቁም	**STOP**

Road Safety   የመንገድ ላይ ጥንቃቄ

It's a good idea to ask local authorities about safety conditions before setting out.

Are there problems on the road?
    meun·geud lai chig·gər al·leu?   መንገድ ላይ ችግር አለ?
No problem. It's safe.
    chig·gər yeul·leum. seu·lam nō   ችግር የለም፡ ሰላም ነው·
There are problems. It's not safe.
    chig·gər al·leu. seu·lam yeul·leum   ችግር አለ፡ ሰላም የለም

You can't pass this way.
  beuz·zi beu·kul ma·leuf
  kəl·kəl nō

በዚህ በኩል ማለፍ
ክልክል ነው.

Is there another way?
  le·la meun·geud al·leu?

ሌላ መንገድ አለ?

Which road is better?
  yeu·tə·nyow meun·geud
  yi·sha·lal?

የትኛው መንገድ ይሻላል?

Do we need police protection?
  yeu po·lis ər·da·ta
  yas·feul·lə·geu·nal?

የፖሊስ እርዳታ
ያስፈልገናል?

Are there likely to be bandits?
  shəf·ta yi·no·ral?

ሽፍታ ይኖራል?

Car Problems

የመኪና ችግሮች

Where can I find a mechanic?
  meu·ka·nik yeut yi·geu·nyal?

መካኒክ የት ይገኛል?

There's something wrong with
this car.
  meu·ki·now teu·beu·lash·twal

መኪናው ተበላሽቷል

The battery's flat.
  bat·ryu al·ḳwal

ባትሪው አልቋል

The radiator's leaking.
  ra·di·ya·teu·ru ya·feu·sal

ራዲያተሩ ያፈሳል

I have a flat tyre.
  gom·ma·ye teun·fəss·wal

ጎማዬ ተንፍሷል

It's overheating.
  mo·teu·ru mo·ḳwal

ሞተሩ ሞቋል

I've lost my car keys.
  yeu·meu·ki·na·ye ḳulf
  ṭeuf·to·bə·nyal

የመኪናዬ ቁልፍ
ጠፍቶብኛል

I've run out of petrol.
  ben·zin al·ḳo·bə·nyal

ቤንዚን አልቆብኛል

Please check the ...
  ... ə·ba·ḳəh ə·yō (m)

... እባከህ እየው.

accelerator	ben·zin meus·cha	ቤንዚን መስጫ
battery	ba·tri	ባትሪ
brakes	fren	ፍሬን
clutch	fri·si·yon	ፍሪስዮን
drivers licence	meun·ja feu·kad	መንጃ ፈቃድ
engine	mo·teur	ሞተር
fan belt	chən·ge	ችንጌ
indicator	fre·cha	ፍሬቻ
lights	meu·brat	መብራት
number plate	tar·ga	ታርጋ
oil	yeu meu·ki·na zayt	የመኪና ዘይት
puncture (tyre)	yeu·teu·neu·feu·seu gom·ma	የተነፈስ ጎማ
radiator	ra·di·ya·teur	ራዲያተር
tyres	gom·ma	ጎማ
water	wu·ha	ውሃ
windscreen	yeu fit meus·ta·weut	የፊት መስታወት

BICYCLE

ብስክሌት

Where can I hire a bicycle?

bəs·klet yeut meu·keu·ra·yeut
ə·cha·lal·lō?

ብስክሌት የት
መከራየት እችላለሁ-?

Is it within cycling distance?

beu bəs·klet kərb nō?

በብስክሌት ቅርብ ነው-?

I have a flat tyre.

gom·ma·ye teun·feuss·wal

ጎማዬ ተንፍሷል

bike	bəs·klet	ብስክሌት
helmet	hel·met	ሄልሜት
inner tube	keu·leu·meu·da·ri·ya	ከለመዳሪያ
lights	meub·rat	መብራት
padlock	yeu kulf gan	የቁልፍ ጋን
pump	yeu gom·ma meun·fi·ya	የጎማ መንፊያ
puncture	keu·da·da/ yeu·teu·neu·feu·seu	ቀዳዳ/ የተነፈስ
tyre repairer	go·mis·ta	ጎሚስታ

HITCHHIKING   መኪና እየጠበቁ በነጻ መጓዝ

While hitchhiking is risky, it's sometimes the only way to reach places off the beaten track. Always hitch in pairs. For a lift, wave your hand or hold it out in a thumbs-up gesture. Don't forget pick-ups often function as buses or taxis, so you may have to pay for the ride.

Are you going to ...?
    weu·deu ... tə·he·dal·leuh? (m)   ወደ ... ትሄዳለህ?
Can I get a lift with you please?
    ə·ba·kəh a·sa·freuny? (m)   እባክህ አሳፍረኝ?
Please stop here.
    ə·ba·kəh əz·zi a·ḳum (m)   እባክህ እዚህ አቁም

TALKING ABOUT TRAVELLING   ስለ ጉዞዎ ማውራት

Your fellow passengers will love hearing about where you're going and where you've been. See First Encounters, page 40, for basics.

I'm a tourist.
    tu·rist/go·beu·nyi neuny   ቱሪስት/ጎብኚ ነኝ
Where are you heading?
    weu·det nō?   ወዴት ነው?
I'm returning to ... (tomorrow).
    (neu·geu) weu·deu ...   (ነገ) ወደ ...
    ə·meul·leu·sal·lō   እመለሳለሁ
(Today) I arrived from ...
    (za·re) keu ... geu·bow   (ዛሬ) ከ ... ገባሁ
I'll stay around here.
    əz·zi ə·seu·neu·bə·tal·lō   እዚህ እሰነብታለሁ
How long have you been travelling?
    gu·zo keu·jeu·meurk   ጉዞ ከጀመርክ
    sənt gi·ze ho·neuh? (m)   ስንት ጊዜ ሆነህ?
    gu·zo keu·jeu·meursh   ጉዞ ከጀመርሽ
    sənt gi·ze ho·neush? (f)   ስንት ጊዜ ሆነሽ?

I've been travelling for (two) months.
gu·zo keu·jeu·meur·ku
(hu·leutt) weur ho·neuny
ጉዞ ከጀመርኩ
(ሁለት) ወር ሆነኝ

Where have you been?
yeut a·geur neub·beurk/
neub·beursh? (m/f)
የት አገር ነበርክ/
ነበርሽ?

I've been to (Egypt).
(gəbṣ) neub·beur·ku
(ግብጽ) ነበርኩ

How was it?
ən·det neub·beur?
እንዴት ነበር?

It was ...   ... neub·beur   ... ነበር
  amazing   as·deu·na·ḳi   አስደናቂ
  beautiful   ḳon·jo   ቆንጆ
  boring   deu·ba·ri   ደባሪ
  expensive   wədd   ውድ
  historical   ta·ri·ka·wi   ታሪካዊ
  interesting   yeu·mi·yas·deu·sət   የሚያስደስት
  unique   lə·yu   ልዩ
  very crowded   sō beu·ṭam   ሰው በጣም
                   yeu·beu·za·beut   የበዛበት

They're good people.
ṭə·ru sō·woch na·chō
ጥሩ ሰዎች ናቸው

What's there to see in ...?
... mən yeu·mi·tai neu·geur al·leu?
... ምን የሚታይ ነገር አለ?

When's the best time to go there?
weu·deu·zi·ya leu meu·hed
ṭə·ru gi·ze meu·che nō?
ወደዚያ ለመሄድ ጥሩ
ጊዜ መቼ ነው?

Is it difficult for women travelling on
their own?
leu set tu·ris·toch
as·cheu·ga·ri nō?
ለሴት ቱሪስቶች
አስቸጋሪ ነው?

ማረፊያ ቦታ ACCOMMODATION

Ask for an extra tə·rass, 'pillow', and sink back into the al·ga, 'bed' – hotels are great places for practising your Amharic.

FINDING ACCOMMODATION   ማረፊያ ቦታ መፈለግ

See In the Country, page 161, for words and phrases on camping.

Where can I find a ...?	... yeut yi·geu·nyal?	... የት ይገኛል?
hotel	ho·tel	ሆቴል
good hotel	tə·ru ho·tel	ጥሩ ሆቴል
cheap hotel	rə·kash ho·tel	ርካሽ ሆቴል
hotel nearby	kərb ho·tel	ቅርብ ሆቴል
luxury hotel	təl·lək ho·tel	ትልቅ ሆቴል
place to sleep	ma·reu·fi·ya bo·ta	ማረፊያ ቦታ

Is it near the city centre/
bus station?
leu (meu·hal keu·teu·ma;   ለ (መሃል ከተማ/
ow·to·bəs ṭa·bi·ya) yi·keur·bal?   አውቶብስ ጣቢያ) ይቀርባል?

BOOKING AHEAD   በቅድሚያ ቦታ መያዝ

A 'single' often means a room with a double bed, and a 'double' a room with two beds. The Amharic word for bed, al·ga, is often used in place of kə·fəl, 'room'.

I'd like to book a room (please).
(ə·ba·kon) al·ga   (እባክዎን) አልጋ
meu·yaz ə·feul·lə·gal·lō   መያዝ እፈልጋለሁ

| double | hu·leutt | ሁለት |
| single | and | አንድ |

ACCOMMODATION

How much is it per (night/week)?
leu and (ma·ta/sam·mənt)
sənt nō?

ለ (አንድ ማታ/ሳምንት)
ስንት ነው?

Does the price include (breakfast)?
(ḳur·sə·nəm) yi·cheu·mə·ral?

(ቁርስንም) ይጨምራል?

I'll/We'll be arriving at ... o'clock.
beu ... seu'at ə·deur·sal·lō/
ən·deur·sal·leun

በ ... ሰዓት እደርሳለሁ/
እንደርሳለን

My name's ...
sə·me ... nō

ስሜ ... ነው

CHECKING IN አልጋ መያዝ

See Paperwork, page 89, for assistance with forms.

Are there any rooms available?
al·ga al·leu?

አልጋ አለ?

We're full.
al·ga yeul·leu·nəm

አልጋ የለንም

I want to see the room.
kəf·lun ma·yeut ə·feul·lə·gal·lō

ክፍሉን ማየት እፈልጋለሁ

Can I see a different room?
le·la kə·fəl ma·yeut ə·cha·lal·lō?

ሌላ ክፍል ማየት እችላለሁ?

I/We want a room with a ...	... yal·lō kə·fəl ə·feul·lə·gal·lō/ ən·feul·lə·gal·leun	... ያለው ክፍል እፈልጋለሁ/ እንፈልጋለን
bathroom	méu·ta·ṭeu·bi·ya bet	መታጠቢያ ቤት
TV	ti·vi	ቲ.ቪ.

How long will you be staying?
sənt gi·ze tə·ḳo·yal·leuh? (m)
sənt gi·ze tə·ḳo·yal·leush? (f)

ስንት ጊዜ ትቆያለህ?
ስንት ጊዜ ትቆያለሽ?

I'm staying for ...	... ə·ḳo·yal·lō	... እቆያለሁ
(one) night	(and) ma·ta	(አንድ) ማታ
(two) weeks	(hu·leutt) sam·mənt	(ሁለት) ሳምንት
(three) days	(sost) ḳeun	(ሶስት) ቀን

I leave (tomorrow morning).
   (neu·geu teu·wat) ə·he·dal·lō   (ነገ ጠዋት) እሂዳለሁ·
I don't know yet.
   geu·na a·la·weu·kum   ገና አላወኩም

BATHROOM BASICS

Showers in cheaper hotels could be either bal·di, 'bucket', or yeu bwam·bwa wu·ha, 'running water'. You can buy soft, 'toilet paper', from local kiosks. There's often a waste basket beside toilets, as putting paper down the drain can block plumbing.

Do you have hot water (all day)?
   muḳ wu·ha   ሙቅ ውሃ
   (ḳeu·nun mu·lu) al·leu?   (ቀኑን ሙሉ) አለ?
The plumbing is blocked.
   tu·bō teu·deuf·nwal   ቲቦው ተደፍኗል

Where's the ...?	... yeut nō?	... የት ነው·?
toilet	shənt bet	ሽንት ቤት
bathroom	meu·ta·teu·bi·ya bet	መታጠቢያ ቤት
shower	sha·weur	ሻወር
wash basin	yeu fit	የፊት
	meu·ta·teu·bi·ya	መታጠቢያ
soap	sa·mu·na	ሳሙና
towel	fo·ṭa	ፎጣ
water for bathing	meu·ta·teu·bi·ya wu·ha	መታጠቢያ ውሃ
water for laundry	yeu·ləbs ma·ṭeu·bi·ya wu·ha	የልብስ ማጠቢያ ውሃ
water for toilet	leu shənt bet wu·ha	ለሽንት ቤት ውሃ

ACCOMMODATION

REQUESTS & QUERIES   ጥያቄዎች

Please clean my room.
ə·ba·kəh kəf·len aṣ·da·ləny (m)   እባክህ ክፍሌን አጽዳልኝ
ə·ba·kəsh kəf·len aṣ·jə·ləny (f)   እባክሽ ክፍሌን አጽጂልኝ

Please change the bed sheets.
an·so·la ḳeu·yə·rə·ləny (m)   አንሶላ ቀይርልኝ
an·so·la ḳeu·yə·ri·ləny (f)   አንሶላ ቀይሪልኝ

Where's the dining room?
mə·gəb be·tu yeut nō?   ምግብ ቤቱ የት ነው?

Is there somewhere to wash clothes?
ləbs ma·ṭeu·bi·ya bo·ta al·leu?   ልብስ ማጠቢያ ቦታ አለ?

Is there a laundry service?
yeu·lown·deu·ri a·geul·glot al·leu?   የላውንደሪ አገልግሎት አለ?

Can I use the telephone?
səlk meu·ṭeu·ḳeum ə·cha·lal·lō?   ስልክ መጠቀም እችላለሁ?

I've locked myself out of my room.
ḳul·fen kəf·lu wəst reu·sow   ቁልፌን ከፍሉ ውስጥ እረሳሁ

Please wake me up at (one o'clock).
ə·ba·ḳəh (and seu'at)   እባክህ (አንድ ሰዓት)
lai ḳeuss·kəs·seuny (m)   ላይ ቀስቀሰኝ
ə·ba·ḳəsh (and seu'at)   እባክሽ (አንድ ሰዓት)
lai ḳeuss·kə·shiny (f)   ላይ ቀስቅሺኚ

Do you arrange tours to ...?
weu·deu ... gub·bə·nyit   ወደ ... ጉብኝት
ta·zeu·ga·jal·la·chu?   ታዘጋጃላችሁ?

Can you recommend a guide/
translator?
yeu·mə·tow·ḳut as·gob·nyi/   የምታወቁት አስጎብኚ/
as·teur·gwa·mi al·leu?   አስተርጓሚ አለ?

Is there a message for me?
leu·ne meu·lə·kət al·leu?   ለኔ መልእክት አለ?

Could I have a receipt please?
ə·ba·kon deu·reu·seuny?   እባክዎን ደረሰኝ?

I want another ...   le·la ... ə·feul·lə·gal·lō   ሌላ ... እፈልጋለሁ
blanket   bərd ləbs   ብርድ ልብስ
pillow   tə·rass   ትራስ

COMPLAINTS

ቅሬታ

I can't open/ close the ...	... meuk·feut/ meuz·gat al·chəl·ləm	... መክፈት/ መዝጋት አልቻልም
door	beu·run	በሩን
window	meus·ko·tun	መስኮቱን

The ... doesn't work.	... ai·seu·ram	... አይሰራም
electricity	e·le·tri·ku	ኤሌትሪኩ
light	meub·ra·tu	መብራቱ
tap	bwan·bwow	ባንቧው

This room's (very) ...	kəf·lu (beu·țam) ...	ክፍሉ (በጣም) ...
cold	yi·beur·dal	ይበርዳል
hot	yi·mo·ķal	ይሞቃል
noisy	a·ka·ba·bi	አካባቢ
	cha·cha·ta al·leu	ጫጫታ አለ
smelly	wəsţ meuţ·fo	ውስጥ መጥፎ
	shə·ta al·leu	ሽታ አለ

This room's not clean.

kəf·lu nə·ṣuh ai·deul·leum   ክፍሉ ንጹህ አይደለም

I want another room.

le·la kə·fəl ə·feul·lə·gal·lō   ሌላ ክፍል እፈልጋለሁ

ACCOMMODATION

OUT IN THE COLD

Some hotels lock the grounds before midnight. If you're planning a big night out drinking a·reu·ķi (a local liquor) with friends, it's worth checking with reception and the zeu·beu·nya, 'security guard', before you go out.

What time do you lock the grounds?

beu sənt seu'at beur   በስንት ሰዓት በር
tə·zeu·gal·la·chu?   ትዘጋላችሁ?

Can I get back in after (midnight)?

keu (ə·ku·leu le·lit) bo·hal·lạ   ከ (እኩለ ሌሊት) በኋላ
meum·meu·leus ə·cha·lal·lō?   መመለስ እችላለሁ?

I'm a hotel guest.

əz·zi ho·tel nō ya·reuf·kut   እዚህ ሆቴል ነው ያረፍኩት

ACCOMMODATION

CHECKING OUT

ከሆቴል መውጣት

I'd like to check out today/tomorrow.

kəf·lun za·re/neu·geu ə·leu·kal·lō

ክፍሉን ዛሬ/'ነገ እለቃለሁ

I want to pay the bill (now).

(a·hun) meuk·feul
ə·feul·lə·gal·lō

(አሁን) መክፈል
እፈልጋለሁ

I have already paid.

keu·fə·yal·lō

ከፍያለሁ

There's a mistake in the bill.

deu·reu·seu·nye lai
sə·hə·teut al·leu

ደረሰኜ ላይ ስህተት አለ

I'm returning in (one) week.

keu (and) sam·mənt bo·hal·la
ə·meul·leu·sal·lō

ከ (አንድ) ሳምንት በኋላ
እመለሳለሁ

Can I leave my luggage here?

shan·ṭa·yen əz·zi
mas·keu·meuṭ ə·chə·lal·lō?

ሻንጣዬን እዚህ
ማስቀመጥ እችላለሁ?

How much per day?

beu keun sənt nō?

በቀን ስንት ነው?

Please call me a taxi.

ə·ba·kəh tak·si ṭə·ral·ləny (m)
ə·ba·kəsh tak·si ṭə·ril·ləny (f)

እባክህ ታክሲ ጥራልኝ
እባክሽ ታክሲ ጥሪልኝ

SNOOZE TIME

I'm tired.

deu·ka·mo·nyal

ደክሞኛል

I'm/We're going to sleep now.

lə·teu·nya/lən·teu·nya nō

ልተኛ/ልንተኛ ነው።

I want to rest.

ma·reuf ə·feul·lə·gal·lō

ማረፍ እፈልጋለሁ

I dreamt a lot.

bə·zu həlm ai·yō

ብዙ ሕልም አየሁ

LONG-TERM ACCOMMODATION

የረጅም ጊዜ መኖሪያ

I'd like to rent a room near (the university).

   (yu·ni·veur·si·ti) a·ţeu·geub
and kə·fəl meu·keu·ra·yeut
ə·feul·lə·gal·lō

(ዩኒቨርስቲ) አጠገብ አንድ
ክፍል መከራየት እፈልጋለሁ·

Do you have a special rate for (one month)?

   leu (and weur) ķə·nash
al·la·chu?

ለ (አንድ ወር)
ቅናሽ አላችሁ?

I want to rent a house.

   bet meu·keu·ra·yeut
ə·feul·lə·gal·lō

ቤት መከራየት
እፈልጋለሁ·

How much per (month)?

   leu (weur) sənt nō?

ለ (ወር) ስንት ነው?

Useful Words

ጠቃሚ ቃሎች

candle	sha·ma	ሻማ
chair	weun·beur	ወንበር
cupboard	ķum sa·ţən	ቁም ሳጥን
curtains	meu·ga·reu·ja	መጋረጃ
iron	kow·ya	ካው·ያ
key	ķulf	ቁልፍ
light	meub·rat	መብራት
matches	kəb·rit	ክብሪት
mattress	fə·rash	ፍራሽ
mosquito net	yeu bim·bi meu·reub	የቢምቢ መረብ
padlock	meu·ķo·leu·fi·ya gan	መቆለፊያ ጋን
porter	teu·sheu·ka·mi	ተሸካሚ
power socket	soket	ሶኬት
safe	ya·deu·ra ə·ķa	ያደራ ዕቃ
	mas·ķeu·meu·cha sa·ţən	ማስቀመጫ ሳጥን
security guard	zeu·beu·nya	ዘበኛ
sheet	an·so·la	አንሶላ
worker	seu·ra·teu·nya	ሰራተኛ

ACCOMMODATION

STAYING WITH A FAMILY ከቤተሰብ ጋር መሰንበት

Staying with a family is a great way to experience local life. Ethiopian households have a regular stream of visitors, including go·reu·bet, 'neighbours', teu·keu·rai, 'lodgers', zeu·meud, 'relatives', giggling yeu seu·feur lə·joch, 'local children' and yeu bet seu·ra·teu·nya, 'domestic helpers'.

Please come and stay with us.
    ə·nya ga ə·reuf (m)   እኛ ጋ እረፍ
    ə·nya ga ə·reu·fi (f)   እኛ ጋ እረፊ
    ə·nya ga yi·reu·fu (pol)   እኛ ጋ ይረፉ
Where do you live?
    yeut tə·no·ral·leuh? (m)   የት ትኖራለህ?
    yeut tə·no·ri·yal·leush? (f) የት ትኖሪያለሽ?
I'm leaving today/tomorrow.
    za·re/neu·geu ə·he·dal·lō   ዛሬ/ነገ እሄዳለሁ
I'll visit you on my way back.
    sə·meul·leuss ə·meu·ṭal·lō ስመለስ እመጣለሁ
Thank you for your hospitality.
    a·meu·seu·gə·nal·lō sə·leu   አመሰግናለሁ ስለ
    meus·teun·gə·dō   መስተንግዶው

AROUND TOWN

Whether you're searching for a səlk, 'phone', or in dire need of a şi·meu·la·cheut, 'shave', you'll be a·ra·da, 'street wise', with some Amharic.

LOOKING FOR ...   ... መፈለግ

Is there a	əz·zi a·ka·ba·bi	እዚህ አካባቢ
... nearby?	... al·leu?	... አለ?
bank	bank	ባንክ
hotel	ho·tel	ሆቴል
market	geu·bi·ya	ገቢያ
restaurant	mə·gəb bet	ምግብ ቤት
post office	pos·ta bet	ፖስታ ቤት
toilet	shənt bet	ሽንት ቤት
travel agency	yeu gu·zo weu·kil	የጉዞ ወኪል

| Where is it? | yeut nō | የት ነው-? |

Where's the ...?	... yeut nō?	... የት ነው-?
city centre	meu·hal keu·teu·ma	መሃል ከተማ
... embassy	yeu ... em·bas·si	የ ... ኤምባሲ
tourist office	yeu tu·rist bi·ro	የቱሪስት ቢሮ
university	yu·ni·veurs·ti	ዩኒቨርስቲ

What time does it open/close?
beu sənt seu'at yi·keu·feu·tal/ | በስንት ሰዓት ይከፈታል/
yiz·zeu·gal? | ይዘጋል?

AT THE BANK   ባንክ

You'll find banks and international exchange facilities in major town centres, but credit card services are more limited. Don't forget to hold on to currency declaration/exchange forms and receipts in case you need to show them on departure.

Where can I change money?
  geun·zeub meu·ḳeu·yeu·ri·yow yeut nō?   ገንዘብ መቀየሪያው የት ነው?

I want to change money/ travellers cheques.
  geun·zeub/trav·leur chek meu·ḳeu·yeur ə·fetul·lə·gal·lō   ገንዘብ/ትራቨሎር ቼክ መቀየር እፈልጋለሁ

What's the rate?
  beu sənt wa·ga?   በስንት ዋጋ?

Can I use my credit card to withdraw money?
  geun·zeub beu kre·dit kard mow·ṭat ə·chə·lal·lō?   ገንዘብ በክሬዲት ካርድ ማውጣት እችላለሁ?

I'd like to get some money transferred to me from ...
  geun·zeub keu ... ən·diz·za·weur·liny ə·feul·lə·gal·lō   ገንዘብ ከ ... እንዲዛወርልኝ እፈልጋለሁ

How long will it take?
  sənt gi·ze yi·weus·dal?   ስንት ጊዜ ይወስዳል?

I'm expecting a money transfer from ...
  geun·zeub keu ... ə·ṭeu·bə·ḳal·lō   ገንዘብ ከ ... እጠብቃለሁ

Has my money transfer from ... arrived?
  geun·zeub keu ... meu·to·lə·nyal?   ገንዘብ ከ ... መጥልኛል?

coins	san·tim	ሳንቲም
currency	yeu geun·zeub ai·neut	የገንዘብ ዓይነት
exchange bureau	yeu geun·zeub meu·ḳeu·yeu·ri·ya bi·ro	የገንዘብ መቀየሪያ ቢሮ

AROUND TOWN

AT THE POST OFFICE   ፖስታ ቤት

Postal staff read and write English. Words such as 'postcard',
'telegram' and 'telex' retain their English names. See Stationery &
Publications, page 133, for other useful words.

Where can I post this?
yeut las·geu·bow?   የት ላስገባው?

I'd like to send a ...	... meu·lak ə·feul·lə·gal·lō	... መላክ እፈልጋለሁ
gift	sə·ţo·ta	ስጦታ
letter	deub·dab·be	ደብዳቤ
package	ţə·ķəl	ጥቅል

How much is it to ...?
weu·deu ... sənt nō?   ወደ ... ስንት ነው?
(Three) stamps please.
ə·ba·kon (sost) tem·bər   እባክዎን (ሶስት) ቴምብር
A (three)-birr stamp.
ba·leu (sost) bərr tem·bər   ባለ (ሶስት) ብር ቴምብር
Am I allowed to send (this)?
(yi·hen) meu·lak ə·cha·lal·lō?   (ይሄን) መላክ እችላለሁ?
Could I borrow a pen please?
əs·krip·to an·de lə·was?   እስክሪፕቶ አንዴ ልዋስ?
Where's the (poste restante) section?
(post res·tant) al·leu?   (ፖስት ሬስታንቴ) አለ?
Do you have mail for me?
My name's ...
leu·ne deub·dab·be al·leu?   ለኔ ደብዳቤ አለ?
sə·me ... nō   ስሜ ... ነው

airmail	ya·yeur meul'əkt	የአየር መልእክት
box	sa·ţən	ሳጥን
envelope	pos·ta	ፖስታ
express post/EMS	as·cheu·kwai/i·em·es	አስቸኳይ/ኢኤምኤስ
mailbox	yeu pos·ta sa·ţən	የፖስታ ሳጥን
registered post	ya·deu·ra deub·dab·be	ያደራ ደብዳቤ
stamp	tem·bər	ቴምብር
surface mail	yeu·yeubs meul'əkt	የየብስ መልእክት

AROUND TOWN

ADDRESSES   አድራሻ

What's the address?
ad·ra·show yeut nō?   አድራሻው የት ነው-?

Is that the postal/residential
address?
yeu (pos·ta; meu·no·ri·ya bet)   የ (ፖስታ/መኖሪያ ቤት)
ad·ra·sha nō?   አድራሻ ነው-?

Use roman script for writing postal addresses. Many Ethiopian
postal addresses are PO boxes, but you'll sometimes see words
like *woreda* (wo·reu·da, 'region'), *kebele* (ḳeu·beu·leu, 'local
administration') and a suburb name.

    Lakiya Tasew
    PO Box: 6122
    Woreda 17, Kebele 25, Gerj
    Addis Ababa, Ethiopia

TELECOMMUNICATIONS   ስልክ ቤት

You can make long-distance/international calls and send/receive
faxes from a *səlk bet*, where telecommunications staff generally
speak English. You can also use public phones and local shops for
local/national calls.

Is there a	əz·zi a·ka·ba·bi	እዚህ አካባቢ
... nearby?	... al·leu?	... አለ?
fax service	yeu faks	የፋክስ
	a·geul·glot	አገልግሎት
public telephone	yeu həzb səlk	የሕዝብ ስልክ
shop with	səlk yal·lō suḳ	ስልክ ያለው ሱቅ
a telephone		
telecommunications	səlk bet	ስልክ ቤት
building		

I want to make a local/international call.
(a·geur wəsṭ; wəch a·geur) səlk   (አገር ውስጥ/ውጭ አገር)
meu·deu·weul ə·feul·lə·gal·lō   ስልክ መደወል እፈልጋለሁ-

ITEM CHARGED

LIB#: *1000214393*
GRP: STUDENT

Due: 1/22/2013 08:00 PM

Title: Ethiopian Amharic phrasebook /
Tilahun Kebede
Auth: Kebede, Tilahun
Call #: 492.8 KEBEDE 2002
Enum
Chron
Copy: 1
Item *0042988V*

I want to send/receive a fax.
   faks meu·lak/meu·ḳeu·beul ፋክስ መላክ/መቀበል
   ə·feul·lə·gal·lō እፈልጋለሁ

I want to call ...
   weu·deu ... meu·deu·weul ወደ ... መደወል
   ə·feul·lə·gal·lō እፈልጋለሁ

The number is ...
   ḳu·ṭru ... nō ቁጥሩ ... ነው

I want to reverse the charges/
make a collect call.
   teu·zeu·wa·wa·ri ə·feul·lə·gal·lō ተዘዋዋሪ እፈልጋለሁ

How much does it cost
for ... minute(s)?
   leu ... deu·ḳi·ḳa sənt nō? ለ ... ደቂቃ ስንት ነው?

How much is it for ... page(s)?
   leu ... geuṣ sənt nō? ለ ... ገጽ ስንት ነው?

I want to speak to the operator.
   o·pə·re·teur ə·feul·lə·gal·lō ኦፐሬተር እፈልጋለሁ

The number for ... (please).
   (ə·ba·kon) yeu ... ḳu·ṭər (እባክዎን) የ ... ቁጥር

I'd like to speak to ...
   ... ma·neu·ga·geur ... ማነጋገር እፈልጋለሁ
   ə·feul·lə·gal·lō

The number is ...
   ḳu·ṭru ... nō ቁጥሩ ... ነው

It's engaged.
   tay·zwal ተይዟል

Nobody answered.
   ma·nəm a·ya·neu·sa·wəm ማንም አያነሳውም

I've been cut off.
   meus·meur teu·ḳwar·ṭwal መስመር ተቋርጧል

deposit	meu·ya·zha	መያዣ
mobile phone	mo·bail fon	ሞባይል ፎን
phone book	yeu səlk mow·cha	የስልክ ማውጫ
urgent	as·cheu·kwai	አስቸኳይ

Making a Call   ስልክ መደወል

When using the polite form, use a·to, 'Mr', or way·zeu·ro, 'Mrs', before a person's first name.

Hello, is ... there?
  al·lo ... al·leu/   አሎ ... አለ/አለች/አሉ?
  al·leuch/al·lu? (m/f/pol)
Who's calling?
  man lə·beul?   ማን ልበል?
It's ... speaking.
  ... ə·ba·lal·lō   ... እባላለሁ
One moment (please).
  and gi·ze (ə·ba·kon)   አንድ ጊዜ (እባክዎን)
He's/She's gone out.
  weu·ṭa bə·leu·wal   ወጣ ብለዋል

ሰላም ደህና ነህ?

ደህና ነኝ

He's/She's not here.
  yeul·leum/yeul·leu·chəm   የለም/የለችም
Can I leave a message?
  meul'əkt meu·tō ə·chə·lal·lō?   መልእክት መተው እችላለሁ?
Please tell him/her ... called.
  ... deu·wəl·lo neub·beur   ... ደውሎ ነበር ይበሉልኝ
  yi·beu·lu·ləny
My number is ...
  səlk ku·ṭre ... nō   ስልክ ቁጥሬ ... ነው
I'll call back later.
  bo·hal·la ə·deu·wə·lal·lō   ቢኋላ እደውላለሁ
What time should I call?
  beu sənt seu'at lə·deu·wəl?   በስንት ሰዓት ልደውል?

COMPUTING SERVICES

የኮምፒዩተር
አገልግሎት

Terms like kom·pyu·teur and mo·deum are easy to recognise, being so similar to English. There are few Internet services outside Addis. See Stationery & Publications, page 133, and Business, page 215, for document services.

Is there an internet café?
yeu in·teur·net a·geul·glot al·leu?

የኢንተርኔት አገልግሎት አለ?

Is there a place to send email?
i·mel meu·la·ki·ya bo·ta al·leu?

ኢሜል መላኪያ ቦታ አለ?

I'd like to receive/send email.
i·mel meu·ķeu·beul/meu·lak ə·feul·lə·gal·lō

ኢሜል መቀበል/
መላክ እፈልጋለሁ

How much for (10 minutes)?
leu (a·sər deu·ķi·ķa) sənt nō?

ለ (አስር ደቂቃ) ስንት ነው?

SIGHTSEEING

አገር ማየት

Castles, historical ruins and island monasteries are amongst Ethiopia's key attractions. Ethiopians are happy to share their unique heritage with others, but ask people before taking their photograph or before wandering into areas that may be off limits. There are restrictions on photographing certain sights.

Where's the tourist office?
yeu tu·rist bi·rō yeut nō?

የቱሪስት ቢሮው የት ነው?

Do you have a map?
kar·ta al·leuh/al·leush? (m/f)

ካርታ አለህ/አለሽ?

What are the main attractions?
meu·ta·yet ya·leu·ba·chō bo·ta·woch yeu·tə·nyo·chu na·chō?

መታየት ያለባቸው
ቦታዎች የትኞቹ ናቸው?

How much is the entry fee?
meug·bi·ya sənt nō?

መግቢያ ስንት ነው?

Is there a discount for (children)?
   leu (lə·joch) kə·nash al·leu?   ለ (ልጆች) ቅናሽ አለ?
Am I allowed to take
photographs here?
   əz·zi fo·to man·sat yi·cha·lal?   እዚህ ፎቶ ማንሳት ይቻላል?
How much is it to take
a video/picture?
   vi·di·yo/fo·to leu man·sat   ቪድዮ/ፎቶ ለማንሳት
   sənt nō?   ስንት ነው?
Can I take your photograph?
   fo·to lan·sah? (m)   ፎቶ ላንሳህ?
   fo·to lan·sash? (f)   ፎቶ ላንሳሽ?
   fo·to lan·sa·chu? (pl)   ፎቶ ላንሳችሁ?
Can you please take my
photograph?
   ə·ba·kəh fo·to an·sany? (m)   እባክህ ፎቶ አንሳኝ
   ə·ba·kəsh fo·to an·shiny? (f)   እባክሽ ፎቶ አንሽኚ
I'll send you the photo.
   fo·to·wən ə·lə·kal·lō   ፎቶውን አልካለሁ

The Sights   የሚነበቡ ቦታዎች

Can you show me ...?
   ... li·ya·sa·yuny yi·chi·lal·lu?   ... ሊያሳዩኝ ይችላሉ?
Can I have a look at ...?
   ... ma·yeut yi·cha·lal?   ... ማየት ይቻላል?
Can I touch/hold it?
   meun·kat/meu·yaz yi·cha·lal?   መንካት/መያዝ ይቻላል?
Can I see inside?
   wəst ma·yeut yi·cha·lal?   ውስጥ ማየት ይቻላል?
Excuse me, what's this/that?
   yi·kər·ta, yi·he/ya   ይቅርታ ይህ/ያ
   mən·dən nō?   ምንድን ነው?
What's this/that called?
   yeuz·zi/yeuz·za səm   የዚህ/የዛ
   mən·dən nō?   ስም ምንድን ነው?

building	hən·ṣa/foḳ	ሕንፃ/ፎቅ
church	be·teu krəs·ti·yan	ቤተ ክርስቲያን
court (of law)	fərd bet	ፍርድ ቤት
hall	a·da·rash	አዳራሽ
hot spring baths	fəl wu·ha	ፍል ውሃ
library	be·teu meu·ṣa·haf	ቤተ መጻሐፍ
market area	meur·ka·to/a·ra·da	መርካቶ/አራዳ
monastery	deu·bər	ደብር
museum	be·teu meu·zeu·kər	ቤት መዘከር
national (theatre)	bə·he·ra·wi (ti·ya·tər)	ብሔራዊ (ትያትር)
parliament	par·la·ma; mə·kər bet	ፓርላማ/ምክር ቤት
park/gardens	meu·na·feu·sha	መናፈሻ
swimming pool	meu·wa·nya bo·ta	መዋኛ ቦታ
sports	sport	ስፖርት
square	ad·deu·ba·bai	አደባባይ
stadium	sta·di·yeum	ስታዲየም
statue/monument	ha·wəlt	ሐውልት
tourist office	yeu tu·rist bi·ro	የቱሪስት ቢሮ
university	yu·ni·veurs·ti	ዩኒቨርስቲ
wall	gəd·gəd·da	ግድግዳ
zoo	zu	ዙ

AROUND TOWN

NAME DROPPING

Emperor Menelik	a·ṣe mi·ni·lik	አጼ ሚኒሊክ
Lion of Judah	yeu yi·hu·da	የይሁዳ
	an·beus·sa	አንበሳ
Lucy	dənḳ·neush	ድንቅነሽ
(the hominoid)		
Mohammed	grany	ግራኝ ሃመድ
the Left-Handed	meu·ham·meud	
Prince Taferi	ras teu·feu·ri	ራስ ተፈሪ
Queen of Sheba	nə·gəst sa·ba	ንግስት ሳባ

TALKING HISTORY

How old is it?		
əd·ma·yō sənt nō?		እድሜው· ስንት· ነው·?
What period is it from?		
keu·yeu·tə·nyow		ከየትኛው· ክፍል
kə·fə·leu zeu·meun nō?		ዘመን· ነው·?

the Stone Age	yeu dən·gai zeu·meun	የድንጋይ ዘመን
civilization	sə·lə·ta·ne	ስልጣኔ
(Aksum)	yeu (ak·sum)	የ(አክሱም)
(Zagwe)	(za·gō) zeu·meu·neu	(ዛግዌ·)
dynasty	meun·gəst	ዘመነ መንግስት
(20th) century	ha·ya·nyow kəf·leu	ሃያኛው
	zeu·meun	ክፍለ ዘመን
time of Italian	beu tal·yan	በጣልያን
occupation	weu·reu·ra gi·ze	ወረራ ጊዜ

ancestor	kəd·meu a·yat	ቅድመ አያት
ancient buildings	tən·ta·wi gəmb	ጥንታዊ ግምብ
antique	tən·ta·wi	ጥንታዊ
Aksum monoliths	yeu ak·sum ha·wəl·toch	የአክሱም ሐወልቶች
castle	gəmb	ግምብ
emperor	nə·gu·seu neu·geust	ንጉስ ነገስት
excavation	ku·feu·ra	ቁፈራ
feudalism	ba·la·ba·ta·wi a·geu·zaz	ባላባታዊ አገዛዝ
fortress	təl·lək mə·shəg	ትልቅ ምሽግ
fossil/remains	a·səm/kə·rit	አፅም/ቅሪት
fragments	sə·bər·ba·ri	ስብርባሪ
grave/tomb	meu·ka·bər	መቃብር
history	ta·rik	ታሪክ
monarchy	nə·gu·sa·wi a·geu·zaz	ንጉሳዊ አገዛዝ
palace	be·teu meun·gəst	ቤተ መንግስት
patriot	ar·beu·nya	አርበኛ
revolution	a·bə·yot	አቦት
rock hewn	keu a·leut yeu·teu·seu·ru	ከአለት የተሰሩ
churches	be·teu krəs·ti·ya·noch	ቤተ ክርስቲያኖች
ruins	fə·rash	ፍራሽ
stele	ha·wəlt	ሐወልት
tools	meu·sa·ri·ya·woch	መሳሪያዎች

AROUND TOWN

TOURS, GUIDES & TRANSLATORS

ጉብኝቶች፤ አስጎብኚዎችና
አስተርጓሚዎች

Are there regular tours to ...?
  weu·deu ... kwa·mi yeu·ho·nu
  gu·bə·nyi·toch al·lu?

ወደ ... ቋሚ የሆኑ
ጉብኝቶች አሉ?

Is there a guide/translator available?
  as·gob·nyi/as·teur·gwa·mi
  al·leu? (m)

አስጎብኚ /አስተርጓሚ
አለ?

How much for (one hour/
two hours)?
  leu (and seu'at/hu·leutt seu'at)
  sənt nō?

ለ (አንድ ሰዓት/
ሁለት ሰዓት) ስንት ነው?

How long is the tour?
  gu·bə·nyi·tu sənt gi·ze
  yi·weus·dal?

ጉብኝቱ ስንት
ጊዜ ይወስዳል?

Does the tour go to ...?
  gu·bə·nyi·tu weu·deu ...
  yi·hed·al?

ጉብኝቱ ወደ ...
ይሄዳል?

I've lost my group.
  a·breu·wəny yeu·meu·ṭut
  sō·woch ṭeu·fu·bəny

አብረውኝ የመጡት
ሰዎች ጠፉብኝ

ON THE STREET

መንገድ ላይ

Ethiopian streets attract a fascinating crowd of street vendors,
beggars, shoe cleaners and roaming orators. Many have migrated
from country areas in search of work or more stability. Never refuse
a beggar – simply say əg·zər yis·ṭəh/yis·ṭəsh/yis·ṭə·ləny (m/f/pol),
'May God give you', if you don't want to give money.

I want it.
  ə·feul·lə·gal·lō

እፈልጋለሁ

I don't want it.
  al·feul·lə·gəm

አልፈልግም

Sorry, I don't have any change.
  az·nal·lō zər·zər yeul·leu·nyəm

አዝናለው ዝርዝር የለኝም

AROUND TOWN

beggar	məs·kin	ምስኪን
city dweller	keu·teu·me	ከተሜ
footpath	yeu·gər meun·geud	የግር መንገድ
hawkers	suk beu·deu·reu·te	ሱቅ በደረቴ
newspaper seller	ga·ze·ṭa shaçh	ጋዜጣ ሻጭ
shoe shiner	lis·tro	ሊስትሮ
snack seller	ḳo·lo shaçh	ቆሎ ሻጭ
street	meun·geud	መንገድ
street children	yeu go·da·na teu·da·da·ri	የጎዳና ተዳዳሪ
	hə·ṣa·nat	ሕፃናት
street lamp	yeu meun·geud meub·rat	የመንገድ መብራት
street stall	gul·lət	ጉልት
traffic lights	yeu tra·fik meub·rat	የትራፊክ መብራት

AROUND TOWN

THEY MAY SAY ...

mən ho·neu?	What's happening?
əbd!	Crazy!
ba·leu·ge!	You're rude!
and gi·ze!	Just a minute!
le·ba!	Thief!
ḳoy!/ḳo·yi! (m/f)	Wait!
na!/nay! (m/f)	Come!
hid!/hij!/hi·du! (m/f/pl)	Go!

UNWANTED ATTENTION   ሰው-ን ማስቸገር

Often the most difficult part of travelling in Ethiopia is dealing with unwanted attention, ranging from an occasional 'You! You! You!' to a steady crescendo of feu·reunj! feu·reunj!, 'Foreigner!/ White person!', from groups of giggling children. Try to remember that no malice is intended – it's usually a sign of curiosity or excitement. Saying hid! (m) or hij! (f), 'Go away!', or zəm·beul!, 'Shut up!', often only makes things worse. The best approach is to either ignore it, or to use some friendly Amharic phrases like sə·ma·chu man nō?, 'What are your names?'. See also Talking with Children, page 105.

PAPERWORK   የሚሞሉ ፎርሞች

While officials generally speak English, and official forms show English translations, the following may be useful:

I'd like ...   ... ə·feul·lə·gal·lō   ... እፈልጋለሁ
   to extend   vi·za·yen   ቪዛዬን ማሳደስ
   my visa   ma·sa·deuss
   to visit the   (bə·he·ra·wi park)   (ብሔራዊ ፓርክ)
   (National Park)   meu·go·bə·nyeut   መጉብኘት

Is a/an ... required?   ... yas·feul·lə·gal?   ... ያስፈልጋል?
I have a/an ...   ... al·leuny   ... አለኝ
   entry permit   meug·bi·ya feu·ḳad   መግቢያ ፈቃድ
   form   ḳəṣ (form)   ቅፅ (ፎርም)
   letter of   yeu feu·ḳad   የፈቃድ ደብዳቤ
   permission   deub·dab·be
   pass/permit   yeu yi·leuf feu·ḳad   የይለፍ ፈቃድ
   police report   yeu po·lis ri·port   የፖሊስ ሪፖርት
   proof of   yeu meu·ta·weu·ḳi·ya   የመታወቂያ
   identity   weu·reu·ḳeut   ወረቀት
   receipt   deur·reu·seuny   ደረሰኝ

Forms

ፎርሞች

name	səm	ስም
address	a·dra·sha	አድራሻ
age	əd·me	እድሜ
sex	şo·ta	ፆታ
nationality	ze·gə·neut	ዜግነት
religion	hai·ma·not	ሃይማኖት
occupation	sə·ra	ስራ
date of arrival	yeu geu·bu·beut ķeun	የገቡበት ቀን
date of birth	yeu tu·ləd ķeun	የትውልድ ቀን
date of departure	yeu weu·ţu·beut ķeun	የወጡበት ቀን
country of birth	yeu tu·ləd a·geur	የትውልድ አገር
domicile	meu·no·ri·ya	መኖሪያ
duration of stay	yeu mi·ķo·yu·beut gi·zay	የሚቆዩበት ጊዜ
passport number	yeu pas·port ķu·ţər	የፓስፖርት ቁጥር
valid until	yeu·mi·şeu·na·beut gi·zay	የሚፀናበት ጊዜ
purpose of stay	yeu mi·ķo·yu·beut mək·ni·yat	የሚቆዩበት ምክኒያት

SIGNS

ማስታወቂያ	INFORMATION
እንግዳ መቀበያ	RECEPTION
ክፍት ነው	OPEN
ተዘግቷል	CLOSED
መግቢያ	ENTRANCE
መውጫ	EXIT
መግባት ክልክል ነው	ENTRY PROHIBITED
ዝግ ነው	NO ENTRY
ማቆም ክልክል ነው	NO PARKING
ፎቶ ማንሳት ክልክል ነው	NO PHOTOGRAPHS
ማጨስ ክልክል ነው	NO SMOKING
ሽንት ቤት	TOILETS
የወንዶች	MALE
የሴቶች	FEMALE
አደገኛ	DANGER
ተጠንቀቅ	CAUTION

AROUND TOWN

HAIR STYLES

Elaborate ornaments and manicuring objects often support traditional hair designs. In some areas in the south, wooden headrests instead of pillows are used to keep clay caps, feathers or jewellery in place. Butter or fat is often used to moisturise dry hair. See also Souvenirs, page 128.

hair braids (traditional afro)	shu·ru·ba	ሹሩባ
hair braids (Tigre style, tight to head, then frizzed out)	ḳun·dal·la	ቀንዳላ
shaved head with tuft (on children)	ḳun·cho	ቀንጮ
wooden comb	mi·do	ሚዶ

ለመዝናናት መውጣት

Ethiopia enjoys a vibrant night-time bar and music scene. While az·ma·ri bet, 'music clubs', bubble with wine and song, local bun·na bet, 'coffee houses', serve up drinks, conversation and casual entertainment. In the city, you'll also find nightclubs and theatres.

WHERE TO GO

ወዴት ነው።

What's there to do in the evenings here?
mə·shət lai mən ai·neut meuz·na·nya bo·ta al·leu?

ምሽት ላይ ምን አይነት መዝናኛ ቦታ አለ?

I'm/We're thinking of going to ...
weu·deu ... meu·hed feul·lə·ge/ feul·lə·geun neub·beur

ወደ ... መሄድ ፈልጌ/ፈልገን ነበር

Where can I find a good ...?	tə·ru ... yeut yi·geu·nyal?	ጥሩ ... የት ይገኛል?
bar/coffee house	bun·na bet	ቡና ቤት
cinema	si·ni·ma bet	ሲኒማ ቤት
nightclub	dans bet	ዳንስ ቤት
restaurant	mə·gəb bet	ምግብ ቤት
theatre	ti·ya·tər bet	ትያትር ቤት
traditional music venue	az·ma·ri bet	አዝማሪ ቤት

Where can I see a good film/play?
tə·ru si·ni·ma/dra·ma yeut yi·ta·yal?

ጥሩ ሲኒማ/ድራማ የት ይታያል?

What's showing?
mən yi·ta·yal?

ምን ይታያል?

Is it in English/Amharic?
beu ən·gli·zə·nya/ a·ma·rə·nya nō?

በ እንግሊዝኛ/ አማርኛ ነው?

Are there any tickets for ...?
leu ... ti·ket al·leu?   ለ ... ትኬት አለ?

I want (three) tickets.
(sost) ti·ket ə·feul·lə·gal·lō   (ሶስት) ትኬት እፈልጋለሁ

What's the entry fee/cover charge?
meug·bi·ya sənt nō?   መግቢያ ስንት ነው?

How much is a (first-class ticket)?
(an·deu·nya ma·ə·reug)   (አንደኛ ማዕረግ)
sənt nō?   ስንት ነው?

We're sold out.
ti·ket al·kwal   ትኬት አልቋል

ሰላም ደህና ነህ?

ደህና ነኝ

INVITATIONS   ግብዣ

It's common to 'shout' someone a few drinks or a meal when
you invite them out. A common phrase is yeu·ne gəb·zha nō!,
'My treat!'.

Let's go for (a) ...	leu ... ən·hid	ለ ... እንሂድ
coffee	bun·na	ቡና
dance	dans	ዳንስ
dinner	ə·rat	እራት
drink (beer)	bi·ra	ቢራ

We're having a party (tonight).
(za·re ma·ta) par·ti al·leun   (ዛሬ ማታ) ፓርቲ አለን

Please come!
ə·ba·kəh na! (m)   እባክህ ና!
ə·ba·kəsh nay! (f)   እባክሽ ነይ!
ə·ba·ka·chu nu! (pl)   እባካችሁ ኑ!

We'll have a great time!
tə·ru gi·ze ə·na·sa·lə·fal·leun!   ጥሩ ጊዜ እናሳልፋለን!

NIGHTCLUBS & BARS

ዳንስ ቤትና መጠጥ ቤት

What would you like?
   mən lə·ta·zeuz?

ምን ልታዘዝ?

How about a game of (billiards)?
   (bil·yard) ə·nə·cha·weut?

(ቢልያርድ) እንጫወት?

Are there any good (nightclubs) around here?
   əz·zi a·ka·ba·bi tə·ru
   (dans bet) al·leu?

እዚህ አካባቢ ጥሩ
(ዳንስ ቤት) አለ?

What should I wear?
   mən ləl·beus?

ምን ልልበስ?

What kind of music do they have?
   mən ai·neut mu·zi·ka al·la·chō?

ምን አይነት መዚቃ አላቸው?

Do you want to dance?
   meu·da·neus tə·feul·lə·gal·leuh/
   tə·feul·lə·gi·yal·leush? (m/f)

መደነስ ትፈልጋለህ/
ትፈልጊያለሽ?

What type of music do you prefer?
   mən ai·neut mu·zi·ka
   tə·weud·dal·leuh/
   tə·wa·ja·leush? (m/f)

ምን አይነት መዚቃ
ትወዳለህ/ትወጃለሽ?

I really like (reggae).
   (re·ge) beu·tam ə·weud·dal·lō

(ሬጌ) በጣም እወዳለሁ

This place is great!
   kon·jo bet!

ቆንጆ ቤት!

The music here isn't very good.
   mu·zi·kow tə·ru ai·deu·leum

መዚቃው ጥሩ አይደለም

Shall we go somewhere else?
   le·la bo·ta ən·hid?

ሌላ ቦታ እንሂድ?

THEY MAY SAY ...

ən·det nō?	How is it?
a·rif nō!	It's cool!
keul·den nō	Just joking!
⟨…⟩·jo!	My baby!
a·bo at·deub·reun/ at·deub·rin! (m/f)	Don't be boring!

GOING OUT

DATING & ROMANCE   ቀጠሮ መያያዝና ፍቅር

People often use the English terms for boyfriend/girlfriend.
Usually, yeu weund gwa·deu·nya (lit: boy friend) just means
a male friend, and yeu set gwa·deu·nya, a female friend.

Do you have anywhere
to go (tomorrow)?
    (neu·geu) yeu·mat·he·də·beut   (ነገ) የምትሄድበት
    bo·ta al·leu? (m)   ቦታ አለ?
    (neu·geu) yeu·mat·he·jə·beut   (ነገ) የምትሄጂበት
    bo·ta al·leu? (f)   ቦታ አለ?
Can we meet?
    meu·geu·na·nyeut ən·chə·lal·leun?   መገናኘት እንችላለን?

See also Invitations and Arranging to Meet, pages 92 and 93.

Classic Pick-Up Lines   የመማባቢያ ቃሉች

What can I get you?
   mən lə·gab·zəh? (m)   ምን ልጋብዝህ?
   mən lə·gab·zəsh? (f)   ምን ልጋብዝሽ?

Do you have a light?
   lai·teur al·leuh/al·leush? (m/f)   ላይተር አለህ/አለሽ?

Do you mind if I sit here?
   sō al·leu?   ሰው አለ?

Shall we get some fresh air?
   weu·deu wəʧ weu·ṭa ən·beul?   ወደ ውጭ ወጣ እንበል?

You have a beautiful smile.
   ḳon·jo feu·geug·ta al·leuh/   ቆንጆ ፈገግታ አለህ/
   al·leush (m/f)   አለሽ

Do you have a girlfriend/boyfriend?
   geurl frend al·leuh? (m)   ገርል ፍሬንድ አለህ?
   boy frend al·leush? (f)   ቦይ ፍሬንድ አለሽ?

She's just a friend; He's just a friend.
   əs·swa gwa·deu·nya·ye nat;   እሷ ጓደኛዬ ናት/
   əs·su gwa·deu·nya·ye nō   እሱ ጓደኛዬ ነው።

Can I take you home?
   bet la·dər·səh? (m)   ቤት ላድርስህ?
   bet la·dər·səsh? (f)   ቤት ላድርሰሽ?

Classic Rejections   ግብዣን አለመቀበል

In Ethiopia, you may come across meug·deur·deur, the concept
of modestly declining an offer (such as a date) even though you
would like to accept. To ensure 'No thanks' is not misinterpreted
as 'OK', be polite but insistent.

No, thank you.
   aiy a·meu·seu·gə·nal·lō   አይ አመሰግናለሁ።

I don't drink.
   meu·ṭeuṭ al·ṭeu·ṭam   መጠጥ አልጠጣም

I don't smoke.
   a·la·cheu·səm   አላጨስም

I don't chew *chat*.
   chat al·ḳə·məm   ጫት አልቅምም

I have another appointment.
le·la ķeu·ţeu·ro al·leuny   ሌላ ቀጠሮ አለኝ

Excuse me, I'm with someone.
yi·ķər·ta ķeu sō gar neuny   ይቅርታ ከሰው ጋር ነኝ

I'm waiting for (my husband/wife).
(ba·leu·be·ten)   (ባለቤቴን)
ə·yeu·ţeu·beu·ku nō   እየጠበኩ ነው

Excuse me, I have to go now.
yi·ķər·ta a·hun meu·hed   ይቅርታ አሁን መሄድ
al·leu·bəny   አለብኝ

Leave me/us alone!
a·bo teu·weun!   አቦ ተወን!

DATE SAFE

I don't want to.
al·feul·lə·gəm   አልፈልግም

I've had enough.
beu·ķany   በቃኝ

I don't feel well. *(after food or drink)*
al·teus·ma·ma·nyəm   አልተሰማማኝም

Please call me a taxi.
ə·ba·ķeh tak·si ţe·ral·leny (m)   እባክህ ታክሲ ጥራልኝ
ə·ba·ķesh tak·si ţe·ril·leny (f)   እባክሽ ታክሲ ጥሪልኝ

Let's use a condom.
kon·dom ə·nə·ţeu·ķeum   ኮንዶም እንጠቀም

Love   ፍቅር

I love you.
ə·weud·də·hal·lō (m)   እወድሃለሁ
ə·weud·də·shal·lō (f)   እወድሻለሁ

Do you love me?
tə·weud·deu·nyal·leuh? (m)   ትወደኛለህ?
tə·weu·jə·nyal·leush? (f)   ትወጀኛለሽ?

Do you want to be with me?
keu·ne gar meu·hon
tə·feul·lə·gal·leuh/
tə·feul·lə·gi·yal·leush? (m/f)

ከኔ ጋር መሆን
ትፈልጋለህ/
ትፈልጊያለሽ?

Let's move in together.
ab·reun ə·nə·nur

አብረን እንኑር

Will you marry me?
ta·geu·ba·nyal·leuh? (m)
ta·geu·bi·nyal·leush? (f)

ታግባኛለህ?
ታግቢኛለሽ?

date	keu·teu·ro	ቀጠሮ
to date	meuk·teur	መቅጠር
to go out with	ab·ro mō·tat	አብሮ መወጣት
relationship	yeu fə·kər gə·nu·nyə·neut	የፍቅር ግንኙነት

LEAVING & BREAKING UP

መሰናበትና መለያየት

I have to leave (tomorrow).
(neu·geu) meu·hed al·leu·bəny

(ነገ) መሄድ አለብኝ

I'll miss you.
ə·na·fə·kə·hal·lō (m)
ə·na·fə·kə·shal·lō (f)

እናፍቅሃለሁ·
እናፍቅሽአለሁ·

Let's write to/phone each other.
ə·nə·ṣa·ṣaf/ə·nə·deu·wa·weul

እንጻጻፍ/እንደዋወል

I don't think it's working out.
fə·kə·ra·chən yeu·mi·keu·təl
ai·meu·səl·leu·nyəm

ፍቅራችን የሚቀጥል
አይመስለኝም

I want to stay friends.
gwa·deuny·neu·ta·chə·nən
ba·na·kom deus yi·leu·nyal

ጓደኝታችንን ባናቆም
ደስ ይለኛል

HOUSE OF EVERYTHING

bet, 'house', is used to refer to all sorts of places, from the divine to the everyday, including:

cinema	si·ni·ma bet
coffee house	bun·na bet
heaven	seu·mai bet
hut	go·jo bet
post office	pos·ta bet
prison	ə·sər bet
toilet	shənt bet

Ethiopians love chatting about lə·joch, 'children', and zeu·meud, 'relatives'. Even if you've never met an acquaintance's family, it's courteous to ask be·teu·seub deu·na nō?, 'Is your family well?'.

FAMILY

QUESTIONS   ጥያቄዎች

Are you married?
   a·gəb·teu·hal? (m)   አግብተሃል?
   a·gəb·teu·shal? (f)   አግብተሻል?
Do you have any children?
   lə·joch al·luh? (m)   ልጆች አሉህ?
   lə·joch al·lush? (f)   ልጆች አሉሽ?
How many children do you have?
   sənt lə·joch al·luh/al·lush? (m/f)   ስንት ልጆች አሉህ/አሉሽ?
How many brothers and sisters
do you have?
   sənt weun·də·moch na   ስንት ወንድሞችና እህቶች
   ə·hə·toch al·luh/al·lush? (m/f)   አሉህ/አሉሽ?

Do you have family photos?
   yeu be·teu·seub fo·to·graf   የቤተሰብ ፎቶግራፍ
   al·leuh/al·leush? (m/f)   አለህ/አለሽ?
Who's this?
   yi·he man nō? (m)   ይሄ ማነው-?
   yi·chi man neuch? (f)   ይቺ ማነች?
Do you miss them?
   tə·na·fə·kal·leuh? (m)   ትናፍቃለህ?
   tə·na·fə·ki·yal·leush? (f)   ትናፍቂያለሽ?
Where do they live?
   yeut nō yeu·mi·no·rut?   የት ነው የሚኖሩት?

FAMILY

REPLIES

መልሶች

I'm married.
ag·bə·chal·lō
አግብቻለሁ

I'm engaged.
ə·cho·nya al·leuny
እጮኛ አለኝ

I'm not married.
a·la·geu·ba·hum
አላገባሁም

I'm divorced.
keu ba·leu·be·te gar
teu·fa·tə·chal·lō
ከባለቤቴ ጋር
ተፋትቻለሁ

I have one child.
and ləj al·leuny
አንድ ልጅ አለኝ

I have (three) children.
(sost) lə·joch al·luny
(ሶስት) ልጆች አሉኝ

I don't have any children.
lə·joch yeul·lu·nyeum
ልጆች የሉኝም

I have a daughter/son.
and (set ləj; weund ləj)
al·leuny
አንድ (ሴት ልጅ/
ወንድ ልጅ) አለኝ

I have one (brother).
and (weun·dəm) al·leuny
አንድ (ወንድም) አለኝ

I have two (sisters).
hu·leutt (ə·hə·toch) al·luny
ሁለት (እህቶች) አሉኝ

I'm the oldest/youngest child.
yeu meu·jeu·meu·ri·yow/
meu·cheu·reu·show ləj neuny
የ መጀመሪያው/
መጨረሻው ልጅ ነኝ

My ... died.
yeu·ne ... mo·teu·wal
የኔ ... ሞተዋል

My parents are divorced.
ə·nat·na ab·ba·te teu·fa·teu·wal
እናትና አባቴ ተፋትተዋል

FAMILY MEMBERS የቤተሰብ አባላ‐ች

Family terms are used with great flexibility. For example, ə·hat, 'sister', can be used to refer to female nieces, cousins and friends.

aunt	a·kəst	አክስት
brother	weun·dəm	ወንድም
(younger) brother	(tən·nish) weun·dəm	(ትንሽ) ወንድም
child/children	ləj/lə·joch	ልጅ/ልጆች
cousin	ya·got ləj (m)	ያጎት ልጅ/
	ya·kəst ləj (f)	ያክስት ልጅ
daughter	set ləj	ሴት ልጅ
family	be·teu·seub	ቤተሰብ
father	ab·bat	አባት
fiance/e	ə·cho·nya	እጮኛ
foster child	yeu ma·deu·go ləj	የማደጎ ልጅ
friend	gwa·deu·nya	ጓደኛ
god(child)	yeu kə·ras·tən·na (ləj)	የክርስትና (ልጅ)
grandchildren	yeu ləj lə·joch	የልጅ ልጆች
grandfather	weund a·yat	ወንድ አያት
grandmother	set a·yat	ሴት አያት
husband	bal	ባል
man/men	sō/sō·woch	ሰው/ሰዎች
mother	ə·nat	እናት
sister	ə·hat	እህት
(older) sister	(təl·ləķ) ə·hat	(ትልቅ) እህት
step (mother)	ən·jeu·ra (ə·nat)	እንጀራ (እናት)
uncle	a·got	አጎት
wife	mist	ሚስት
woman/women	set/se·toch	ሴት/ሴቶች

WHOSE WHOSE?

To form the possessive 'my', add e or use yeu·ne:

ab·ba·te	my father
yeu·ne ə·nat	my mother

To form a possessive like 'my friend's brother' add yeu:
yeu gwa·deu·nya·ye weun·dəm
(lit: of friend-my brother)

FAMILY

TALKING WITH PARENTS

ከወላጆች ጋር ማውራት

How old are your children?
yeu lə·jo·chu əd·me sənt nõ?

የልጆቹ ዕድሜ ስንት ነው?

How many (girls/boys) are there?
sənt (se·toch/weun·doch) al·lu?

ስንት (ሴቶች/ወንዶች) አሉ?

Does he/she attend school?
təm·hərt bet jeu·mə·rwal/
jeu·mə·ral·leuch?

ትምህርት ቤት ጀምሯል/
ጀምራለች?

What's the baby's name?
yeu hə·ṣa·nu səm man nõ?

የሕፃኑ ስም ማነው?

Is it a boy or a girl?
weund nõ ways set neuch?

ወንድ ነው ወይስ ሴት ነች?

What a beautiful baby/child!
beu·ṭam ḳon·jo ləj!

በጣም ቆንጆ ልጅ!

Who does he/she look like?
ma·nən yi·meus·lal/
tə·meus·lal·leuch?

ማንን ይመስላል/
ትመስላለች?

He looks like you.
an·teun yi·meus·lal

አንተን ይመስላል

She looks like you.
an·chən tə·meus·lal·leuch

አንችን ትመስላለች

EMIGRATION BLUES

(My brother) lives in ...
(weun·də·me) ... yi·no·ral

(ወንድሜ) ... ይኖራል

Yes, there are many Ethiopians in (Toronto).
ow (to·ron·to) bə·zu
i·ta·yo·pi·ya·noch yi·no·ral·lu

አዎ (ቶሮንቶ) ብዙ
ኢትዮጵያኖች ይኖሩሉ

I want to go to your country.
weu·deu (an·teu/an·chi) a·geur
meu·hed ə·feul·lə·gal·lõ (m/f)

ወደ (አንተ/አንቺ) አገር
መሄድ እፈልጋለሁ

TALKING WITH CHILDREN ከልጆች ጋር ማውራት

Ethiopian children are a mixed bunch – some work, some go to school and some do both! Whichever the case, most kids love sport and games, are proud of their religion and cultural heritage and have a terrific sense of humour. Chatting to them will sometimes take the heat out of 'foreigner frenzy' (see Unwanted Attention in Around Town, page 88).

FAMILY

What's your name?
  sə·məh/sə·məsh man nō? (m/f)   ስምህ/ስምሽ ማነው·?

How old are you?
  əd·meh/əd·mesh sənt nō? (m/f)   ዕድሜህ/ዕድሜሽ ስንት ነው·?

Do you have brothers and sisters?
  weun·də·mə·na ə·hət
  al·leuh/al·leush? (m/f)   ወንድምና እህት
  አለህ/አለሽ?

Do you go to school?
  təm·hərt bet tə·he·dal·leuh/
  tə·he·jal·leush? (m/f)   ትምህርት ቤት ትሄዳለህ/
  ትሄጃለሽ?

Do you have a good teacher?
  tə·ru as·te·ma·ri al·leuh? (m)   ጥሩ አስተማሪ አለህ?
  tə·ru as·te·ma·ri al·leush? (f)   ጥሩ አስተማሪ አለሽ?

Do you study English?
  ən·gli·zə·nya tə·ma·ral·leuh? (m)   እንግሊዝኛ ትማራለህ
  ən·gli·zə·nya tə·ma·ri·yal·leush? (f)   እንግሊዝኛ ትማሪያለሽ?

What's your favourite game?
  yeu·mət·weud·dō/
  yeu·meut·weu·ju cheu·wa·ta
  mən·dən nō? (m/f)   የምትወደው·/
  የምትወጅው· ጨዋታ
  ምንድን ነው·?

What will we play?
  mən ə·nə·cha·weut?   ምን እንጫወት?

I like ...	... ə·weud·dal·lō	... እወዳለሁ·
football	ə·gər kwass	እግር ኳስ
hide and seek	də·bəb·bə·kosh	ድብብቆሽ
hopscotch	seu·nyo mak·seu·nyo	ሰኞ ማክሰኞ
skipping	geu·meud zə·lai	ገመድ ዝላይ
swings	zhə·wa·zhə·we	ዥዋዥዌ

FAMILY

BIRTHDAYS

ልደቶች

Birthdays are only celebrated during childhood in Ethiopia.

When's your birthday?
| la·deu·təh/lə·deu·təsh | ልደትህ/ልደትሽ |
| meu·che nō? (m/f) | ሙቼ ነው? |

My birthday is on (25 January).
| lə·deu·te beu | ልደቴ በ |
| (ha·ya a·məst ja·nu·wa·ri) nō | (ሃያ አምስት ጁነዋሪ) ነው |

Happy birthday!
| meul·kam lə·deut! | መልካም ልደት! |

LIFE STAGES

baby	hə·şan	ሕፃን
child	ləj	ልጅ
boy	weund ləj	ወንድ ልጅ
girl	set ləj	ሴት ልጅ
youth	weu·ṭat	ወጣት
middle age	gol·ma·sa	ጎልማሳ
old man	shə·ma·gə·le	ሽማግሌ
old woman	a·ro·git	አሮጊት

INTERESTS

Radios blaring with mu·zi·ka, 'music', cafés abuzz with weu·re, 'chatter', and walls adorned with sə'əl, 'art' – Ethiopians love their home-grown entertainment. Sport (see Activities, page 179) and theatre are also very popular.

COMMON INTERESTS

የጋር ፍላጎቶች

What do you do in your spare time?

beu tərf gi·zeh mən ta·deur·gal·leuh? (m)	በትርፍ ጊዜህ ምን ታደርጋለህ?
beu tərf gi·zesh mən ta·deur·gi·yal·leush? (f)	በትርፍ ጊዜሽ ምን ታደርጊያለሽ?

I like/I don't like ...	... ə·weud·dal·lō/ al·weud·dəm	... እወዳለሁ/ አልወድም
cooking	mə·gəb meus·rat	ምግብ መስራት
gardening	at·kəlt	አትክልት
	meun·keu·ba·keub	መንከባከብ
listening to music/the radio	mu·zi·ka/ra·di·yo meus·mat	ሙዚቃ/ራድዮ መስማት
meeting friends	keu·gwa·deu·nyoch gar meu·geu·na·nyeut	ከጓደኞች ጋር መገናኘት
painting	sə'əl meu·sal	ስዕል መሳል
photography	fo·to man·sat	ፎቶ ማንሳት
playing (cards)	(kar·ta) meu·cha·wot	(ካርታ) መጫወት
reading	meu·sə·haf	መጽሐፍ
	man·beub	ማንበብ
sport	sport	ስፖርት
theatre	ti·ya·teur	ትያትር
travelling	a·geur meu·go·bə·nyeut	አገር መጎብኘት
visiting relatives	zeu·meud meu·ţeu·yeuk	ዘመድ መጠየቅ
watching movies	film ma·yeut	ፊልም ማየት
watching TV	ti·vi ma·yeut	ቲቪ ማየት
writing (letters)	(deub·dab·be) meu·şaf	(ደብዳቤ) መፃፍ

INTERESTS

MUSIC & RADIO መዚቃና ራዲዮ

Ethiopia has a thriving home-grown music industry that includes jazz, pop and traditional tunes. Music also has an important community function – on the farm, during special events and in the church. Radio is the most popular form of broadcast entertainment in Ethiopia.

Which is a good station for ...?	leu ... yeu·tə·nyow ra·di·yo ṭa·bi·ya yi·sha·lal?	ለ ... የተሻ̱ናው ራድዮ ጣቢያ ይሻ̱ላል?
traditional music	ba·həl mu·zi·ḳa	ባህል መዚ̱ቃ
Western music	feu·reunj mu·zi·ḳa	ፈረንጅ መዚ̱ቃ
the news in English	ən·gli·zə·nya ze·na	እንግሊዝኛ ዜና

Which is the English station?
yeu ən·gli·zə·nya ḳwan·ḳwa ṭa·bi·ya yeu·tə·nyow nō? የእንግሊዝኛ ቋንቋ ጣቢያ የትኛው· ነው·?

What frequency is it on?
beu·yeu·tə·nyow mo·geud lai nō? በየትኛው· ሞገድ ላይ ነው·?

What music do you like?
mən ai·neut mu·zi·ḳa tə·weud·dal·leuh/ tə·weu·jal·leush? (m/f) ምን አይነት መዚ̱ቃ ትወዳለህ/ትወጃለሽ?

Who's your favourite (singer)?
yeu·mət·weud·dō/ yeu·mət·weu·ju (zeu·fany) man nō? (m/f) የምትወደው·/ የምትወጀው· (ዘፋኝ) ማን ነው·?

My favourite singer is (Bob Marley).
yeu·mə·weud·dō zeu·fany (bob mar·li) nō የምወደው· ዘፋኝ (ቦብ ማርሊ) ነው·

What instrument do you play?
mən ai·neut yeu mu·zi·ḳa meu·sa·ri·ya tə·cha·wo·tal·leuh/ tə·cha·wo·chal·leush? (m/f) ምን አይነት የመዚ̱ቃ መሳሪያ ትጫወታለህ/ ትጫወቻለሽ?

I play the ...
| ... ə·cha·weu·tal·lō | ... እጫወታለሁ· |

Shall we try it together?
| ab·reun ən·mo·kər? | አብረን እንሞክር? |

Do you like ...?	... tə·weud·dal·leuh? (m)	... ትወዳለህ?
	... tə·weu·jal·leush? (f)	... ትወጃለሽ?
dancing	meu·da·neus	መደነስ
listening to music	mu·zi·ḳa meus·mat	ሙዚቃ መስማት
singing	meuz·feun	መዝፈን
playing music	mu·zi·ḳa meu·cha·wot	ሙዚቃ መጫወት

band	yeu mu·zi·ḳa gwad	የሙዚቃ ጓድ
guitar	gi·tar	ጊታር
musician	mu·zi·ḳeu·nya	ሙዚቀኛ
show/concert	zə·gə·jət	ዝግጅት
singer	zeu·fany	ዘፋኝ
song	zeu·feun	ዘፈን
stage	meud·reuk	መድረክ
voice	dəmş	ድምፅ
whistling	fu·cheut	ፉጨት

INTERESTS

For traditional instruments, dancing and music venues, see page 93.

ART ኪነ ጥበብ

Church art is Ethiopia's most famous traditional art form. See also Religion, page 191.

Where can I see some good ...?	tə·ru ... yeut ma·yeut ə·cha·lal·lō?	ጥሩ ... የት ማየት እችላለሁ?
church art	yeu be·teu krəs·ti·yan sə'ə·loch	የቤተክርስቲያን ስዕሎች
modern painting	zeu·meu·na·wi sə'ə·loch	ዘመናዊ ስዕሎች
painting by (Afwerke Tekle)	yeu (af·weurḳ teuk·len) sə'ə·loch	የ (አፈወርቅ ተክሌን) ስዕሎች
traditional painting	yeu ba·həl sə'ə·loch	የባህል ስዕሎች

INTERESTS

Who's the painter?
man nō seu·al·yu? ማን ነው· ሰዓሊው·?
When was it done/painted?
meu·che nō yeu·teu·seu·row/ መቼ ነው· የተሰራው·/
yeu·teu·sa·lō? የተሳለው·?

architecture	yeu hən·ṣa a·seu·rar	የሕንፃ አሰራ·ር
art (painting)	sə'əl	ስዕል
artwork	yeu ki·neu ṭə·beub	የኪነ· ጥበብ
	sə·ra·woch	ስራ·ዎች
artist	yeu ki·neu ṭə·beub sō	የኪነ· ጥበብ ሰው·
calligraphy	yeu ḳum ṣeu·ha·fi	የቁም ፀሐፊ
canvas	sheu·ra	ሸራ
exhibition	eg·zi·bi·shən	ኤግዚቢሽን
paintbrush	yeu ḳeu·leum bu·rəsh	የቀለም ቡርሽ
paints	ḳeu·leum	ቀለም
photographer	fo·to an·shi	ፎቶ አንሺ
print	ə·tem	እትም
sculpture	ḳər·ṣa ḳərṣ	ቅርፃ ቅርፅ
style	sta·yil/zeu·de	ስታይል/ዘዴ

CINEMA   ሲኒማ

What's on at the cinema tonight?
za·re mən·dən nō ዛሬ ምንድነው·
yeu·weu·ṭow? የወጣው·?
What type of movie is it?
mən ai·neut film nō? ምን አይነት ፊልም ነው·?
Have you seen ...?
... ai·teu·hal/ai·teu·shal? (m/f) ... አይተሃል/አይተሻል?
What films do you like?
mən ái·neut film ምን አይነት ፊልም
tə·wéud·dal·leuh/ ትወዳለህ/ትወጃለሽ?
tə·weu·jal·leush? (m/f)

I like/I don't like ...	... ə·weud·dal·lō/ al·weud·dəm	... እወዳለሁ/ አልወድም
action	ak·shən film	አክሽን ፊልም
comedy	yeu·mi·ya·səḳ film	የሚያስቅ ፊልም
drama	ta·rik ya·lō film	ታሪክ ያለው· ፊልም
films from (India)	yeu (hənd) film	የ (ሀነድ) ፊልም

WAXING LYRICAL

Allusion and double meanings play a major role in Amharic verse and literature, which are said to have səm əna weurḳ (wax and gold). The wax is the apparent meaning, and the gold, the hidden but true meaning.

INTERESTS

THEATRE, LITERATURE & STORIES
ትያትር፡ ስነ ጽሑፍና ታሪኮች

Ethiopia's rich literary tradition finds expression in theatre, poetry, song and the novel. Oral narratives are also popular. You can see these at various entertainment venues. Even if you don't understand a word that's said, the colourful gestures, expressions and clever use of pauses and intonation should keep you entertained.

I want to go to the theatre.

| weu·deu ti·ya·tər bet | ወደ ትያትር ቤት |
| meu·hed ə·feul·lə·gal·lō | መሄድ እፈልጋለሁ· |

I'd like to see a ...	... ma·yeut ə·feul·gal·lō	... ማየት እፈልጋለሁ·
comedy	yeu·mi·ya·səḳ dra·ma	የሚያስቅ ድራማ
(historical) drama	(yeu ta·rik) dra·ma	(የታሪክ) ድራማ
variety show	yeu·teu·leu·ya·yu tər'i·toch	የተለያዩ ትርኢቶች

Renton Tech Coll Library

Can you recommend one?
  yeu·tə·nyow yi·sha·lal   የትኛው ይሻላል
  tə·la·lah/tə·ya·leush? (m/f)   ትሳለህ/ት.ያለሽ?

Did you like it?
  weu·deud·kō? (m)   ወደድከው?
  weu·deud·shyu? (f)   ወደድሽው?

I really liked it!
  beu·tam weud·də·jeu·wal·lō!   በጣም ወድጀዋለሁ!

The main actor was great!
  wan·now ak·teur   ዋናው አክተር
  as·deu·na·ki̱ neub·beur!   አስደናቂ ነበር!

I didn't understand much.
  bə·zu al·geu·ba·nyəm   ብዙ አልገባኝም

COLOURFUL CHARACTERS

Amharic is full of colourful words to describe people's status and characters.

big man	təl·ləḵ sō	ትልቅ ሰው
commoner	teu·ra sō	ተራ ሰው
a gossip	a·lu·bal·teu·nya	አሉ·ባልተኛ
jealous	ḵeu·na·teu·nya	ቀናተኛ
loyal	ta·many	ታማኝ
modern person	zeu·meu·na·wi	ዘመናዊ
nice/gentle	cheu·wa	ጨዋ
poor	deu·ha	ደሃ
rich	hab·tam	ሃብታም
rude	ba·leu·ge	ባለጌ
shy	ai·neu a·far	አይነ አፋር
talkative	weu·re·nya	ወሬኛ
worldly	a·leu·ma·wi	ዓለማዊ

READING

ማንበብ

See also Stationery & Publications, page 133.

Do you like reading?
   man·beub tə·weud·dal·leuh/   ማንበብ ትወዳለህ/
   tə·weu·jal·leush? (m/f)   ትወጃለሽ?
I like/I don't like it.
   ə·weud·dal·lō/al·weud·dəm   እወዳለሁ/አልወድም
What do you like to read?
   mən man·beub   ምን ማንበብ
   tə·weud·dal·leuh/   ትወዳለህ/
   tə·weu·jal·leush? (m/f)   ትወጃለሽ?

I like to read ...	... man·beub	... ማንበብ
	ə·weud·dal·lō	እወዳለሁ
books	meu·ṣə·haf	መጽሐፍ
comics	a·sə·ḳiny	አስቂኝ
	meu·ṣə·haf	መጽሐፍ
crime novels	yeu weun·jeul ləb	የወንጀል
	weu·leud	ልብ ወለድ
fables	teu·reut	ተረት
fiction/novels	ləb weu·leud	ልብ ወለድ
magazines	meu·ṣə·het	መጽሔት
newspapers	ga·ze·ṭa	ጋዜጣ
non-fiction	ləb weu·leud	ልብ ወለድ
	yal·ho·neu meu·ṣə·haf	ያልሆነ መጽሐፍ
poetry	gə·ṭəm	ግጥም
romance	yeu fə·ḳər	የፍቅር
	ləb weu·leud	ልብ ወለድ
short stories	a·cha·chər	አጫጭር
	ta·ri·koch	ታሪኮች

INTERESTS

Do you have any books (in English)?
   beu (ən·gli·zə·nya) yeu·teu·ṣa·feu   በ (እንግሊዝኛ)
   meu·ṣə·haf al·la·chu?   የተጻፈ መጽሐፍ አላችሁ?
Can I borrow it?
   meu·was yi·cha·lal?   መዋስ ይቻላል?

OPINIONS

አስተያየት

It looks ...	... yi·meus·lal	... ይመስላል
crowded	sō yeu·beu·za·beut	ሰው የበዛበት
empty	ba·do	ባዶ
(like) a painting	sə'əl	ስዕል

It smells ...	... shə·ta al·lō	... ሽታ አለው
awful	a·ṣeu·ya·fi	አጸያፊ
beautiful	ḳon·jo	ቆንጆ
like (butter)	yeu (ḳə·be)	የ (ቅቤ)
	ai·neut	አይነት

It's ...	... nō	... ነው
rough	sheu·ka·ra	ሻካራ
soft/smooth	leus·las·sa	ለስላሳ

It's noisy.
bə·zu cha·cha·ta al·leu — ብዙ ጫጫታ አለ

It's quiet.
ṣeuṭ ya·leu nō — ጸጥ ያለ ነው

Did you like it?
weu·deud·kō? (m) — ወደድከው?
weu·deud·shyu? (f) — ወደድሽው?

It was ...	... neub·beur	... ነበር
boring	deu·ba·ri	ደባሪ
entertaining	yeu·mi·yaz·na·na	የሚያዝናና
sad	yeu·mi·ya·sa·zən	የሚያሳዝን
very funny	beu·ṭam	በጣም
	yeu·mi·ya·səḳ	የሚያስቅ

| ... is better. | ... yi·sha·lal | ... ይሻላል |

INTERESTS

ማሕበራዊ ጉዳዮች SOCIAL ISSUES

Ethiopians have a strong interest in the world around them, and may ask questions about your home country. Be discreet about discussing politics and sensitive social issues, particularly in relation to cultural practices.

EXPRESSING OPINIONS   አስተያየትን መግለጽ

What do you think of ...?
  sə·leu ... mən as·teu·ya·yeut
  al·leuh/al·leush? (m/f)

ስለ ... ምን አስተያየት
አለህ/አለሽ?

It's good/bad.
  tə·ru/meut̞·fo nō

ጥሩ/መጥፎ ነው-

I think/believe ...
  ə·ne ən·deu·ma·sə·bō ...

እኔ እንደማስበው ...

Do you like ...?
  ... tə·weud·dal·leuh? (m)
  ... tə·weu·jal·leush? (f)

... ትወዳለህ?
... ትወጃለሽ?

I like/don't like ...
  ... ə·weud·dal·lō/al·weud·dəm

... እወዳለሁ-/አልወድም

IN THE NEWS   ዜና

Did you hear today's news?
  yeu za·re ze·na seum·teu·hal/
  seum·teu·shal? (m/f)

የዛሬ ዜና ሰምተሃል/
ሰምተሻል?

There are problems in
(the Middle East).
  (meu·ha·keu·leu·nyow məs·rak̞)
  wəs̞t chig·gər alleu

(መካከለኛው ምስራቅ)
ውስጥ ችግር አለ

Yes, it's a serious matter.
  ow a·sa·sa·bi gu·dai nō

አዎ አሳሳቢ ጉዳይ ነው-

affair/issue	gu·dai	ጉዳይ
bomb	bomb	ቦምብ
civil war	yeurs beurs ṭor·neut	የርስ በርስ ጦርነት
civilian	seu·la·ma·wi sō	ሰላማዊ ሰው·
conflict	wə·gi·ya	ውጊያ
crime	weun·jeul	ወንጀል
demonstration	seu·la·ma·wi seulf	ሰላማዊ ሰልፍ
headline	ar'əs·teu ze·na	አርእስተ ዜና
hijacking	yeu ai·ro·plan	የአይሮፕላን
	ṭeu·leu·fa	ጠለፋ
international	a·leum a·ḳeuf	አለም አቀፍ
landmine	feunj	ፈንጅ
newspaper	ga·ze·ṭa	ጋዜጣ
Organisation for	yeu af·ri·ka	የአፍሪካ
African Unity	an·də·neut də·rə·jat	አንድነት ድርጅት
peace	seu·lam	ሰላም
peace agreement	yeu seu·lam	የሰላም
	sə·mə·mə·neut	ስምምነት
radio	ra·di·yo	ራዲዮ
refugees	sə·deu·teu·nyoch	ስደተኞች
soldier	weu·ta·deur	ወታደር
terrorism	shə·bar	ሽብር
the United	yeu·teu·ba·beu·rut	የተባበሩት
Nations	meun·gə·stat	መንግስታት
	də·rə·jat	ድርጅት
war	ṭor·neut	ጦርነት

SOCIAL ISSUES

THEY MAY SAY ...

əw·neut nō	It's true.
weu·re nō	It's a rumour.
wu·sheut nō	It's a lie.
əw·neut ai·deul·leum	It's not true.

DEVELOPMENT ISSUES

የእድገት ጉዳዮች

What do people think about ...?

sə·leu ... sō·woch mən
ya·sə·ba·lu?

ስለ ... ሰዎች ምን
ያስባሉ?

(Agriculture) is important
for development.

(gəb·rən·na) leu əd·geut
as·feul·la·gi nō

(ግብርና) ለእድገት
አስፈላጊ ነው።

It's good for ...	leu ... ţə·ru nō	ለ ... ጥሩ ነው።
It's not good	leu ... ţə·ru	ለ ... ጥሩ
for ...	ai·deul·leum	አይደለም
developed countries	ya·deu·gu a·geu·roch	ያደጉ አገሮች
developing countries	ta·da·gi a·geu·roch	ታዳጊ አገሮች
ordinary people	teu·ra sō	ተራ ሰው።
rich people	hab·tam sō	ሃብታም ሰው።
poor people	deu·ha sō	ደሃ ሰው።

aid organisation	yeu ər·da·ta də·rə·jat	የርዳታ ድርጅት
aid worker	yeu ər·da·ta də·rə·jat seu·ra·teu·nya	የርዳታ ድርጅት ሠራተኛ
air pollution	yeu ai·yeur meu·beu·keul	የአየር መበከል
charity	beu·go ad·ra·got	በጎ አድራጎት
colonialism	kəny a·geu·zaz	ቅኝ አገዛዝ
development	əd·geut	እድገት
foreign aid	yeu wəch ər·da·ta	የውጭ እርዳታ
foreign culture	yeu wəch ba·həl	የውጭ ባህል
foreign debt	yeu wəch ə·da	የውጭ እዳ
foreign investment	yeu wəch meu·wa·leu nə·wai	የውጭ መዋለ ንዋይ
free trade	neu·şa nəgd	ነፃ ንግድ
human rights	yeu sō·woch neu·şa·neut	የሰዎች ነፃነት

SOCIAL ISSUES

illiteracy	meu·ha·yə·mə·neut	መሀይምነት
money	geun·zeub	ገንዘብ
poverty	də·hə·neut	ድህነት
privatisation	keu meun·gəst	ከመንግስት
	weu·deu gəl nə·breut	ወደ ግል
	ma·zeu·wa·weur	ንብረት ማዘዋወር
slums	ko·sha·sha seu·feur	ቆሻሻ ሰፈር
standard of living	yeu·nu·ro deu·reu·ja	የኑሮ ደረጃ
tourism	tu·ri·zəm	ቱሪዝም
underprivileged	chig·gə·reu·nya	ችግረኛ
unemployment	sə·ra a·tə·neut	ስራ አጥነት
urbanisation	yeu keu·teu·moch	የከተሞች
	meus·fa·fat	መስፋፋት
World Bank	yeu a·leum bank	የአለም ባንክ

የዛሬ ዜና ሰምተሻል?

አም አሳሳቢ ጉዳይ ነው።

TELL TAILS

Remember Amharic verbs have the subject attached in the form of affixes. In the case of 'you', there are male, female and polite forms. Listen for these sounds at the beginning and end of verbs:

tə...al·leuh (m)   (for addressing males)
tə...al·leush (f)   (for addressing females)
yi...al·lu (pol)   (for addressing older people)

POLITICS   ፖለቲካ

You'll find that words like prez·dant, 'president', and so·sha·list, 'socialist', are almost identical to English.

Who is your country's
(prime minister)?
   ya·geu·ra·chu (ṭeuḳ·lai   ያገራችሁ (ጠቅላይ
   mi·nis·ter) man nō?   ሚኒስትር) ማን ነው?
What is the main political party?
   wan·now yeu po·leu·ti·ka   ዋናው የፖለቲካ
   par·ti man nō?   ፓርቲ ማን ነው?
What are conditions for
(immigrants) like?
   yeu (sə·deu·teu·nyoch) hu·ne·ta የ (ስደተኞች)
   ən·det nō?   ሁኔታ እንዴት ነው?
(The cost of living) is/isn't high.
   (nu·ro) wəd nō;   (ኑሮ) ውድ ነው-/
   (nu·ro) wəd ai·deu·leum   (ኑሮ) ውድ አይደለም
(Education) is free/expensive/cheap.
   (təm·hərt) neu·ṣa/wədd/   (ትምህርት) ነፃ/ውድ/
   rə·kash nō   ርካሽ ነው-
Does the government provide
(social security)?
   meun·gəst yeu·mi·seu·ṭō   መንግስት የሚሰጠው-
   (də·go·ma) al·leu?   (ድጎማ) አለ?

conservative	a·ṭə·ba·ḳi	አጥባቂ
democracy	di·mok·ra·si	ዲሞክራሲ
economy	i·ko·no·mi	ኢኮኖሚ
education	təm·hərt	ትምህርት
election	mər·cha	ምርጫ
equality	ə·ku·lə·neut	እኩልነት
free (not bound)	neu·ṣa	ነፃ
free speech	yeu meu·na·geur	የመናገር
	neu·ṣa·neut	ነፃነት
government	meun·gəst	መንግስት
health care	yeu ṭe·na a·geul·glot	የጤና አገልግሎት

homeless	yeu go·da·na teu·da·da·ri	የጎዳና ተዳዳሪ
immigration	sə·deut	ስደት
(new) jobs	(ad·dis) sə·ra·woch	(አዲስ) ስራዎች
opposition	teu·ka·wa·mi	ተቃዋሚ
parliament	mə·kər bet	ምክር ቤት
policy	a·meu·rar	አመራር
politician	po·leu·ti·keu·nya	ፖለቲከኛ
previous	yeu keud·mō	የቀድሞው
government	meun·gəst	መንግስት
racism	zeu·reu·nyə·neut	ዘረኝነት
tax	gə·bər	ግብር
unemployment	sə·ra meu·ta·ṭat	ስራ መታጣት

SOCIAL ISSUES

ወደ ገቢያ መሄድ SHOPPING

LOOKING FOR ... ... መፈለግ
At the Market & Street Stalls ገቢያና መደብሮች

Ethiopian geu·bi·ya, 'markets', operate daily in major towns and once a week in rural areas. People from miles around congregate to buy and sell their wares and catch up on the latest news. Use Amharic to find your way through the colourful maze of clothing, baskets, spices, trinkets and livestock. Local gul·lət, 'street stalls', are great for vegetables, eggs and small household items.

When's market day?
    yeu geu·bi·ya ḵeun meu·che nō?   የገቢያ ቀን መቼ ነው?
Where's the market area?
    wan·now geu·bi·ya yeut nō?   ዋናው ገቢያ የት ነው?
Where can I find ...?
    ... yeut yi·geu·nyal?   ... የት ይገኛል?
Do you have any (sandals)?
    (neu·ṭeu·la cham·ma) al·leu?   (ነጠላ ጫማ) አለ?
I would like to buy (this/that).
    (yi·hen/yan) meug·zat   (ይሄን/ያን) መግዛት
    ə·feul·lə·gal·lō   እፈልጋለሁ

Where is the ... stall/section?	yeu ... teu·ra yeut nō?	የ ... ተራ የት ነው?
clothes	ləbs	ልብስ
fruit and vegetable	fə·ra·fə·re na at·kəlt	ፍራፍሬና አትክልት
grains	ə·həl	እህል
pottery	sheuk·la	ሽክላ
spices	ḵə·meu·ma ḵə·meum	ቅመማ ቅመም

At the Shops

ሱቆች አካባቢ

Where's the nearest ...?	keuz·zi yeu·mi·keur·bō ... yeut nō?	ከዚህ የሚቀርበው ... የት ነው·?
bakery	dab·bo bet	ዳቦ ቤት
barber	şeu·gur as·teu·ka·kai	ፀጉር አስተካካይ
bookshop	meu·şə·haf bet	መጽሐፍ ቤት
butcher	sə·ga bet	ስጋ ቤት
camera shop	fo·to bet	ፎቶ ቤት
chemist	far·ma·si bet	ፋርማሲ ቤት
clothes shop	yeu ləbs suk	የልብስ ሱቅ
curio/souvenir shop	yeu ba·həl ə·ka·woch meu·deu·bər	የባህል ዕቃዎች መደብር
electronics shop	yeu e·le·trik ə·ka·woch meu·deu·bər	የኤሌትሪክ ዕቃዎች መደብር
fruit shop	fə·ra·fə·re bet	ፍራፍሬ ቤት
general store	sheu·keu·ta sheu·keut meu·deu·bər	ሸቀጣ ሸቀጥ መደብር
grocery	gro·seu·ri	ግሮሰሪ
hairdresser	kun·jə·na sa·lon	ቀንጀና ሳሎን
jewellery shop	ge·ţa geţ suk	ጌጣ ጌጥ ሱቅ
laundry	lown·deu·ri	ላውንደሪ
market	geu·bi·ya	ገቢያ
music shop	mu·zi·ka bet	ሙዚቃ ቤት
service station	neu·daj ma·deu·ya	ነዳጅ ማደያ
shop	suk	ሱቅ
tailor	ləbs seuf·fi	ልብስ ሰፊ
travel agent	yeu gu·zo weu·kil	የጉዞ ወኪል

SIGNS	
ክፍት ነው·	OPEN
ተዘግቷል	CLOSED

MAKING A PURCHASE

መግዛት

How much is it?
   sənt nō?

ስንት ነው-?

I'm just looking.
   ə·ya·yō nō

እያየሁ ነው-

That's all/enough.
   yi·beu·ḳal

ይበቃል

What is it?
   mən·dən nō?

ምንድን ነው-?

I'll come back later.
   ə·meul·leu·sal·lō

እመለሳለሁ

I want (three).
   (sost) ə·feul·lə·gal·lō

(ሶስት) እፈልጋለሁ

Do you have (something better/any others)?
   (yeu·teu·shal·leu/lę·la) al·leu?

(የተሻለ/ሌላ) አለ?

I want a (larger/smaller) ...
   (teu·leuḳ ya·leu/an·neus ya·leu) ... ə·feul·lə·gal·lō

(ተለቅ ያለ/አነስ ያለ) ... እፈልጋለሁ

I want one like this.
   ən·deuz·zi ai·neut ə·feul·lə·gal·lō

እንደዚህ አይነት እፈልጋለሁ

I want it./I don't want it.
   ə·feul·lə·gal·lō/al·feul·lə·gəm

እፈልጋለሁ-/አልፈልግም

Can I pay using credit card/cheques?
   beu (kre·dit kard; chek) meuk·feul yi·cha·lal?

በ (ክሬዲት ካርድ/ቼክ) መክፈል ይቻላል?

Could I have a receipt please?
   deu·reu·seuny ə·ba·kon?

ደረሰኝ እባክዎን?

Keep the change.
   yan·teu/yan·chi gur·sha nō (m/f)

ያንተ/ያንቺ ጉርሻ ነው-

I want my change.
   meuls ə·feul·lə·gal·lō

መልስ እፈልጋለሁ

Please wrap it.
   ə·ba·kon yi·ṭeuḳ·lə·lu·ləny

እባክዎን ይጠቅልሉልኝ

OK, thank you!
   ə·shi, a·meu·seu·gə·nal·lō!   እሽ አመሰግናለሁ!

I want something like this/that.
   yeuz·zi/yeuz·za ai·neut   የዚህ/የሃ አይነት
   ə·feul·lə·gal·lō   እፈልጋለሁ

It's too short/long.
   beu·ṭam a·chər/reu·jim nō   በጣም አጭር/ረጂም ነው

Returning Items   እቃዎችን መመለስ

Can I return it?
   meum·meu·leus ə·cha·lal·lō?   መመለስ እችላለሁ?

I'd like a refund.
   geun·zeu·ben meul·lə·su·liny   ገንዘቤን መልሱልኝ

It's not good quality.
   ṭə·rat yeu·leu·wəm   ጥራት የለውም

It's broken.
   teu·seub·rwal   ተሰብሯል

THEY MAY SAY ...

yeul·leum
   We don't have any available.

beu·ḳa?
   Is that all?

sənt tə·feul·lə·gal·leuh? (m)
sənt tə·feul·lə·gi·yal·leush? (f)
   How many/much do you want?

yeu·tə·nya·wən?
yi·he·nya·wən?
   Which one? This one?

a·ya·wa·ṭam!
   I'll lose on that!
   (said by shopkeepers when bargaining)

deun·beu·nya ən·ho·nal·leun
   We'll deal more in future.

BARGAINING   መከራ·ከር

You may need to bargain for souvenirs, clothes and similar items, though some shops have fixed prices.

How much is it?	
sənt nō?	ስንት ነው·?
That's expensive.	
wədd nō	ው·ድ ነው·
I'll pay ... birr	
... bərr ə·keuf·lal·lō	... ብር እከፍላለሁ·
Do you have anything cheaper?	
rə·kash al·leu?	ርካሽ አለ?
(Please) give me a discount.	
(ə·ba·kəh) wa·ga keu·nəs (m)	(እባክህ) ዋጋ ቀንስ
(ə·ba·kəsh) wa·ga keu·nəsh (f)	(እባክሽ) ዋጋ ቀንሽ
Is that your last price?	
yeu·meu·cheu·reu·sha wa·ga nō?	የመጨረሻ ዋጋ ነው·?
(OK), I'll take it.	
(ə·shi), ə·weus·deu·wal·lō	(እሺ) እወስደዋለሁ·

ESSENTIAL GROCERIES   አስፈላጊ ሸቀጣ ሸቀጦች

Do you have ...	... al·leu?	... አለ?
batteries	ba·tri dən·gai	ባትሪ ድን·ጋይ
bread	dab·bo	ዳቦ
candle(s)	sha·ma	ሻማ
egg(s)	ən·ku·lal	እንቁላል
flour	du·ket	ዱቄት
margarine	mar·ga·rin	ማርጋሪን
matches	kəb·rit	ክብሪት
milk	weu·teut	ወተት
salt	chō	ጨው·
soap	sa·mu·na	ሳሙና
sugar	sə·kwar	ስኳር
tea (leaf)	shai kə·teul	ሻይ ቅጠል
toilet paper	soft; yeu shənt bet ·	ሶፍት/የሽንት
	weu·reu·keut	ቤት ወረቀት
washing powder	o·mo	አሞ

CLOTHING

ልብሶች

bra	ṭut ma·si·ya·zha	ጡት ማስያዣ
clothes	ləbs	ልብስ
dress	ķeu·miss	ቀሚስ
jacket	ja·ket	ጃኬት
jeans	jəns	ጅንስ
jumper/sweater	shu·rab	ሹራብ
leather jacket	ķo·da kot	ቆዳ ኮት
rain clothes	yeu zə·nab ləbs	የዝናብ ልብስ
singlet	ka·na·te·ra	ካናቴራ
shirt	sheu·miz	ሸሚዝ
shorts	ķum·ṭa su·ri	ቁምጣ ሱሪ
socks	kal·si	ካልሲ
trousers	su·ri	ሱሪ
underpants	wəsṭ su·ri	ወስጥ ሱሪ

Do you have something in my size?
  leu·ne yeu·mi·hon al·leu?

ሰኔ የሚሆን አለ?

Can I see some samples?
  na·mu·na ma·yeut yi·cha·lal?

ናሙና ማየት ይቻላል?

I want you to take my measurements.
  meul·leu·kat ə·feul·lə·gal·lō

መለካት እፈልጋለሁ

Can I try it on?
  lə·leu·kow?

ልለካው?

Is there a mirror?
  meus·ta·weut al·leu?

መስታወት አለ?

It fits well.
  lə·ke nō

ልኬ ነው

Can it be altered?
  lə·tas·teu·ka·kəl·lō
  tə·cha·lal·leuh? (m)

ልታስተካክለው ትችላለህ?

Can you mend this?
  yi·hen sə·fal·liny? (m)

ይሄን ስፋልኝ

When will it be ready?
  meu·che yi·deur·sal?

መቼ ይደርሳል?

I'll come back later.
  bo·hal·la ə·meul·leu·sal·lō

በኋላ እመሳሳለሁ

button	yeu ləbs ḳulf	የልብስ ቁልፍ
fabric	cheurḳ	ጨርቅ
hem	ṭeurz	ጠርዝ
needle and thread	meur·fe·na kər	መርፌና ክር
safety pin	meur·fe ḳulf	መርፌ ቁልፍ
(long) sleeves	(reu·jim) ə·jə·ge	(ረጅም) እጅጌ
zip	zip/teu·fe·tə·leuk	ዚፕ/ተፈትለክ

Traditional Dress & Body Decorations

የአገር ባህል ልብስና
የሰው·ነት ጌጦች

beur·nos	woollen cape	በርኖስ
bu·lə·ko	grey-white cloth used as blanket or body wrap	ቡ·ልኮ
də·rə·ya	colourful cloth (worn by Harari women)	ድርያ
ə·jeu ṭeu·bab	men's long shirt	እጅ ጠባብ
ga·bi	thick shawl normally worn over clothing	ጋቢ
ḳeu·miss	dress	ቀሚስ
ku·ta	white cotton toga, thicker than neu·ṭeu·la	ኩ·ታ
neu·ṭeu·la	shawl worn over a ḳeu·miss	ነጠላ
shash	female head cloth	ሻሽ
sheu·ma	light white shawl worn over clothing	ሸማ
shi·riṭ	Somali and Afar wrap	ሸርጥ
ṭə·beub	traditional women's dress, normally white; also refers to embroidered borders on material	ጥበብ
ṭəlf ṭeu·la·fi	embroidery	ጥልፍ ጠላፊ
yeu ba·həl ləbs	traditional dress/ clothing	የባሀል ልብስ

SOUVENIRS

የስጦታ ዕቃዎች

Ethiopian souvenirs range from authentic carvings and paintings to items still used in Ethiopian homes. You may need a permit to export cultural items like parchments and antiques (or even things that look old!). See also Jewellery & Accessories, page 130.

candle-stick	yeu sha·ma	የሻማ
holder	mas·keu·meu·cha	ማስቀመጫ
carpet	mən·ṭaf	ምንጣፍ
carving	kər·ṣa ḳərṣ	ቅርጻ ቅርጽ
comb	mi·do	ሚዶ
cross	meus·ḳeul	መስቀል
fly whisk	chə·ra	ጭራ
knife	seun·ṭi	ሰንጢ
painting	(yeu ba·həl)	(የባህል)
(traditional)	sə'əl	ስዕል
parchment	bə·ran·na	ብራና
(of animal hide)		
pottery	yeu sheuk·la ə·ḳa·woch	የሸክላ ዕቃዎች
rug	yeu·gər mən·ṭaf	የገር ምንጣፍ
rug (sheepskin)	a·go·za	አጎዛ
stool (wooden)	du·ka/beur·chu·ma	ዱካ/በርጩማ
straw mat	seu·len	ሰሌን
umbrella	jan·ṭə·la	ጃንጥላ
vase	yeu a·beu·ba	የአበባ
	mas·ḳeu·meu·cha	ማስቀመጫ

WHERE'D YEU GET IT?

Each region has its own distinctive style and speciality. Dorze is known for colourful cotton clothes, Harar for quality basketry, Debre Birhan for carpets, Gonder for crosses and other areas for jewellery and pottery. To indicate the region of origin for a requested item, simply add yeu before the region and item.

yeu (dor·ze) ləbs — cloth from (Dorze)
yeu (gon·deur) meus·ḳeul — cross from (Gonder)

Baskets   ቅርጫቶች

Baskets in Ethiopia have different names depending on their design and purpose.

kər·chat/kər·cha·toch   ቅርጫት/ቅርጫቶች
  basket/baskets

a·geul·gəl   አገልግል
  leather/animal skin food storage basket (often round, deco-
  rated and tied with leather straps)

meu·sob   መሶብ
  large multi-coloured basket used for keeping ən·jeu·ra, sometimes used as a traditional eating table (meu·sob weurk)

mu·dai   ሙዳይ
  small, round, often coloured/decorated basket

seu·fed   ሰፈድ
  flat basket used for winnowing grain

yeu ha·rar kər·cha·toch   የሐረር ቅርጫቶች
  baskets from the Harar region

zeun·bil   ዘንቢል
  basket for carrying goods (usually shopping)

Cooking &   የምግብ መስሪያና
Eating Implements   መመገቢያ እቃዎች

bə·rə·le	for drinking honey wine (ṭeuj)	ብርሌ
geu·beu·te	wooden bowl	ገበቴ
geun·bo	clay pot	ገንቦ
ən·sə·ra	large clay pot/pitcher used for storing and carrying water	እንስራ
jeu·beu·na	traditional coffee pot	ጀበና
kəl	gourd	ቅል
sheuk·la dəst	clay saucepan/pot	ሸክላ ድስት
wan·cha	traditional cup (horn/clay)	ዋንጫ
yeu sheuk·la ə·ḳa	earthenware pot	የሸክላ ዕቃ

SHOPPING

JEWELLERY & ACCESSORIES   ጌጣ ጌጥ

anklet	al·bo	አልቦ
belt	keu·beu·to	ቀበቶ
bracelet	am·bar	አምባር
cap	ko·fə·ya	ኮፍያ
earrings	gu·tə·cha	ጉትቻ
engraving	kərş	ቅርፅ
handkerchief	meu·ha·reub	መሃረብ
hat	kob	ቆብ
jewellery	ge·ta get	ጌጣ ጌጥ
necklace	kə·tab	ክታብ
necklet	ha·bəl	ሃብል
purse	por·sa	ፖርሳ
ring	keu·leu·beut	ቀለበት
sandals	kəft cham·ma	ክፍት ጫማ
shoelaces	yeu cham·ma ma·seu·ri·ya	የጫማ ማሰሪያ
shoes	cham·ma	ጫማ
sunglasses	yeu şeu·hai meu·neu·şar	የፀሃይ መነፅር
sun hat	bar·ne·ţa	ባርኔጣ
wallet	yeu kis por·sa	የኪስ ፖርሳ

BODY BEAUTIFUL

Unique facial and body markings are used by different groups in Ethiopia. In the north, delicate neck and
facial tattoos set off traditional white clothing and
elaborate hair designs. In the south-west, some groups
pattern themselves with intricate scarification and body
painting. Henna (hen·na) patterns are used all over
Ethiopia to enhance beauty.

kul	ኩል
eyeliner	
ən·so·səl·la	አንሶስላ
hand and foot decoration, made from plant extracts	
nə·kə·sat	ንቅሳት
tattoo on the forehead, neck or hands (of women), or	
used to darken the gums of the mouth	

MATERIALS

ጨርቃ ጨርቅና የሽክላ እቃዎች

What's it made of?
keu mən·dən nō
yeu·teu·seu·row?

ከምንድን ነው የተሰራው?

Is it pure (gold)?
nə·ṣuh (weurk̩) nō?

ንፁህ (ወርቅ) ነው?

bronze	neu·has	ነሐስ
calico	a·bu·jeu·did	አቡጀዲድ
copper	meu·dab	መዳብ
cotton	ṭəṭ	ጥጥ
(handmade)	(beu əj yeu·teu·seu·ra)	(በእጅ የተሰራ)
glass	bər·chə·k̩o	ብርጭቆ
gold	weurk̩	ወርቅ
leather	k̩o·da	ቆዳ
metal	bə·reut	ብረት
rubber	las·tik/gom·ma	ላስቲክ/ጎማ
silk	harr	ሐር
silver	bərr	ብር
stainless steel	yeu·mai·zəg bə·reut	የማይዝግ ብረት
synthetic	sō seu·rash	ሰው ሰራሽ
velvet	keu·fay	ከፈይ
wax	seum	ሰም
wood	ən·cheut	እንጨት
wool	suf	ሱፍ

COLOURS

ቀለሞች

black	ṭə·k̩ur	ጥቁር
blue	seu·ma·ya·wi	ሰማያዊ
brown	bun·na ai·neut	ቡና አይነት
green	a·reun·gwa·de	አረንጓዴ
orange	bər·tu·kan ai·neut	ብርቱካን አይነት
pink	roz	ሮዝ
purple	ham·ra·wi	ሐምራዊ
red	k̩ai	ቀይ
white	neuch	ነጭ
yellow	bi·cha	ቢጫ

TOILETRIES   የመታጠቢያ ቤትና የመኪኪያ እቃዎች

If you can't find the word for something you need in this list, try using the English for it.

brush	bu·rəsh	ቡርሽ
comb	ma·beu·ṭeu·ri·ya	ማበጠሪያ
condom	kon·dom	ኮንዶም
cosmetics	meu·kwa·kwa·ya	መኪኪያ
insect repellent	yeu bim·bi	የቢምቢ
	meu·keu·la·keu·ya krem	መከላከያ ክሬም
mirror	meus·ta·weut	መስታወት
nail clippers	yeu ṭə·fər meu·ku·reu·cha	የጥፍር መቀረጫ
perfume	shə·to	ሽቶ
razor	yeu ṣim mə·lach	የጺም ምላጭ
sanitary pads	mo·deuss	ሞደስ
shampoo	sham·po	ሻምፖ
skin oil	yeu sō·neut ḳə·bat	የሰውነት ቅባት
soap	sa·mu·na	ሳሙና
tampons	tam·pon	ታምፖን
toilet paper	soft; yeu shənt	ሶፍት/ የሽንት
	bet weu·reu·ḳeut	ቤት ወረቀት
toothbrush	yeu ṭərs bu·rəsh	የጥርስ ቡርሽ
traditional	yeu ṭərs	የጥርስ
wooden	meu·fa·ḳi·ya	መፋቂያ
toothbrush		
toothpaste	yeu ṭərs	የጥርስ
	sa·mu·na/kol·get	ሳሙና/ኮልጌት

FOR THE BABY   ለሕፃናት

... for babies	leu hə·ṣan yeu·mi·hon ...	ለሕፃን የሚሆን ...
nappy rash cream	yeu ko·da ḳə·bat/krem	የቆዳ ቅባት/ክሬም
powdered milk	yeu kor·ḳo·ro weu·teut	የቅርቅሮ ወተት
tinned baby food	yeu kor·ḳo·ro mə·gəb	የቅርቅሮ ምግብ
feeding bottle	ṭu·ṭo	ጡጦ

STATIONERY & PUBLICATIONS

የጽሕፈት ዕቃዎችና
መጽሐፍት

Ethiopian newspapers in English include the *Addis Tribune*, the *Monitor* and the *Ethiopian Herald*. See Reading, page 113, for additional book-related words.

Where are newspapers sold?
  ga·ze·ta yeut yi·sheu·tal?   ጋዜጣ የት ይሸጣል?

I want it in (English/Amharic).
  beu (ən·gli·zə·nya/   በ (እንግሊዝኛ/አማርኛ)
  a·ma·rə·nya) ə·feul·lə·gal·lō   እፈልጋለሁ

Do you have any books by ...?
  yeu ... meu·ṣə·haf al·la·chu?   የ ... መጽሐፍ አላችሁ?

I want a book	sə·leu i·tə·yo·pi·ya ...	ስለ ኢትዮጵያ
about Ethiopian ...	meu·ṣə·haf	... መጽሐፍ
	ə·feul·lə·gal·lō	እፈልጋለሁ
art	ki·neu ṭə·beub	ኪነ ጥበብ
cookery	mə·gəb a·seu·rar	ምግብ አሰራር
history	ta·rik	ታሪክ
wildlife	dur a·ra·wit	ዱር አራዊት

I want a/an ...	... ə·feul·lə·gal·lō	... እፈልጋለሁ
(Ethiopian/	yeu (i·tə·yo·pi·ya/	የ (ኢትዮጵያ/
foreign)	feu·reunj) ḳeun	ፈረንጅ) ቀን
calendar	meu·ḳu·ṭeu·ri·ya	መቁጠሪያ
dictionary	meuz·geu·beu ḳa·lat	መዝገበ ቃላት
(English to	(keu ən·gli·zə·nya	(ከእንግሊዝኛ
Amharic)	weu·deu a·ma·rə·nya)	ወደ አማርኛ)

book	meu·ṣə·haf	መጽሐፍ
box	sa·ṭən	ሳጥን
card	kard	ካርድ
envelope	pos·ta	ፖስታ
exercise book	deub·teur	ደብተር
fountain pen	bə'ər	ብዕር
glue	ma·ṭa·beu·ḳi·ya	ማጣበቂያ

magazine	meu·ṣə·het	መጽሔት
... map	yeu ... kar·ta	የ ... ካርታ
city	keu·teu·ma	ከተማ
region/zone	kəl·ləl	ክልል
road	meun·geud	መንገድ
masking tape	plas·teur	ፕላስተር
newspaper	(yeu wəč)	(የውጭ)
(foreign)	ga·ze·ṭa	ጋዜጣ
pen	əs·krip·to	እስክሪፕቶ
pencil	ər·sass	እርሳስ
scissors	meu·ḳeuss	መቀስ
string	si·ba·go	ሲባጎ
writing paper	meu·ṣa·fi·ya	መጻፊያ ወረቀት
	weu·reu·ḳeut	

Do you provide	yeu ... a·geul·glot	የ... አገልግሎት
a ... service?	al·la·chu?	አላችሁ?
Is there a	əz·zi a·ka·ba·bi	እዚህ አካባቢ የ
... service nearby?	... a·geul·glot al·leu?	... አገልግሎትአለ?
computer	kom·pyu·teur	ኮምፒዉተር
photocopying	fo·to ko·pi	ፎቶ ኮፒ
translation	as·teur·gwa·mi	አስተርጓሚ
(English) typing	(ən·gli·zə·nya)	(እንግሊዝኛ)
	taip	ታይፕ

How much to print (one) page?
(and) geuṣ print leu mad·reug   (አንድ) ገፅ ፕሪንት
sənt nō?   ለማድረግ ስንት ነው-?

MUSIC

መ·ዚ·ቃ

For music types, see page 108 in Interests. You can buy tapes and sometimes CDs at a mu·zi·ka bet.

I want to buy a/an ...	... meug·zat ə·feul·lə·gal·lō	... መግዛት እፈል·ጋለሁ·
audio cassette	ka·set	ካሴት
blank cassette	yal·teu·keu·da·beut yeu tep ka·set	ያል·ተ·ቀዳበት የቴፕ ካሴት
cassette by ...	yeu ... ka·set	የ ... ካሴት
CD by ...	yeu ... si·di	የ ... ሲ·ዲ
song by ...	yeu ... zeu·feun	የ ... ዘፈን
traditional Ethiopian music cassette	ya·geur ba·hal ka·set	ያገር ባህል ካሴት

What's her/his best recording?
yeus·swa/yeus·su yeu·ta·weu·kō ka·set yeu·tə·nyow nō?

የሷ/የሱ የታወቀው ካሴት የትኛው ነው?

Can I listen to this (cassette) here?
yi·hen (ka·set) meus·mat ə·cha·lal·lō?

ይህን (ካሴት) መስማት እችላለሁ?

PHOTOGRAPHY

ፎቶግራፍ

For photographic goods and services, ask for a fo·to bet. English is used for many photographic terms, like 'lens' and 'flash'.

How much is it for developing/enlarging?
mat·ko·ri·ya/ma·sa·teu·bi·ya sənt nō?

ማጥቆሪያ/ማሳጠቢያ ስንት ነው?

Can you fix my camera?
ka·me·ra·yen lət·seu·row tə·cha·lal·leuh? (m)

ካሜራዬን ልትሰራው ትችላለህ?

When will it be ready?
meu·che yi·deur·sal?

መቼ ይደርሳል?

I want to buy	... meug·zat	... መግዛት
a/an ...	ə·feul·lə·gal·lō	እፈልጋለሁ
battery	ba·tri dən·gai	ባትሪ ድንጋይ
camera	ka·me·ra; fo·to man·sha	ካሜራ/ፎቶ ማንሻ
film	film	ፊልም
B&W film	tə·k̲ur na neuçh film	ጥቁርና ነጭ ፊልም
colour film	keu·leur film	ከለር ፊልም
(24/36) film	ba·leu (ha·ya a·rat; seu·las·sa sə·dəst) film	ባለ (ሃያ አራት/ ሰላሳ ስድስት) ፊልም
flash	flash	ፍላሽ
videotape	vi·di·yo ka·set	ቪድዮ ካሴት

SMOKING
ሲ.ጋራ ማጨስ

Is it OK if I smoke here?
əz·zi si·ga·ra ma·çheus yi·cha·lal? — እዚህ ሲ.ጋራ ማጨስ ይቻላል?

No smoking.
ma·çheus kəl·kəl nō — ማጨስ ክልክል ነው.

Excuse me, do you have a light?
yi·k̲ər·ta kəb·rit al·leuh/ al·leush? (m/f) — ይቅርታ ክብሪት አለህ/ አለሽ?

Please don't smoke.
ə·ba·kəh a·ta·çhəs (m) — እባክህ አታጭስ
ə·ba·kəsh a·ta·çhə·shi (f) — እባክሽ አታጭሺ.

I'm trying to give up.
leu·ma·k̲om ə·yeu·mo·keur·ku nō — ለማቆም እየሞከርኩ ነው.

ashtray	yeu si·ga·ra meu·teur·ko·sha	የሲ.ጋራ መተርኮሻ
cigarette (packet)	(pa·ko) si·ga·ra	(ፓኮ) ሲ.ጋራ
cigars	si·ga·ra	ሲ.ጋራ
lighter	lai·teur	ላይተር
matches	kəb·rit	ክብሪት
pipe	pi·pa	ፒፓ
tobacco	təm·ba·ho	ትምባሆ

SIZES & COMPARISONS · ልክና ማመሳሰል

another	le·la	ሌላ
big	təl·ləḵ	ትልቅ
bigger	teu·leuḵ ya·leu	ተለቅ ያለ
biggest	beu·ṭam təl·ləḵ	በጣም ትልቅ
enough	beu·ḵi	በቂ
few	tən·nish	ትንሽ
heavy	keu·bad	ከባድ
many/a lot	bə·zu	ብዙ
more	beu·za ya·leu	በዛ ያለ
small	tən·nish	ትንሽ
smaller (less)	an·neus ya·leu	አነስ ያለ
smallest	beu·ṭam tən·nish	በጣም ትንሽ
some	an·dand	አንዳንድ
too much/many	beu·ṭam bə·zu	በጣም ብዙ

WEIGHTS & MEASURES · ሚዛንና መለኪያዎች

Ethiopia uses the metric measurement system. Amharic metric terms sound almost exactly the same as they do in English.

centimetre	sən·ti me·tər	ሴንቲ ሜትር
metre	me·tər	ሜትር
kilometre	ki·lo me·tər	ኪሎ ሜትር
gram	gram	ግራም
half a kilogram	gə·mash ki·lo	ግማሽ ኪሎ
kilogram	ki·lo gram	ኪሎ ግራም
100 kilograms	kun·tal	ኩንታል
millilitre	mil·li li·tər	ሚሊ ሊትር
half a litre	gə·mash li·tər	ግማሽ ሊትር
litre	li·tər	ሊትር

SHOPPING

USEFUL WORDS   ጠቃሚ ቃሎች

agent (commission)	deu·lal·la	ደላላ
to bargain	meu·keu·ra·keur	መከራከር
change	meuls	መልስ
cheap	rə·kash	ርካሽ
clean	nə·suh	ንጹህ
dirty	ko·sha·sha	ቆሻሻ
discount	kə·nash	ቅናሽ
expensive	wədd	ውድ
to export	weu·deu wəch meu·lak	ወደ ውጭ መላክ
fixed price	yeu teu·weu·seu·neu wa·ga	የተወሰነ ዋጋ
to import	keu·wəch mas·meu·ṭat	ከውጭ ማስመጣት
long	reu·jim	ረጅም
new	ad·dis	አዲስ
old	a·ro·ge	አሮጌ
packet	pa·ko	ፓኮ
plastic bag	keu·reu·ṭit	ከረጢት
receipt	deur·reu·seuny	ደረሰኝ
shop/kiosk	suk	ሱቅ
short	a·chər	አጭር
street stalls	gul·lət	ጉልት
surcharge	teu·cheum·ma·ri wa·ga	ተጨማሪ ዋጋ
trade	nəgd	ንግድ

SHOPPING

Most Ethiopian meals consist of ən·jeu·ra, a local flat bread, topped with a spicy meat or vegetable weuṭ, 'sauce'. Wash it all down with ṭeuj, 'honey wine', and a pot of fresh bun·na, 'coffee' – meul·kam mə·gəb!, 'Enjoy your meal!'.

THROUGH THE DAY   በቀን ውስጥ

Ethiopians usually take a light breakfast and have a solid lunch and/or dinner.

breakfast	ḳurs	ቁርስ
lunch	mə·sa	ምሳ
dinner	ə·rat	እራት
snack (evening)	meuk·seus	መክሰስ

PLACES TO EAT   መመገቢያ ቦታዎች

Eating places are generally open from early morning until late in the evening, with meal times flexible.

Is there a good/cheap (restaurant)
near here?
   əz·zi a·ka·ba·bi ṭə·ru/rə·kash   እዚህ አካባቢ ጥሩ/ርካሽ
   (mə·gəb bet) al·leu   (ምግብ ቤት) አለ?
What's the name of the restaurant?
   yeu mə·gəb be·tu səm   የምግብ ቤቱ ስም
   man nō?   ማነው?
Where's (the restaurant)?
   (mə·gəb be·tu) yeut nō?   (ምግብ ቤቱ) የት ነው?

I want to	yeu ... mə·gəb	የ ... ምግብ
eat ... food.	ə·feul·lə·gal·lō	እፈልጋለሁ
Ethiopian	i·tə·yo·pi·ya	ኢትዮጵያ
Italian	ṭal·yan	ጣሊያን
Western	feu·reunj	ፈረንጅ

FOOD

The main places for eating out are mə·gəb bet and bun·na bet, but there are plenty of other great places to eat, drink and unwind. Most neighbourhoods have at least one of the following:

az·ma·ri bet   አዝማሪ ቤት
    traditional music and entertainment bar, serving drinks and
    light snacks
bun·na bet   ቡና ቤት
    'coffee house', serving coffee, tea, soft drinks, alcoholic drinks,
    light snacks and sometimes full meals
kek bet or pes·tri   ኬክ ቤት
    bakery or tea shop selling cakes, pastries, tea and coffee
jus bet   ጁስ ቤት
    snack bar specialising in fresh fruit juices so thick and delicious
    your spoon will stand up in them
mə·gəb bet   ምግብ ቤት
    restaurant or eating house (refers to any place serving full meals)
meu·sheu·ta bet   መሸታ ቤት
    similar to a bun·na bet or az·ma·ri bet, with drinks and
    entertainment
țeul·la bet/țeuj bet   ጠላ ቤት/ጠጅ ቤት
    traditional bars serving Ethiopian beer, spirits and wine (usually
    a male domain)

EATING OUT   ውጭ መብላት

Menus aren't always available, so ask the a·sa·la·fi, 'waiter', about dishes and prices. The menu decoder on page 148 will help you decipher what the dishes mean. To attract the waiter's attention, say yi·ķər·ta, 'Excuse me', or hold up your hand.

Do you serve (food) here?
    (mə·gəb) al·leu?   (ምግብ) አለ?
A table for (two).
    leu (hu·leutt) sō bo·ta   ለ (ሁ·ለት) ሰው ቦታ
Is this seat free?
    sō al·leu?   ሰው አለ?

Do you have a menu (in English)?
  me·nu (beu ən·gli·zə·nya) al·leu?　ሜኑ (በእንግሊዝኛ) አለ?

What's on the menu today?
  za·re mən al·la·chu?　ዛሬ ምን አላቸሁ?

Do you have (vegetables)?
  (at·kəlt) al·leu?　(አትክልት) አለ?

Where can I wash my hands?
  əj meu·ta·ṭeu·bi·ya yeut nō?　እጅ መታጠቢያ የት ነው?

I want (another) ...
  (le·la) ... ə·feul·lə·gal·lō　(ሌላ) ... እፈልጋለሁ

I'm hungry.
  ra·beuny　ራበኝ

I'm thirsty.
  wu·ha ṭeu·many　ውሃ ጠማኝ

I'm full/satisfied.
  ṭeu·gəb·yal·lō　ጠግቤአለሁ

The bill please.
  hi·sab ə·ba·kəh/ə·ba·kəsh (m/f)　ሂሳብ እባክህ/እባክሽ

Please bring a/an ...　ə·ba·kəh ... am·ṭa (m)　እባክህ ... አምጣ
　　　　　　　　　ə·ba·kəsh ... am·chi (f)　እባክሽ ... አምጪ

ashtray	meu·teur·ko·sha	መተርኮሻ
cup	ku·ba·ya	ኩባያ
fork	shu·ka	ሹካ
glass	bər·chə·ḳo	ብርጭቆ
knife	bil·la·wa	ቢላዋ
plate	sa·hən	ሳህን
spoon	man·ki·ya	ማንኪያ
towel	fo·ṭa	ፎጣ

FOOD

THEY MAY SAY ...

mən lə·ta·zeuz?
　What would you like?
le·la mə·gəb yəm·ṭa?
　Do you want more food?

FOOD

Describing Your Meal

ስለ ምግብዎ መናገር

This food is delicious.
kon·jo mə·gəb nō
ቆንጆ ምግብ ነው‐

We love Ethiopian cuisine.
yeu i·tə·yo·pi·ya mə·gəb
ən·weud·dal·leun
የኢትዮጵያ ምግብ
እንወዳለን

Our compliments to the chef.
ba·leu mu·ya nō yeu seu·row
ባለሙያ ነው‐ የሰራው‐

This food is off/not good.
məg·bu teu·beu·lash·twal
ምግቡ ተበላሽቷል

This food is too spicy.
məg·bu beur·beu·re
beuz·to·beu·tal
ምግቡ በርበሬ
በዝቶበታል

I want it mild/hot.
a·lə·cha/beur·beu·re
yi·hu·nə·ləny
አልጫ/በርበሬ
ይሁንልኝ

I don't want ...
... al·feul·lə·gəm
... አልፈልግም

I want only ...
... bə·cha ə·feul·lə·gal·lō
... ብቻ እፈልጋለሁ‐

It's ...	... nō	... ነው‐
bitter	meu·ra·ra	መራራ
cold	keuz·kaz·za	ቀዝቃዛ
cooked	yeu beu·seu·leu	የበሰለ
dry	deu·reuk	ደረቅ
heated	mok ya·leu	ሞቅ ያለ
hot	muk	ሙቅ
salty	chō yeu·beu·za·beut	ጨዉ የበዛበት
stale	yeu teu·beu·la·sheu	የተበላሸ
sweet	ta·fach	ጣፋጭ

VEGETARIAN & SPECIAL MEALS

አትክልትና ልዩ ምግቦች

In fasting season, vegetarian dishes are always available. Local markets are great for raw food to supplement your diet. See the menu decoder for popular vegetarian dishes.

I don't eat meat.
sə·ga al·beul·lam
ስጋ አልበላም

Do you have fasting food (vegetarian dishes)?
yeu şom mə·gəb al·leu?
የጾም ምግብ አለ?

I don't eat (fish).
(a·sa) al·beul·lam
(አሳ) አልበላም

I can't eat dairy products.
weu·teut neuk məg·bo·chən al·beul·lam
ወተት ነክ ምግቦችን አልበላም

Do you have any vegetable dishes?
yeu at·kəlt mə·gəb al·la·chu?
የአትክልት ምግብ አላችሁ?

Does it contain (eggs)?
(ən·ķu·lal) al·lō?
(እንቁላል) አለው-?

I'm allergic to (peanuts).
(o·cho·lo·ni) ais·ma·ma·nyəm
(አቾሎኒ) አይስማማኝም

USEFUL WORDS

ጠቃሚ ቃሎች

bottle opener	yeu ţeur·mus meuk·feu·cha	የጠርሙስ መክፈቻ
chair	weun·beur	ወንበር
cooking oil	yeu mə·gəb zayt	የምግብ ዘይት
to eat	meub·lat	መብላት
food	mə·gəb	ምግብ
jug	ţa·sa	ጣሳ
mortar and pestle	mu·ķeu·cha·na zeu·neu·zeu·na	ሙቀጫና ዘነዘና
napkin	yeu aff meuţ·reu·gi·ya	የአፍ መጥረጊያ
pot	sheuk·la	ሽክላ
recipe	mə·gəb a·seu·rar zeu·de	ምግብ አሰራር ዘዴ
saucepan	yeu weuţ sa·hən	የወጥ ሳህን
table	ţeu·reu·pe·za	ጠረጴዛ
teaspoon	yeu shai man·ki·ya	የሻይ ማንኪያ
waiter	a·sa·la·fi	አሳላፊ

FOOD

FOOD

EATING WITH FRIENDS   ከጓደኞች ጋር መብላት

Ethiopians often ask friends and visitors to join them for a meal –
usually a communal experience with several people eating from the
one large plate of ən·jeu·ra. If you're not hungry, take a little food
to thank them for the invitation, or pat your stomach and say
a·meu·seu·gə·nal·lō, ṭeu·gəb·yal·lō, 'Thank you, I'm satisfied'.

While mealtimes are relaxed and friendly, there are a few points
on etiquette to note. Try to avoid using your left hand for eating
to respect cultural sensitivities. Never pick at food, lick your
fingers, or eat food from the other side of the plate. If your hosts
raise parcels of food to your mouth, a friendly gesture known as
gur·sha, accept the mouthful. People will urge you to keep eating
until you reassure them with ṭeu·gəb·yal·lō, 'I'm satisfied'.

Please join us!	ə·nə·bla!	እንብላ!
Please eat!	bə·la/biy! (m/f)	ብላ/ብይ!
Please have a drink!	ṭeu·ṭa/ṭeu·chi! (m/f)	ጠጣ/ጠጪ!
I'll pay/My treat!	yeu·ne gəb·zha nō!	የኔ ግብዣ ነው·
It was an enjoyable	ḳon·jo mə·gəb	ቆንጆ ምግብ ነው·
meal.	neub·beur	ነበር

FEAST OF FASTS

Religion has a big influence on Ethiopian eating habits.
Devoted Orthodox Christians fast around 165 to 250
days a year, including Lent in the lead-up to Easter.
During this time, they abstain from all animal products
(meat, dairy, eggs). The main Muslim fast is Ramadan,
in which followers eat nothing between sunrise and sun-
down. Both Orthodox Christians and Muslims only eat
meat slaughtered by their own kind.

fasting	ṣom	ፆም
fasting food	yeu ṣom mə·gəb	የፆም ምግብ
feast	meu·feu·seuk	መፈሰክ

BREAKFAST
ቁርስ

The most common light breakfast is dab·bo beu shai, 'bread and tea'. Most eateries also serve honey, eggs and coffee. Spicy traditional cereals are sometimes served in people's homes.

bread/bread rolls	dab·bo	ዳቦ
coffee (with sugar/ without sugar)	bun·na (beu sə·kwar; ya·leu sə·kwar)	ቡና (በስኳር/ ያለ ስኳር)
coffee (with milk/ without milk)	bun·na (beu weu·teut; ya·leu weu·teut)	ቡና (በወተት/ ያለ ወተት)
egg(s)	ən·ku·lal	እንቁላል
boiled eggs	kə·kəl ən·ku·lal	ቅቅል እንቁላል
fried eggs	ən·ku·lal ṭəbs	እንቁላል ጥብስ
scrambled eggs	ən·ku·lal fər·fər	እንቁላል ፍርፍር
honey	mar	ማር
juice	chə·ma·ķi	ጭማቂ
margarine	mar·geu·rin	ማርገሪን
milk	weu·teut	ወተት
sugar	sə·kwar	ስኳር
tea (strong/weak)	(weuf·ram/ķeu·chən) shai	(ወፍራም/ቀጭን) ሻይ

FOOD

Traditional Breakfast Dishes
የአገር ባህል የቁርስ ምግቦች

fət·fət
ፍትፍት
chopped up ən·jeu·ra or bread mixed with chilli or butter

geun·fo
ገንፎ
barley or wheat porridge, often served with Ethiopian butter and a spicy hot sauce

ka·teu·nya/də·rəb·rə·bosh
ቃተኛ/ድርብርቦሽ
ən·jeu·ra cooked in a paste of chilli and Ethiopian butter

kən·che
ቅንጬ
boiled crushed wheat porridge with traditional butter

FOOD

TYPICAL DISHES   ዋና ምግቦች

To eat Ethiopia's main dish, *injera* (ən·jeu·ra), break a corner off
with the fingers and use it to wrap or scoop up the spicy meat or
vegetable topping. If you like your food on the mild side, ask for
a·lə·ça food. See also the menu decoder, page 148.

The most common meats are chicken, lamb and beef. Seafood,
other than fish, is rare. Pork is also rare, as it is forbidden to both
Christians and Muslims.

Traditional Condiments   የአገር ባህል ቅመማ ቅመም

Powdered herb and spice mixtures are added during cooking or
used as a seasoning for the main meal. The combination of the
spices in beur·beu·re and spiced butter is what gives sauces their
distinct Ethiopian flavour.

a·frinj   አፍሪንጅ
  mixture of red pepper seeds, ginger and garlic

a·wa·ze/də·leuh   አዋዜ/ድለህ
  butter and beur·beu·re sauce; usually eaten with raw meat

beur·beu·re   በርበሬ
  crushed chilli, garlic, ginger, basil, rue seed, cloves, cinnamon,
  cardamom, Bishop's weed and red onion

miṭ·mi·ṭa   ሚጥሚጣ
  powdered hot small red peppers mixed with garlic, ginger and
  other spices (hotter than beur·beu·re)

seu·na·fəçh   ሰናፍጭ
  Ethiopian mustard

chilli sauce	də·ləh/a·wa·ze	ድለህ/አዋዜ
gravy/broth	meu·reuḳ	መረቅ
salt	çhō	ጨው
sugar	sə·kwar	ስኳር
tomato sauce	yeu ti·ma·tim də·ləh	የቲማቲም ድለህ

Snacks ቀላል ምግቦች

Snacks such as fresh bread or ko·lo, 'fried barley', are eaten with tea, coffee or juices, or on their own. See Staples, page 152, for a list of bread types.

bread/bread rolls	dab·bo	ዳቦ
chips	də·nəch ṭəbs	ድንች ጥብስ
crackers	ki·ṭa	ቂጣ
fried barley	ko·lo	ቆሎ
peanuts	o·cho·lo·ni	አቾሎኒ
popcorn	a·beu·ba ko·lo	አበባ ቆሎ
samosa (lentil)	sam·bo·sa	ሳምቦሳ
wheat snacks	dab·bo ko·lo	ዳቦ ቆሎ
yogurt	ər·go	እርጎ

FOOD

KEY DISHES ዋና ዋና ምግቦች

The main vegetable dishes at eateries are məs·sər weuṭ, shi·ro, at·kəlt and kək weuṭ. The main meat dishes are do·ro weuṭ, kai weuṭ, kət·fo, ṭəbs and zəg·ni. All come with ən·jeu·ra. For a bit of each, ask for beu·yai·neu·tu. For a vegetarian mix, ask for yeu ṣom beu·yai·neu·tu.

You'll notice in the menu decoder that meat and vegetable names are often attached to the following dish types.

a·lə·cha	አልጫ
not too spicy	
mən·cheut a·bəsh	ምንቾት አብሽ
minced, cooked in spices	
shor·ba	ሾርባ
soup, not usually an entree in Ethiopia	
ṭəbs	ጥብስ
cut into pieces and fried in spices	
tə·re	ጥሬ
raw, usually dipped in spices	
weuṭ	ወጥ
spicy stew/sauce	

FOOD

MENU DECODER

aib አይብ
  Ethiopian cheese (similar to cottage cheese). Sometimes mixed with spinach/collard greens (aib beu go·meun)

a·sa አሳ
  fish; either dried, salted or cooked in sauce

a·sa weuṭ አሳ ወጥ
  fish cooked in spicy sauce

at·kəlt (lit: vegetables) አትክልት
  mixture of cooked vegetables; usually spinach, carrots, potatoes

bam·ya a·lə·cha ባምያ አልጫ
  okra in a spicy mild sauce

beu·yai·neu·tu በያይነቱ
  'of each kind'; a mixture of common ən·jeu·ra toppings, usually do·ro weuṭ, ṭəbs, vegetables and spicy pulse mixtures

bid·de·na በዴና
  bread sometimes served in east Ethiopia, similar to ən·jeu·ra, but sweeter and made from millet

də·nəch seu·la·ṭa/də·nəch weuṭ ድንች ሰላጣ/ድንች ወጥ
  potato salad/stew

dab·bo ዳቦ
  bread or bread rolls with similar flavour and texture to Western bread

do·ro weuṭ ዶሮ ወጥ
  a rich and spicy chicken stew, one of Ethiopia's favourite national dishes, often served with a whole boiled egg

du·leut ዱለት
  minced tripe, liver and lean beef fried in onions, butter, chilli, cardamom and pepper

ən·jeu·ra እንጀራ
  large, pancake-like bread made from ṭəf (Ethiopia's native grain), yeast and water. Light and spongy in texture, tangy in flavour, colours vary from white to dark brown, depending on the flour used – sometimes millet or rice flour is used.

ər·go   እርጎ
  yoghurt, a cooling side dish for hot, spicy meals

ən·ḳu·lal weuṭ   እንቁላል ወጥ
  spicy egg sauce

go·meun   ጎመን
  cooked spinach/collard greens

go·meun beu sə·ga   ጎመን በስጋ
  collard greens and meat mixed together

ḳai weuṭ   ቀይ ወጥ
  spicy beef, lamb or goat stew

ḳə·ḳəl   ትቅል
  boiled meat

kək weuṭ   ክክ ወጥ
  spicy split-pea sauce

kət·fo   ክትር
  spicy minced beef often served with aib cottage cheese
  (sometimes served raw – say leub leub if you want it cooked)

ḳi·ṭa   ቂጣ
  crisp chapatti-like bread, often cooked in chilli, butter and
  spices

ḳo·ćho   ቆርጮ
  Southern Ethiopian staple ḳo·ćho (made from the fermented
  roots of the false banana tree), often cooked in a peppery
  sauce with minced meat

ḳwa·li·ma   ቋሊማ
  spicy sausage, from the Harar region

ḳwan·ṭa   ቋንጣ
  strips of beef (usually dried), rubbed in chilli, butter, salt
  and pepper

mən·cheut a·bəsh   ምንቾት አብሽ
  minced meat curry

məs·sər weuṭ   ምስር ወጥ
  lentil 'curry'; lentils cooked in onions, chilli, spices

meu·reuḳ   መረት
  soup/broth (usually spicy lamb or beef)

FOOD

FOOD

nəf·ro ንፍሮ
dry mixture of boiled chick peas, lentils and other legumes

sə·ga weuṭ ስጋ ወጥ
spicy beef stew

seu·la·ṭa ሰላጣ
salad (may be coleslaw or tomato and lettuce, depending on where you are)

shi·ro ሽሮ
spiced chick pea dhal – neuçh shi·ro is mild, and mə·ṭən shi·ro is hot

ṭəbs ጥብስ
pan fried and spiced beef or lamb slices

ṭə·kəl go·meun ጥቅል ጎመን
cooked cabbage and carrots

ṭə·re sə·ga ጥሬ ስጋ
raw beef served with butter, chilli and other spices

ti·ma·tim fəṭ·fəṭ ቲማቲም ፍትፍት
mildly spiced, chopped tomato dish with ən·jeu·ra

yeu a·deun·gwa·re shor·ba የአደንጓሬ ሾርባ
bean soup

yeu do·ro ṭəbs የዶሮ ጥብስ
fried and spiced chicken pieces

yeu dub·ba weuṭ የዱባ ወጥ
spicy pumpkin stew

yeu ka·ri·ya sən·nəny የቃሪያ ስንኝ
uncooked hot peppers stuffed with onion

yeu məs·sər shor·ba የምስር ሾርባ
tasty lentil soup

yeu șom mə·gəb የዓም ምግብ
fasting food; a range of spicy vegetable and legume dishes

zəg·ni a·lə·cha ዝግኒ አልጫ
mild meat stew (usually lamb)

COOKING METHODS   የምግብ አሰራር ዘዴ

Ethiopian meals are time consuming to prepare. The watery ən·jeu·ra dough requires three days of fermentation, and the ubiquitous spices need careful grinding and mixing. Ethiopians are usually happy to demonstrate local cooking techniques and may encourage you to give it a go, a messy but fun experience.

What are you cooking?
mən ə·yeu·seu·rah nō? (m)	ምን እየሰራህ ነው?
mən ə·yeu·seu·rash nō? (f)	ምን እየሰራሽ ነው?

Can I watch?
ma·yeut yi·cha·lal?	ማየት ይቻላል?

Can I help?
meur·dat ə·chəl·lal·lō?	መርዳት እችላለሁ?

It's not cooked.
al·beu·seu·leum	አልበሰለም

baked (in an oven)	yeu·teu·ga·geu·reu	የተጋገረ
boiled	ḳə·ḳəl	ቅቅል
cooked/heated	yeu beu·seu·leu	የበሰለ
fried	yeu teu·ṭeu·beu·seu	የተጠበሰ
raw	ṭə·re	ጥሬ
well done	yeu beu·seu·leu	የበሰለ

SELF-CATERING   ምግብ ማዘጋጀት

You'll find a huge range of fresh fruit, vegetables, eggs, pulses and staples from markets and street stalls. There are also prepared mixtures like shi·ro – just add water and cook! Tinned and imported food is limited to grocery shops in major towns. You can buy meat from a sə·ga bet or a live chicken from the local market – though you might get attached to it on the bus ride home! See also At the Market & Street Stalls, page 121.

FOOD

Staples

ዋና ምግቦች

bread/bread rolls (plain)	dab·bo	ዳቦ
bread (from the false banana tree; a southern staple)	ḳo·cho	ቆጮ
bread (northern Ethiopian round bread)	am·ba·sha	አምባሻ
flour	du·ḳet	ዱቄት
injera	ən·jeu·ra	እንጀራ
injera (dried)	dər·ḳosh	ድርቆሽ
maize (corn)	beu·ḳo·lo	በቆሎ
pasta	pas·ta	ፓስታ
potatoes	də·nach	ድንች
rice	ruz	ሩዝ
roasted barley drink	beu·so	በሶ
spaghetti	spa·ge·ti	ስፓጌቲ
sweet potatoes	sə·kwar də·nach	ስኳር ድንች

Dairy Produce

ወተት ነክ የምግብ ውጤቶች

butter	ḳə·be	ቅቤ
Ethiopian (spiced) butter	yeu teu·neu·ṭeu·reu ḳə·be	የተነካረ ቅቤ
cheese (cottage style)	aib	አይብ
cream (usually skimmed from boiled milk)	səl·ba·bot	ስልባቦት
eggs	ən·ḳu·lal	እንቁላል
margarine	mar·geu·rin	ማርገሪን
milk	weu·teut	ወተት
yogurt	ər·go	እርጎ

Meat & Poultry ስጋና ዶሮ

beef/ox meat	yeu beu·re sə·ga	የበሬ ስጋ
broth	meu·reuķ	መረቅ
chicken	do·ro	ዶሮ
dripping	cho·ma	ጮማ
fish	a·sa	አሳ
goat meat	yeu fə·yeul sə·ga	የፍየል ስጋ
lamb	yeu beug sə·ga	የበግ ስጋ
meat	sə·ga	ስጋ
offal	du·leut	ዱለት
sausage	ķwa·li·ma/so·sej	ቋሊማ/ሶሴጅ
veal	yeu ţə·ja sə·ga	የጥጃ ስጋ

FOOD

Vegetables አትክልቶች

beans	a·deun·gwa·re	አደንጓሬ
beetroot	ķai sər	ቀይ ስር
cabbage	ţə·ķəl go·meun	ጥቅል ጎመን
capsicum	yeu feu·reunj ķa·ri·ya	የፈረንጅ ቃሪያ
carrot	ka·rot	ካሮት
cauliflower	a·beu·ba go·meun	አበባ ጎመን
corn	beu·ķo·lo	በቆሎ
onion	shən·kurt	ሽንኩርት
peas	a·teur	አተር
potato	də·nəch	ድንች
pumpkin/squash	dub·ba	ዱባ
salad	seu·la·ţa	ሰላጣ
spinach	ķos·ţa	ቆስጣ
sweet potato	sə·kwar də·nəch	ስኳር ድንች
tomato	ti·ma·tim	ቲማቲም
vegetables	at·kəlt	አትክልት

FOOD

Legumes, Nuts & Pulses   አተር ባቄላና ለውዝ

barley	geubs	ጐብስ
beans	ba·ḳe·la	ባቄላ
chick peas	shən·bra dub·be	ሽንብራ ዱቤ
kidney beans	ba·ḳe·la	ባቄላ
lentils	məs·sər	ምስር
nuts	leuwz	ለውዝ
peanuts	o·cho·lo·ni	አቾሎኒ
split peas	kək	ክክ
sunflower seeds	yeu suff a·beu·ba feu·re	የሱፍ አበባ ፍሬ

ቆንጆ ምግብ ነው።

ባለሙያ ነው የሰራው።

Fruit   ፍራፍሬ

apple	pom	ፖም
avocado	a·vo·ka·do	አቮካዶ
banana	muz	ሙዝ
dates	teu·mər	ተምር
fruit	fə·ra·fə·re	ፍራፍሬ
grapes	wain	ወይን
guava	zay·tun	ዘይቱን
lemon	lo·mi	ሎሚ
mandarin	meun·deu·rin	መንደሪን
mango	man·go	ማንጎ
melon	bə·ṭih	ብጢ
orange	bər·tu·kan	ብርቱካን
papaya	pa·pa·ya	ፓፓያ
peach	kok	ኮክ
pineapple	a·nan·nas	አናናስ
sugar cane	sheun·ko·ra	ሸንኩራ
sultanas	zeu·bib	ዘቢብ
watermelon	kər·bush	ክርቡሽ

Herbs & Spices ቅመማ ቅመም

See page 146 for traditional ready-made spice mixtures.

basil	beu·so bə·la	በሶ ብላ
Bishop's weed	neuch az·mud	ነጭ አዝሙ·ድ
black cumin	ṭə·ḳur az·mud	ጥቁር አዝሙ·ድ
chilli	ḳa·ri·ya	ቃሪያ
cinnamon	ḳeu·reu·fa	ቀረፋ
cloves	ḳə·rən·fud	ቅርንፉ·ድ
coriander	dəm·bə·lal	ድምብላል
cumin	az·mud	አዝሙ·ድ
fennel	ən·sə·lal	እንስላል
fenugreek	a·bəsh	አበሽ
garlic	neuch shən·kurt	ነጭ ሽንኩ·ርት
ginger	zən·jə·bəl	ዝንጅ·ብል
pepper (black)	ḳun·do beur·beu·re	ቁንዶ በርበሬ
rue	ṭe·na a·dam	ጤና አዳም
spices	ḳə·meu·ma ḳə·meum	ቅመማ ቅመም
turmeric	ərd	እርድ

Sweet Food ጣፋጭ ምግብ

Desserts (other than fruit and yogurt) are uncommon in Ethiopia, but sweet food is a treat between meals. Try cakes and biscuits at your local kek bet. Pastries like hal·wa and bak·la·va are popular in Addis. See also Snacks on page 147.

biscuit	bəs·kut	ብስኩ·ት
cake	kek	ኬክ
chewing gum	mas·ti·ka	ማስቲካ
chocolate	cheu·ko·let	ቸኮሌት
honey	mar	ማር
ice cream	ais krem	አይስ ክሬም
popcorn	a·beu·ba ḳo·lo	አበባ ቆሎ
sugar	sə·kwar	ስኳር
sugar cane	sheun·ko·ra	ሸንኮራ
sweets/lollies/ fudge	keu·reu·me·la	ከረሜላ

FOOD

የቡና አፈላል

yeu bun·na a·feu·lal coffee ceremony

DRINKS

የሚጠጡ

Jus bet and bun·na bet (juice and coffee bars) offer cheap and delicious freshly made drinks as well as bottled drinks. Tap water should be boiled or treated before drinking.

Nonalcoholic

አልኮል ነክ ያልሆኑ

juice	chə·ma·ki	ጭማቂ
mixed fruit	spress	ስፕሬስ
pineapple juice	yeu a·nan·nas chə·ma·ki	የአናናስ ጭማቂ
without water	jus bə·cha ya·leu wu·ha	ጁስ ብቻ ያለ ውሃ
milk	weu·teut	ወተት
mineral water	am·bo wu·ha	አምቦ ውሃ
soda/soft drink	leus·las·sa	ለስላሳ
water	wu·ha	ውሃ
boiled water	yeu feu·la wu·ha	የፈላ ውሃ
sterilised water	yeu teu·ta·ra wu·ha	የተጣራ ውሃ
hot cereal drink	aṭ·mit/beu·so	አጥሚት/በሶ

Tea & Coffee

ሻይና ቡና

Believed to be the original home of the coffee tree, Ethiopia is a coffee lover's dream. Fresh black coffee, cappuccino and latte-style brews are served everywhere in bun·na bet

In the traditional coffee ceremony, held frequently in people's homes, coffee is prepared, step-by-step, over a small charcoal stove. When the roasting beans are passed around for you to savour the aroma, wave the smoke towards your nose. When you're offered snacks or a si·ni (tiny cup) of coffee, nod your head in appreciation. The first round is a·bol, the second hu·leut·teu·nya and the third and most important, beu·reu·ka, which means 'blessing'. The ceremonies are a great time for conversation among friends, families and neighbours, and can last for hours.

FOOD

FOOD

black coffee	ṭə·kur bun·na	ጥቁር ቡና
coffee ...	bun·na ...	ቡና ...
with/without sugar	beu/ya·leu sə·kwar	በ/ያለ ስኳር
with/without milk	beu/ya·leu weu·teut	በ/ያለ ወተት
with a little milk	keu tən·nish	ከትንሽ ወተት
	weu·teut gar	ጋር
coffee beans	ṭə·re bun·na	ጥሬ ቡና
coffee ceremony	yeu bun·na a·feu·lal	የቡና አፈላል
coffee pot	yeu bun·na jeu·beu·na	የቡና ጀበና
incense granules	ə·ṭan	ዕጣን
incense stick	neud	ነድ
coffee leaf tea (rare)	ku·ti/hoj·ja	ቁጢ/ሆጃ
black tea	ṭə·kur shai	ጥቁር ሻይ
tea ...	shai ...	ሻይ ...
with/without sugar	beu/ya·leu sə·kwar	በ/ያለ ስኳር
with/without milk	beu/ya·leu weu·teut	በ/ያለ ወተት
with a little milk	keu tən·nish	ከትንሽ
	weu·teut gar	ወተት ጋር
strong/weak	weuf·ram/keu·chən	ወፍራም/ቀጭን
tea with spices	ba·leu kə·meum shai	ባለ ቅመም ሻይ
tea with lemon	shai beu lo·mi	ሻይ በሎሚ
hot milk	ṭə·kus weu·teut	ትኩስ ወተት

Alcoholic   አልኮል ነክ የሆኑ መጠጦች

The most famous Ethiopian home brews are ṭeul·la and ṭeuj, available at ṭeul·la bet, ṭeuj bet and sometimes restaurants. The main drinking venue is the local bun·na bet (coffee shop/bar) which has local and imported alcoholic and nonalcoholic drinks. Most spirits retain their English or original name.

Let's drink!

ən·ṭeu·ṭa!	እንጠጣ!

Cheers!

leu·ṭe·na·chən!	ለጤናችን!

FOOD

a·reu·ḳi   አረቄ
warming local grain spirit; twice-filtered is da·gəm

ka·ti·ka·la   ካቲካላ
local spirit

ṭeul·la   ጠላ
refreshing mild alcoholic drink made from barley or maize

ṭeuj   ጠጅ
wine made from honey and the local ge·sho plant, drunk out
of bə·rə·le, small flasks with long, narrow necks. Variations
on the main drink include deu·reuḳ (dry), meu·ha·keu·leu·nya
(medium sweet), leus·las·sa or bərz (sweet and mild).

beer	bi·ra	ቢራ
ice	beu·reu·do	በረዶ
whiskey	wis·ki keu	ውስኪ
with (Coke)	(ko·ka ko·la) gar	ከ (ኮካ ኮላ) ጋር
wine	wain	ዋይን

IN THE BAR   ቡና ቤት ውስጥ
What'll you have?
   mən yim·ṭal·ləh? (m)   ምን ይምጣልህ?
   mən yim·ṭal·ləsh? (f)   ምን ይምጣልሽ?
I'll have ...
   ... yim·ṭa·ləny   ... ይምጣልኝ
No ice.
   beu·reu·do al·feul·lə·gəm   በረዶ አልፈልግም
Same again, please.
   yeuz·zi·hu ai·neut ə·ba·kon   የዚሁ አይነት እባክዎን

FOOD

One Too Many?

ብዙ መጠጥ?

I don't drink.
   meu·teuṭ al·ṭeu·ṭam

መጠጥ አልጠጣም

I'm tired, I'd better get home.
   deu·keu·meuny weu·deu
   bet lə·hid

ደክሞኝ ወደ ቤት
ልሂድ

I feel fantastic!
   deus blo·nyal!

ደስ ብሎኛል!

I think I've had one too many.
   bə·zu ṭeu·ṭow

ብዙ ጠጣሁ

Whether hiring a beuk·lo, 'mule', or watching the ko·ko·boch, 'stars', Amharic is great for communicating with geu·beu·re, 'farmers', and a sure way to find the best scenery.

CAMPING   ድንኳን መትከል

There are few designated camp sites in Ethiopia. Always ask permission from landowners or authorities before you pitch your tent. Bury, burn or take away your rubbish.

Is there somewhere to camp nearby?
dən·kwan meut·keu·ya	ድንኳን መትከያ
bo·ta al·leu?	ቦታ አለ?

May I camp here?
əz·zi dən·kwan meut·keul	እዚህ ድንኳን መትከል
ə·cha·lal·lō?	እችላለሁ-?

Yes, you can.
ow, tə·cha·lal·leuh/	አዎ ትቻላለህ/
tə·chi·yal·leush (m/f)	ትችያለሽ

No you can't.
ai·chal·ləm	አይቻልም

How much	leu (and) ...	ለ (አንድ) ...
for (one) ...	sənt nō?	ስንት ነው-?
night	ma·ta	ማታ
tent	dən·kwan	ድንኳን

May I light a fire here?
əz·zi ə·sat man·deud	እዚህ እሳት ማንደድ
yi·cha·lal?	ይቻላል?

IN THE COUNTRY

Where can I find ...?	... yeut yi·geu·nyal?	... የት ይገኛል?
charcoal	keu·seul	ከሰል
firewood	yeu ma·geu·do ən·cheut	የማገዶ እንጨት
kerosene	ke·ro·sin	ኬሮሲን
matches	kəb·rit	ክብሪት
water	wu·ha	ውሃ
bottle opener	yeu teur·mus meuk·feu·cha	የጠርሙስ መክፈቻ
camp site	dən·kwan	ድንኳን መተከያ
	meut·keu·ya bo·ta	ቦታ
canvas	sheu·ra	ሸራ
can opener	yeu kor·ko·ro meuk·feu·cha	የቆርቆሮ መክፈቻ
cooking pot	bə·reut dəst	ብረት ድስት
lamp (oil)	fa·nos	ፋኖስ
matches	kəb·rit	ክብሪት
mosquito net	yeu bim·bi meu·reub	የቢምቢ መረብ
tent	dən·kwan	ድንኳን
torch	yeuj ba·tri	የጅ ባትሪ

ON THE FARM   እርሻ

Most Ethiopians live and work in the country, their lives governed by the seasons, harvests and local religious life. While men and boys tend the animals and labour in the fields, women collect water and wood and take care of the household. Try to respect farmers' privacy, land and customs. Bow and greet people before chatting. Farmers may have a different concept of distance from you: ma·do means 'yonder'.

How has the weather been?	
zeun·də·ro zə·nab ən·det nō?	ዘንድሮ ዝናብ እንዴት ነው?
May I pass this way?	
beuz·zi beu·kul ma·leuf yi·cha·lal?	በዚህ በኩል ማለፍ ይቻላል?
May I cross your property?	
beur·swo meu·ret beu·kul ma·leuf yi·cha·lal?	በርስዎ መሬት በኩል ማለፍ ይቻላል?

agriculture	gəb·rən·na	ግብርና
country person	ba·la·geur	ባላገር
crops	ə·həl	እህል
enclosure (animal)	gur·reu·no	ጉረኖ
farm	ər·sha	እርሻ
farmer	geu·beu·re	ገበሬ
fence	a·ṭər	አጥር
field/paddock	me·da	ሜዳ
granary	go·teu·ra	ጎተራ
harvest (n)	meu·hər	መኸር
hay	dər·ḳosh	ድርቆሽ
hut	go·jo bet	ጎጆ ቤት
livestock	keubt	ከብት
nomad	zeu·lan	ዘላን
planting/ sowing	meut·keul/ meuz·rat	መትከል/ መዝራት
plough	ma·reu·sha	ማረሻ
shepherd	ə·reu·nya	እረኛ
thatch/cover	kə·dan	ክዳን
village	meun·deur/seu·feur	መንደር/ሰፈር
water pump	yeu wu·ha pamp	የውሃ ፓምፕ
well	yeu wu·ha gud·gwad	የውሃ ጉድጓድ

IN THE COUNTRY

HIKING　　　　　　　　　　　　የእግር ጉዞ

From rich green valleys and rivers to spectacular mountain ranges, Ethiopia offers great hiking opportunities. Ask authorities if you'll need a trekking permit, and check the area is safe. Walking long distances is normal for country people – the word for 'trekking' is simply yeu·gər gu·zo, 'to journey by foot'.

Getting Information

መረጃ ማግኘት

Where is the local permit/
government office?
 feu·ḳad yeu·mi·seu·ṭō
 meus·ri·ya bet yeut nō?

ፈቃድ የሚሰጠው መስሪያ
ቤት የት ነው-?

I want to trek (in this area).
 (əz·zi a·ka·ba·bi) beu·gər
 meu·gwaz ə·feul·lə·gal·lō

(እዚህ አካባቢ) በግር
መጓዝ እፈልጋለሁ

Do I need a permit?
 yeu yi·leuf feu·ḳad
 yas·feul·lə·gal?

የዪለፍ ፈቃድ
ያስፈልጋል?

Are there bandits/land mines?
 shəf·ta/feunj al·leu?

ሽፍታ/ፈንጅ አለ?

I want to go from ... to ...
 keu ... weu·deu ... meu·hed
 ə·feul·lə·gal·lō

ከ ... ወደ ... መሄድ
እፈልጋለሁ

Are there marked trails?
 yeu·gər meun·geud al·leu?

የግር ጐዞ መንገድ አለ?

Do you know this area well?
 yi·hen bo·ta beu·deunb
 yō·ḳu·tal?

ይኸን ቦታ በደንብ
ያውቁታል?

How long will it take?
 sənt gi·ze yi·weus·dal?

ስንት ጊዜ ይወስዳል?

Is there anything interesting to
see on the way?
 meun·geud lai yeu·mi·tai
 neu·geur al·leu?

መንገድ ላይ የሚታይ
ነገር አለ?

Is access difficult?
 leu·ma·leuf as·cheu·ga·ri nō?

ለማለፍ አስቸጋሪ ነው-?

How high is the climb?
 weu·deu lai leu mō·ṭat mən
 ya·həl yi·rə·ḳal?

ወደ ላይ ለመውጣት ምን
ያህል ይርቃል?

Which is the shortest route?
 yeu·tə·nyow meun·geud
 ya·ḳwar·ṭal?

የትኛው- መንገድ
ያቁርጣል?

Which is the easiest route?
yeu·tə·nyow meun·geud
yi·keu·lal?

የትኛው መንገድ ይቀላል?

Where can we buy supplies?
yeu gu·zo sənk yeut
meug·zat yi·cha·lal?

የጉዞ ስንቅ የት
መግዛት ይቻላል?

Is there a (rest house) on the route?
meun·geud lai (ma·reu·fi·ya
bet) al·leu?

መንገድ ላይ
(ማረፊያ ቤት) አለ?

Guides, Porters & Hiring Animals

አስጎብኚዎች፣ ሠራተኞችና
ለኪራይ የሚሆኑ እንስሳት

We are thinking of going to ...
weu·deu ... meu·hed a·sə·beu·nal

ወደ ... መሄድ አስበናል

How many hours will we
travel per day?
beu keun leu sənt seu'at
ə·nə·gwa·zal·leun

በቀን ለስንት ሰዓት
እንንዛለን?

Can you recommend a ...	yeu·mə·tow·kut ... al·leu?	የምታወቁት ... አለ?
guide	as·gob·nyi	አስጎብኚ
interpreter	as·teur·gwa·mi	አስተርጓሚ
porter	teu·sheu·ka·mi	ተሸካሚ
worker	seu·ra·teu·nya	ሰራተኛ

Where can I hire a ...?	... yeut meu·keu·ra·yeut ə·cha·lal·lō?	... የት መከራየት እችላለሁ·?
donkey	a·hə·ya	አህያ
horse	feu·reus	ፈረስ
mule	beuk·lo	በቅሎ

How much is it for ...?	leu ... sənt nō?	ለ ... ስንት ነው·?
(two) days	(hu·leutt) keun	(ሁለት) ቀን
a single journey	and gu·zo	አንድ ጉዞ

I'll pay ...	
... ə·keuf·lal·lō	... እከፍላለሁ
Let's go on foot.	
beu·gər ən·hid	በግር እንሂድ
Go faster! (to mule)	
meuch!	መች!
Go faster! (to horse)	
cha!	ቻ!

On the Path   መንገድ ላይ

Local people are more likely to use terms like 'at daybreak' (goh si·keud) and 'before sunset' (ṣeu·hai sat·geu·ba) instead of specific times.

Let's go!	
ən·hid!	እንሂድ!
How far away is the (next town)?	
(yeu·mi·keu·ṭəl·lō keu·teu·ma)	(የሚቀጥለው ከተማ)
mən ya·həl yi·rə·ḳal?	ምን ያህል ይርቃል?
Can I walk there?	
beu·gər yas·ke·dal?	በግር ያስኬዳል?

Would we reach it ... ?	... ən·deur·sal·leun?	... እንደርሳለን?
before midday	keu ə·ku·leu	ከእኩለ
	keun beu·fit	ቀን በፊት
before nightfall	sai·cheu·ləm	ሳይጨልም

Is this the way to ...?	
... beuz·zi beu·kul nō?	... በዚህ በኩል ነው?
Where are you going?	
yeut tə·he·dal·leuh? (m)	የት ትሄዳለህ?
yeut tə·he·jal·leush? (f)	የት ትሄጃለሽ?
I'm going to ...	
weu·deu ... ə·he·dal·lō	ወደ ... እሄዳለሁ
What is this/that?	
yi·he/ya mən·dən nō?	ይህ/ያ ምንድ ነው?
Look at this/that.	
yi·hen/yan teu·meul·keut (m)	ይህን/ያን ተመልከት
yi·hen/yan teu·meul·keuch (f)	ይህን/ያን ተመልከች

What a beautiful place!
   beu·ṭam deus yeu·mil bo·ta!   በጣም ደስ የሚል ቦታ!
What's the name of this place?
   yi·he bo·ta mən yi·ba·lal?   ይኸ ቦታ ምን ይባላል?
Where are we (on this map)?
   (kar·tow lai)   (ካርታው ላይ)
   yeut nō ya·leu·nō?   የት ነው ያለነው?
We are here (on this map).
   (kar·tow lai) əz·zi lai neun   (ካርታው ላይ) እዚህ ላይ ነን
Can I pass this way?
   beuz·zi beu·kul ma·leuf   በዚህ በኩል ማለፍ
   yi·cha·lal?   ይቻላል?

I'd like to ...	... ə·feul·lə·gal·lō	... እፈልጋለሁ
go to the toilet	weu·deu shənt	ወደ ሽንት ቤት
	bet meu·hed	መሄድ
have a rest	ma·reuf	ማረፍ
have some tea/water	shai/wu·ha	ሻይ/ውሃ

I don't feel comfortable here.
   yi·he bo·ta deus a·la·leu·nyəm   ይኸ ቦታ ደስ አላለኝም
Is there another place?
   le·la bo·ta yi·no·ral?   ሌላ ቦታ ይኖራል?
Is this water safe for drinking?
   wu·how leu meu·ṭeuṭ yi·ho·nal?   ውሃው ለመጠጥ ይሆናል?
(Please) Slow down.
   (ə·ba·kəh) ḳeuss beul (m)   (እባክህ) ቀስ በል
   (ə·ba·kəsh) ḳeuss bay (f)   (እባክሽ) ቀስ በይ
I'm lost.
   meun·geud ṭeuf·to·bə·nyal   መንገድ ጠፍቶብኛል
Where can we spend the night?
   ma·ta yeut ə·nar·fal·leun?   ማታ የት እናርፋለን?
I'll stay overnight in ...
   ... ad·ral·lō   ... አድራለሁ

See also Directions on page 53.

IN THE COUNTRY

altitude	keu·fə·ta	ከፍታ
Amhara duffle bag	jo·nə·ya	ጆንያ
backpack	shan·ṭa	ሻንጣ
bottle (skin)	ko·da	ኮዳ
binoculars	bai·no·ku·lar	ባይኖኩለር
boots	bot cham·ma	ቦት ጫማ
candle	sha·ma	ሻማ
canoe	tan·kwa	ታንኳ
canteen (traditional)	a·geul·gəl	አገልግል
to climb	mō·ṭat	መውጣት
compass	kom·pass	ኮምፓስ
downhill	ḳul·ḳu·leut	ቁልቁለት
drinking bottle	ṭeur·mus	ጠርሙስ
first-aid kit	yeu meu·jeu·meu·ri·ya ər·da·ta sa·ṭən	የመጀመሪያ እርዳታ ሳጥን
hammer	meu·do·sha	መዶሻ
hat	bar·ne·ṭa	ባርኔጣ
hike	yeu·gər gu·zo	የግር ጉዞ
horse ride	feu·reus gəl·bi·ya	ፈረስ ግልቢያ
knife	seun·ṭi	ስንጢ
to load/harness	meu·chan	መጫን
map	kar·ta	ካርታ
mountain climbing	teu·ra·ra mō·ṭat	ተራራ መውጣት
pick	do·ma	ዶማ
rest house	ma·reu·fi·ya bet	ማረፊያ ቤት
rock climbing	ḳwa·ṭəny mō·ṭat	ቋጥኝ መውጣት
rope	geu·meud	ገመድ
saddle	ko·rə·cha	ኮርቻ
steep	ḳeuṭ ya·leu	ቀጥ ያለ
stick	du·la	ዱላ
to unload/ unharness	ma·ra·geuf	ማራገፍ
uphill	a·ḳeu·beut	አቀበት
waterproof clothes	yeu zə·nab ləbs	የዝናብ ልብስ
water purifier	yeu wu·ha ma·ṭa·ri·ya	የውሃ ማጣሪያ

SEASONS   ወቅቶች

Seasons in Ethiopia are divided into dry season and wet season.
There are also other seasonal changes referred to, particularly in
rural areas.

dry season (October to May)	beu·ga	በጋ
wet season (June to September)	kə·reumt	ክረምት
little wet season	beulg	በልግ
harvest time	yeu meu·hər weukt	የመኸር ወቅት
spring	ṣeu·day	ፀደይ

WEATHER   የአየር ሁኔታ

Be prepared for some dramatic weather changes during the wet
season, and carry warm, waterproof gear with you.

What's the temperature?
ai·yeur hu·ne·ta sənt nō?   ያየር ሁኔታ ስንት ነው-?
What will the weather be like
(today/tomorrow)?
yeu (za·re/neu·geu) ai·yeur   የ (ዛሬ/'ነገ) ያየር ሁኔታ
hu·ne·ta mən yi·ho·nal?   ምን ይሆናል?

It'll be ...	... yi·ho·nal	... ይሆናል
Will it be ...?	... yi·ho·nal?	... ይሆናል?
cloudy	deu·meu·na·ma	ደመናማ
cold	bərd	ብርድ
fine	ṭə·ru	ጥሩ
hot	mok ya·leu	ሞቅ ያለ
humid	yi·weu·bək	ይወብቅ
rainy	zə·na·ba·ma	ዝናባማ
stormy	neu·god·gwa·da·ma	ነጎድጓዳማ
sunny	ṣeu·hai·ya·ma	ፀሃያማ
windy	neu·fa·sha·ma	ነፋሻማ

bright	bə·ruh	ብሩህ
dark	cheul·leu·ma	ጨለማ
drought	dərķ	ድርቅ
dry	deu·reuķ	ደረቅ
dust	a·bwa·ra	አቧራ
flood (large)	yeu wu·ha mu·lat	የውሃ ሙላት
flood (small)	gorf	ጎርፍ
fog	gumm	ጉም
hail	beu·reu·do	በረዶ
haze	chi·gag	ጭጋግ
heat wave	ha·rur	ሃሩር
lightning	meub·reuķ	መብረቅ
rain	zə·nab	ዝናብ
rainbow	ķeus·teu deu·meu·na	ቀስተ ደመና
shade	ṭə·la	ጥላ
shelter	meu·ṭeu·leu·ya	መጠለያ
sky	seu·mai	ሰማይ
snow	beu·reu·do	በረዶ
storm (rain)	keu·bad (zə·nab)	ከባድ (ዝናብ)
sun	ṣeu·hai	ፀሃይ
thunder	neu·god·gwad	ነጎድጓድ
weather	ai·yeur hu·ne·ta	ያየር ሁኔታ
wind	neu·fass	ነፋስ

GEOGRAPHICAL TERMS   የጂኦግራፊ ቃሎች

bridge	dəl·dəy	ድልድይ
bush	ķuṭ·ķwa·ṭo	ቁጥቋጦ
burrow	gud·gwad	ጉድጓድ
cave	wa·sha	ዋሻ
clearing	geu·la·ṭa bo·ta	ጋላጣ ቦታ
cliff	geu·deul	ገደል
countryside	a·geur bet	አገር ቤት
creek	jə·reut	ጅረት
dam	gəd·dəb	ግድብ
desert	beu·reu·ha	በረሃ
ditch	gud·ba	ጉድባ
dust	tə·bi·ya	ትቢያ

Earth (the)	meu·ret	መሬት
forest	cha·ka	ጫካ
gorge	geu·deul	ገደል
grass	sar	ሳር
green	a·reun·gwa·de	አረንጓዴ
highlands	keu·fə·teu·nya bo·ta	ከፍተኛ ቦታ
hill	ko·reub·ta	ኮረብታ
horizon	ad·mass	አድማስ
hot springs	fəl wu·ha	ፍል ውሃ
island	deu·set	ደሴት
lake	haik̦	ሐይቅ
lowlands	zə·k̦ə·teu·nya bo·ta	ዝቅተኛ ቦታ
mountain(s)	teu·ra·ra/teu·ra·roch	ተራራ/ተራሮች
mountain peak	yeu teu·ra·ra chaff	የተራራ ጫፍ
mud	chi·k̦a	ጭቃ
national park	bə·he·ra·wi park	ብሔራዊ ፓርክ
pebbles	teu·teur	ጠጠር
plain	leuț ya·leu meu·ret	ለጥ ያለ መሬት
plateau	am·ba	አምባ
pond	ku·re	ኩሬ
region	kəl·ləl	ክልል
river	weunz	ወንዝ
rock	k̦wa·țəny	ቋጥኝ
sand	a·sheu·wa	አሸዋ
stone	dən·gai	ድንጋይ
swamp/marsh	reug reug	ረግ ረግ
track/footpath	yeu·gər meun·geud	የግር መንገድ
valley	sheu·leu·k̦o	ሸለቆ
water	wu·ha	ውሃ
waterfall	fwa·fwa·te	ፏፏቴ

IN THE COUNTRY

ZONED OUT!

cool zone	deu·ga	ደጋ
hot zone	k̦ol·la	ቆላ
temperate zone	way·na deu·ga	ወይና ደጋ

THE ENVIRONMENT

Does (this area) have a problem with ...?	(əz·zi a·ka·ba·bi) yeu ... chig·gər al·leu?	(እዚህ አካባቢ) የ ... ችግር አለ?
air pollution	ai·yeur meu·beu·keul	የአየር መበከል
deforestation	deun meu·meun·ţeur	ደን መመንጠር
drought	dərķ	ድርቅ
famine	reu·hab	ረሃብ
fertilisers	ma·da·beu·ri·ya	ማዳበሪያ
irrigation	meus·no	መስኖ
pesticides	yeu teu·bai meu·keu·la·keu·ya meud·ha·nit	የተባይ ማከላከያ መድሃኒት
soil erosion	a·feur meu·sheur·sheur	አፈር መሸርሸር

See also Expressing Opinions, page 115.

FAUNA   እንስሳት

What wildlife is there in this area?
əz·zi a·ka·ba·bi mən ai·neut
yeu dur a·ra·wi·toch al·lu?

እዚህ አካባቢ ምን አይነት
የዱር አራዊቶች አሉ?

What (animal) is that?
ya (ən·sə·sa) mən·dən nō?

ያ (እንስሳ) ምንድን ነው?

Is it native?
i·tə·yo·pi·ya bə·cha
ye·mi·geuny nō?

ኢትዮጵያ ብቻ የሚገኝ
ነው?

Are there any protected species?
yeu·mi·ţeu·beu·ķu
ən·sə·soch al·lu?

የሚጠበቁ እንስሶች አሉ?

It's a mammal/reptile.
aţ·bi/teu·sa·bi nō

አጥቢ/ተሳቢ ነው።

Domestic   የቤት እንስሳት

With more livestock than virtually any other African country,
you'll see farm animals everywhere – on city streets, in back yards
and, of course, out in the field. A rooster is more likely to step
out of someone's front door than a dog!

camel	gə·meul	ግመል
cat	də·meut	ድመት
chicken	do·ro	ዶሮ
cow	lam	ላም
dog	wu·sha	ውሻ
donkey	a·hə·ya	አህያ
goat	fə·yeul	ፍየል
ox	beu·re	በሬ
rooster	ow·ra do·ro	አውራ ዶሮ
sheep	beug	በግ

Wildlife   የዱር አራዊት

ape	ṭo·ṭa	ጦጣ
bat	yeu le·lit weuf	የሌሊት ወፍ
buffalo	gosh	ጎሽ
bush duiker	mi·da·kwa	ሚዳቋ
bushbuck	də·kwa·la	ድቋላ
chameleon	ə·səst	እስስት
Colobus monkey	gu·re·za	ጉሬዛ
crocodile	a·zo	አዞ
elephant	zə·hon	ዝሆን
Ethiopian mountain goat	wa·li·ya ai·beks	ዋሊያ አይቤክስ
fish	a·sa	አሳ
gazelle	a·ga·zeun	አጋዘን
Gelada baboon	chi·la·da	ጭላዳ
giraffe	ḳeu·chə·ne	ቀጭኔ
hippopotamus	gum·mar·re	ጉማሬ
hyena	jib	ጅብ

jackal	ķeu·beu·ro	ቀበሮ
klipspringer	sass	ሳስ
leopard	neu·bər	ነብር
lion	an·beus·sa	አንበሳ
lizard	ən·shi·la·lit	እንሽላሊት
monkey	zən·jeu·ro	ዝንጀሮ
mouse	aiyṭ	አይጥ
panther	gə·sə·la	ግሰላ
porcupine	jart	ጃርት
rabbit	ṭən·cheul	ጥንቸል
rhinoceros	ow·ra·ris	አውራሪስ
squirrel	shə·ko·ko	ሽኮኮ
snake	ə·bab	እባብ
large snake	zeun·do	ዘንዶ
toad	gurṭ	ጉርጥ
tortoise	e·li	ኤሊ
wildlife	yeu dur a·ra·wit	የዱር አራዊት
zebra	yeu me·da a·hə·ya	የሜዳ አህያ

Birds   ወፎች

I'm looking for a ...

| ... ə·yeu·feul·leu·ku nō | ... እየፈለኩ ነው· |

What do you call that bird?

| ya·nən weuf mən | ያንን ወፍ ምን |
| tə·lu·tal·la·chu? | ትሉታላችሁ? |

bird/birds	ər·gəb/ər·gə·boch	እርግብ/እርግቦች
bird of prey	a·mo·ra	አሞራ
crow/raven	ķu·ra	ቁራ
duck	da·kə·ye	ዳክየ
eagle	nə·sər	ንስር
fowl	jəg·ra	ጅግራ
owl	gug·gut	ጉጉት
vulture (bearded)	chu·leu·le	ጭልሌ
woodpecker	gən·deu ķor·ķur	ግንደ ቆርቆር

Insects ተባይ

Is it poisonous?

    meur·zeu·nya nō?   መርዘኛ ነው?

ant	gun·dan	ጉንዳን
bedbug	tə·hwan	ትኋን
bee/bee hive	nəb; yeu nəb ķeu·fo	ንብ/የንብ ቀፎ
beetle	təl	ትል
butterfly	bi·ra·bi·ro	ቢራቢሮ
caterpillar	a·ba cheu·gwa·re	አባ ጨጓሬ
cockroach	beu·reur·ro	በረሮ
flea	ķu·nə·cha	ቁንጫ
fly	zəmb	ዝምብ
grasshopper	am·beu·ṭa	አምበጣ
insect	teu·bai	ተባይ
lice	ķə·mal	ቅማል
maggot	yeu sə·ga təl	የስጋ ትል
mosquito	bim·bi	ቢምቢ
scorpion	ginṭ	ጊንጥ
spider	sheu·reu·rit	ሸረሪት
wasp	teurb	ተርብ

FLORA & CROPS ዕፅዋትና ሰብል

Ethiopia has a stunning range of native flora. Imports include the ubiquitous ba·hər zaf (eucalyptus tree, literally 'from over the sea'), imported by Emperor Menelik from Australia in the late 19th century. See Food, page 139, and On the Farm, page 162, for related words.

What (tree) is that?

    ya mən ai·neut (zaf) nō?   ያ ምን አይነት (ዛፍ) ነው?

What's it used for?

    leu·mən
    tə·ṭeu·ķeu·mu·beu·tal·la·chu?   ለምን ትጠቀሙበታላችሁ?

acacia tree	gə·rar	ግራር
bamboo	sheum·beu·ḳo	ሽምበቆ
banana tree	yeu muz teu·kəl	የሙዝ ተክል
barley	geubs	ገብስ
branch	ḳə·rən·chaf	ቅርንጫፍ
cactus	ḳul·ḳwal	ቁልቋል
cedar tree	zəg·ba	ዝግባ
chat (mira)	chat	ጫት
coffee plant	yeu bun·na teu·kəl	የቡና ተክል
corn plant	yeu beu·ḳo·lo teu·kəl	የበቆሎ ተክል
cotton	ṭəṭ	ጥጥ
daisy	yeu meus·ḳeul a·beu·ba	የመስቀል አበባ
eucalyptus tree	bahər zaf	ባሕር ዛፍ
false banana tree	ko·ba	ኮባ
flower	a·beu·ba	አበባ
forest	cha·ka/deun	ጫካ/ደን
grass	sar	ሳር
juniper/cedar tree	ṭəd	ጥድ
leaf	ḳə·ṭeul	ቅጠል
log	gənd	ግንድ
millet	ṭef	ጤፍ
mushroom	ən·gu·dai	እንጉዳይ
palm tree	zeu·mə·ba·ba	ዘምባባ
to pick (coffee/fruit)	meul·ḳeum	መልቀም
root	sər	ስር
seed	fə·re	ፍሬ
sorghum	ma·sha·la	ማሽላ
stalk	a·geu·da	አገዳ
tef	ṭef	ጤፍ
thorn	ə·shoh	እሾህ
tree/trees	zaf/za·foch	ዛፍ/ዛፎች
wheat	sən·de	ስንዴ
wood	ən·cheut	እንጨት

IN THE COUNTRY

STAR GAZING

Where's a good place to see
the stars?
　ko·ko·bo·chən leu ma·yeut
　tə·ru bo·ta yeut no?

ኮከቦችን ለማየት
ጥሩ ቦታ የት ነው?

Will it be cloudy tonight?
　za·re ma·ta deu·meu·na·ma
　yi·ho·nal?

ዛሬ ማታ ደመናማ
ይሆናል?

Look! A meteor!
　teu·meul·keut/teu·meul·keuch!
　beu·ra·ri ko·keub! (m/f)

ተመልከት/ተመልከች!
በራሪ ኮከብ!

(full) moon	(mu·lu) çheu·reu·ḳa	(ሙሉ) ጨረቃ
stars	ko·ko·boch	ኮከቦች
universe	a·leu·mat	አለማት

ACTIVITIES

Toss around a kwass, 'ball', dabble in some da·ma, 'checkers', or take a tan·kwa, 'canoe', down the weunz, 'river'. With some of the world's top distance athletes, a great outdoors and a population keen on sports, Ethiopia's a great place for cheu·wa·ta, 'games'.

TYPES OF SPORT የስፖርት አይነቶች

What sport do you play?
mən ai·neut sport	ምን አይነት ስፖርት
tə·cha·weu·tal·leuh/	ትጫወታለህ/
tə·cha·weu·chal·leush? (m/f)	ትጫወቻለሽ?

I play ...	... ə·cha·weu·tal·lō	... እጫወታለሁ
basketball	kər·chat kwass	ቅርጫት ኳስ
handball	əj kwass	እጅ ኳስ
hockey	geun·na	ንና
soccer (football)	ə·gər kwass	እግር ኳስ
table tennis	ṭe·bəl te·nis	ቴብል ቴኒስ
volleyball	meu·reub kwass	መረብ ኳስ

I like ...	... ə·weud·dal·lō	... እወዳለሁ
athletics	at·le·tiks	አትሌቲክስ
boxing	boks/bu·ṭi	ቦክስ/ቡጢ
cycling	bəs·klet meu·ga·leub	ብስክሌት መጋለብ
distance running	reu·jim ru·cha	ረጅም ሩጫ
	meu·roṭ	መሮጥ
weightlifting	kəb·deut man·sat	ክብደት ማንሳት
gymnastics	jəm·na·stik	ጅምናስቲክ
	meus·rat	መስራት
running	ru·cha	ሩጫ
swimming	wa·na	ዋና

TALKING ABOUT SPORT   ስለ ስፖርት ማውራት

People love chatting about Ethiopian distance-running champions and major sporting events like the soccer finals.

Do you like to watch sport?
    sport ma·yeut tə·weud·dal·leuh/   ስፖርት ማየት
    tə·weu·jal·leush? (m/f)   ትወዳለሁ/ትወጃለሽ?
Yes, very much.
    ow beu·tam ə·weud·dal·lō   አዎ በጣም እወዳለሁ
No, not at all.
    aiy al·weud·dəm   አይ አልወድም
What sports do you follow?
    yeu·tə·nyow·ən sport   የትኛውን ስፖርት
    tə·keu·ta·teu·lal·leuh/   ትከታታላለህ/
    tə·keu·ta·teu·yal·leush? (m/f)   ትከታተያለሽ?
I follow ...
    ... ə·keu·ta·teu·lal·lō   ... እከታተላለሁ
What team do you support?
    yeu·tə·nya·wən bu·dən   የትኛውን ቡድን
    tə·deu·gə·fal·leuh/   ትደግፋለህ/
    tə·deu·gə·fi·yal·leush? (m/f)   ትደግፊያለሽ?
I support ...
    ... ə·deu·gə·fal·lō   ... እደግፋለሁ

SOCCER   እግር ኳስ

English terms are often used for words like 'goal' and 'offside'.

Do you follow soccer?
    ə·gər kwass   እግር ኳስ
    tə·keu·ta·teu·lal·leuh/   ትከታታላለህ/
    tə·keu·ta·teu·yal·leush? (m/f)   ትከታተያለሽ?
Who's the best team?
    keu·hul·lu yeu·mi·beul·tow   ከሁሉ የሚበልጠው
    bu·dən man nō?   ቡድን ማን ነው-?
My favourite player is ...
    yeu·mə·weud·dō   የምወደው-
    teu·cha·wach ... nō   ተጫዋች ... ነው-

free kick	ri·go·ri	ሪጎሪ
match	gəṭ·mi·ya	ግጥሚያ
penalty	kə·ṭat	ቅጣት
player	teu·cha·wach	ተጫዋች
team	bu·dən	ቡድን

GOING TO A MATCH

ጨዋታ ለማየት መሄድ

Where can I see a (soccer) match?
  yeu (ə·gər kwass) cheu·wa·ta
  yeut yi·ta·yal?
  የ (እግር ኳስ) ጨዋታ የት
  ይታያል?

What time does it start?
  beu sənt seu'at yi·jeu·mə·ral?
  በስንት ሰዓት ይጀምራል?

Which team is winning/losing?
  yeu·tə·nyow bu·dən
  ə·ya·sheu·neu·feu/
  ə·yeu·teu·sheu·neu·feu nō?
  የትኛው ቡድን እያሸነፈ
  እየተሸነፈ ነው?

What's the score?
  sənt leu sənt na·chō?
  ስንት ለስንት ናቸው?

That was a great game!
  kon·jo cheu·wa·ta neub·beur!
  ቆንጆ ጨዋታ ነበር!

seat (place)	bo·ta	ቦታ
stadium	sta·di·yeum	ስታዲየም
ticket	ti·ket	ትኬት
ticket office	ti·ket meu·sheu·cha	ትኬት መሸጫ

JOINING IN   አብሮ መጫወት

In Ethiopia, all that's required for a great soccer game is space for
playing, a ball (bound rags do the job) and a few willing players.

Can you play (soccer)?
   (ə·gər kwass) meu·cha·wot   (እግር ኳስ)መጫወት
   tə·cha·lal·leuh/   ትችላለህ/ትችያለሽ?
   tə·cha·yal·leush? (m/f)
I don't know how to play.
   meu·cha·wot al·chəl·leum   መጫወት አልችልም
Shall we have a game of (basketball)?
   (kər·chat kwass) ə·nə·cha·weut?   (ቅርጫት ኳስ) እንጫወት?
Is there a ball?
   kwass al·leu?   ኳስ አለ?
Can I join in?
   keun·nan·teu gar meu·cha·wot   ከናንተ ጋር መጫወት
   ə·cha·lal·lō?   እችላለሁ?
Over here!
   weu·deu·zi!   ወደዚህ!
That was a great game!
   kon·jo cheu·wa·ta!   ቆንጆ ጨዋታ!

ball	kwass	ኳስ
boundary	meus·meur	መስመር
goal	gol	ጎል
goal post	yeu gol mə·seu·so	የጎል ምሰሶ
foul	fowl/tə·fat	ፋ‧ወል/ጥፋ‧ት
kick-off	cheu·wa·ta	ጨዋታ
	yeu·mi·jeu·meu·rə·beut	የሚጀመርበት
net	meu·reub	መረብ
referee	da·nya	ዳኛ

KEEPING FIT ስፖርት መስራት

Where's the nearest ...?	yeu·mi·keur·bō ... yeut nō?	የሚቀርበው ... የት ነው-?
recreation centre	meuz·na·nya bo·ta	መዝናኛ ቦታ
swimming pool	meu·wa·nya bo·ta	መዋኛ ቦታ
tennis court	yeu me·da te·nis me·da	የሜዳ ቴኒስ ሜዳ

What's the charge per ...?	leu ... sənt nō?	ለ ... ስንት ነው-?
day	keun	ቀን
game	cheu·wa·ta	ጨዋታ
hour	seu'at	ስዓት

Can I hire ...?	... meu·keu·ra·yeut ə·chə·lal·lō?	... መከራየት እችላለሁ-?
a bicycle	bəs·klet	ብስክሌት
a racquet	ra·ket	ራኬት
(two) racquet(s)	(hu·leutt) ra·ket	(ሁለት) ራኬትና
and a ball	ə·na kwass	ኳስ

Where's the best place to jog/ run around here?
əz·zi a·ka·ba·bi leu ru·cha yeu·mi·hon tə·ru bo·ta yeut nō? እዚህ አካባቢ ለሩጫ የሚሆን ጥሩ ቦታ የት ነው-?

Where are the changing rooms?
ləbs meu·keu·yeu·ri·yow kə·fəl yeut nō? ልብስ መቀየሪያው- ክፍል የት ነው-?

Would you like to play tennis?
te·nis meu·cha·wot tə·feul·lə·gal·leuh/ tə·feul·lə·gi·yal·leush? (m/f) ቴኒስ መጫወት ትፈልጋለህ/ ትፈልጊያለሽ?

ACTIVITIES

MUSIC MOVES

to clap	ma·cheub·cheub	ማጨብጨብ
to jump	meuz·leul	መዝለል
movement	shəb·sheu·ba	ሽብሽባ
shoulder dance	əs·kəs·ta	እስክስታ
ululation	ə·ləl·ta	እልልታ

bicycle	bəs·klet	ብስክሌት
jogging	ru·cha	ሩጫ
massage	meu·ta·sheut	መታሸት
racquet	ra·ket	ራኬት
shower	sha·weur	ሻወር
table tennis bat	yeu teu·reu·pe·za	የጠረጴዛ
	te·nis ra·ket	ቴኒስ ራኬት
tournament	wə·də·dər	ውድድር
towel	fo·ta	ፎጣ
warm-up	sō·neu·tən	ሰውነትን ማማሟቅ
	ma·ma·mwak	
weights	kəb·deut	ክብደት

OUTDOOR SPORTS　　　　　　የውጭ ስፖርቶች

Activities like rafting and rock climbing are usually run by English-speaking guides for Western tourists. Ethiopians may call you deuf·far, 'adventurous'.

I love ...	... ə·weud·dal·lō	... እወዳለሁ
bird watching	yeu weuf	የወፍ
	ai·neu·to·chən	አይኖቻችን ማየት
	ma·yeut	
canoeing/	beu jeul·ba	በጀልባ
rafting	ə·yeu·keu·zeu·fu	እየቀዘፉ መንዝ
	meu·gwaz	
fishing	a·sa mat·meud	አሳ ማጥመድ
mountain/rock	teu·ra·ra/kwa·təny	ተራራ/ቋጥኝ
climbing	mō·tat	መውጣት

Am I allowed to (fish) here?
əz·zi (a·sa mat·meud)　　　　እዚህ (አሳ ማጥመድ)
yi·cha·lal?　　　　　　　　　ይቻላል?
Is there a place I can rent (a canoe)?
(tan·kwa) yeu·mi·ya·keu·rai　　(ታንኳ) የሚያከራይ
sō al·leu?　　　　　　　　　　ሰው አለ?

Can we stop here?
əz·zi ma·ḳom ən·cha·lal·leun? እዚህ ማቆም እንችላለን?

That was great!
beu·ṭam ḳon·jo neub·beur! በጣም ቆንጆ ነበር!

I want to go again!
ən·deu·geu·na meu·hed እንደገና መሄድ
ə·feul·lə·gal·lō! እፈልጋለሁ-!

bank/shore	yeu weunz dar	የወንዝ ዳር
big wave	ma'ə·beul	ማዕበል
boat	jeul·ba	ጀልባ
canoe	tan·kwa	ታንኳ
cliff	geu·deul	ገደል
creek	jə·reut	ጅረት
crocodile	a·zo	አዞ
deep	ṭəlḳ	ጥልቅ
downward slope	ḳul·ḳu·leut	ቁልቁለት
fish	a·sa	አሳ
fish hook	meun·ṭeu·ḳo	መንጠቆ
fisherman	a·sa aṭ·maj	አሳ አጥማጅ
fishing net	a·sa maṭ·meu·ja	አሳ ማጥመጃ
	meu·reub	መረብ
motor	mo·teur	ሞተር
river	weunz	ወንዝ
rock	a·leut	አለት
rope	geu·meud	ገመድ
to row	meuḳ·zeuf	መቅዘፍ
shallow (water)	ṭəlḳ yal·ho·neu	ጥልቅ ያልሆነ
	(wu·ha)	(ውሃ)
strong current	geus·gash wu·ha	ጐሣጐሽ ውሃ
upward slope	da·geut	ዳገት
waterfall	fwa·fwa·te	ፏፏቴ
waterproof	wu·ha yeu·mai·zeul·ḳō	ውሃ የማይዘልቀው-

TRADITIONAL SPORTS   ባህላዊ ስፖርቶች

Almost every region of Ethiopia has a danger sport. Some famous ones include:

geun·na   ገና
> a type of hockey played in some regions at Christmas. Brandishing sticks curved at the ends, two teams compete to whack an i·rur (wooden ball) over their opponent's boundary line.

gugs   ጉግስ
> a type of mock warfare on horseback played in some regions at ṭəm·ḵeut, or the Epiphany. Riders in stunning traditional costumes pursue each other with wooden sticks/clubs and round hide shields.

don·ga   ዶንጋ
Surma/Mursi stick fighting

ACTIVITIES

CYCLING   ብስክሌት መጋለብ

Cycle races are sometimes held in Ethiopian towns. For general terminology on cycling, see page 64 in Getting Around.

Where does the race pass through?
  wə·də·də·ru beu·yeut   ወደድሩ በየት
  beu·kul yal·fal?   በኩል ያልፋል?
Who's winning?
  man ə·yeu·meu·ra nō?   ማን እየመራ ነው?
How many kilometres is
today's race?
  yeu za·re wə·də·dər sant   የዛሬ ውድድር
  ki·lo me·tər nō?   ስንት ኪሎ ሜትር ነው?

Where does it finish?
meu·cheu·reu·show yeut nō?　መጨረሻው የት ነው?
My favourite cyclist is ...
yeu·ma·weud·dō　የምወደው
sai·ka·leu·nya ... nō　ሳይክለኛ ... ነው

cycling	bas·klet meu·ga·leub	ብስክሌት መጋለብ
cyclist	sai·ka·leu·nya	ሳይክለኛ
leg (of race)	zu·ri·ya	ዙሪያ
winner	a·sheu·na·fi	አሸናፊ

GAMES　ጨዋታዎች

Billiards and dominoes are popular games at coffee houses. Around
Ethiopia's streets, you might see people playing geu·beu·ṭa, a
traditional African game using a board and tiny balls.

Do you play ...?　... ta·cha·weu·tal·leuh/　ትጫወታለህ/
... ta·cha·weu·chal·leush? (m/f)　ትጫወቻለሽ?
billiards	bil·yard	ቢልያርድ
bingo	bin·go	ቢንጎ
cards	kar·ta	ካርታ
chess	chez	ቼዝ
checkers	da·ma	ዳማ

Shall we play ...?
... a·na·cha·weut?　... እንጫወት?
How do you play (checkers)?
(dama) an·det nō　(ዳማ) እንዴት ነው
yeum·ta·cha·weu·tut?　የምትጫወቱት?
What are the rules?
ha·gu man·dan nō?　ሕጉ ምንድን ነው?
Whose turn is it?
yeu·man teu·ra nō?　የማን ተራ ነው?
It's my turn.
yeu·ne teu·ra nō?　የኔ ተራ ነው?

I'm winning.	ə·ya·sheu·neuf·ku nō	እያሸነፍኩ·ነው·
I'm losing.	ə·yeu·teu·sheu·neuf·ku nō	እየተሸነፍኩ ነው·
Well done!	gob·bez!	ጎበዝ!
No cheating!	ma·ta·leul ai·chal·ləm!	ማታለል አይቻልም!

Cards

ካርታ

Words like 'bridge' and 'poker' are similar to English.

Do you want to play cards?
  kar·ta meu·cha·wot
  tə·feul·lə·gal·leuh/
  tə·feul·lə·gi·yal·leush? (m/f)

ካርታ መጫወት
ትፈልጋለህ/
ትፈልጊያለሽ?

I don't know how to play.
  meu·cha·wot al·chəl·ləm

መጫወት አልችልም

I'll teach you.
  a·sa·yi·hal·lō/a·sa·yi·shal·lō (m/f)

አሳይሀለሁ/አሳይሻለሁ

It's your turn to pick up a card.
  kar·ta man·sat yan·teu/
  yan·chi teu·ra nō (m/f)

ካርታ ማንሳት ያንተ/
ያንች ተራ ነው·

የኔ ተራ ነው·

ማታለል አይቻልም!

Chess

ቼዝ

Shall we play chess?
  chez ə·nə·cha·weut?

ቼዝ እንጫወት?

White starts.
  neuch yi·jeu·mə·ral

ነጭ ይጀምራል

It's my move.
  yeu·ne teu·ra nō

የኔ ተራ ነው·

bishop	pa·pas	ጳጳስ
black/white pieces	ṭə·ḳur/neuçh weu·ta·deur	ጥቁር/ነጭ ወታደር
castle/rook	ka·səl	ካስል
chessboard	seun·ṭeu·reuzh	ሰንጠረዥ
chess tournament	yeu chez wə·də·dər	የቼዝ ውድድር
king	nə·gus	ንጉስ
knight	feu·reus	ፈረስ
pawn(s)	mi·da·ḳwa	ሚዳቋ
queen	nə·gəst	ንግስት

WHAT ARE YOUR LEGS?

(Deratu Tulu) is amazing!	(deu·rar·tu tu·lu) beu·ṭam as·deu·na·ḳi neuch!	(ደራርቱ ቱሉ) በጣም አስደናቂ ነች!
Ethiopians are great ... runners!	i·tə·yo·pi·ya·noch beu ... ta·wa·ḳi rwa·çhoch na·chō!	ኢትዮጵያኖች በ ... ታዋቂ ሯጮች ናቸው!
marathon	ma·ra·ton	ማራቶን
long distance	reu·jim rə·ḳeut	ረጅም ርቀት
altitude	keu·fə·ta	ከፍታ
bare feet	ba·do ə·gər	ባዶ እግር
endurance	tə·gəst	ትግስት
(gold) medal	(weurk) meu·da·li·ya	(ወርቅ) መዳሊያ
Olympic Games	yeu o·lom·pik çheu·wa·ta	የኦሉምፒክ ጨዋታ
hard training	keu·bad lə·mə·məd	ከባድ ልምምድ
(Boston) marathon	yeu (bos·teun) ma·ra·ton	የ (ቦስተን) ማራቶን
5000 metres	a·məst shi me·tər	አምስት ሺ ሜትር
10,000 metres	a·sər shi me·tər	አስር ሺ ሜትር

ACTIVITIES

TV & VIDEO
ቲቪና ቪዲዮ

Most words related to TV and video, an·te·na for example, sound like their English equivalents.

Where can we hire videos?
yeu vi·di·yo kas·set yeut
meu·keu·ra·yeut ən·chə·lal·leun?

የቪዲዮ ካሴት የት
መከራየት እንችላለን?

How long can I borrow this for?
leu sənt gi·ze meu·keu·ra·yeut
ə·chə·lal·lō?

ለስንት ጊዜ መከራየት
እችላለሁ?

Do you mind if I switch the
TV on/off?
ti·vi·wən lək·feu·tō/
laṭ·fow?

ቲቪውን ልክፈተው/
ላጥፈው?

Do you mind if I turn the
volume up/down?
dəm·ṣun keu·fə/zəķ lar·gō?

ድምፁን ከፍ/ዝቅ ላርገው?

Can I change the channel?
chan·na·lun meu·ķeu·yeur
ə·chə·lal·lō?

ቻናሉን መቀየር
እችላለሁ?

The TV isn't working.
ti·vi·yu ai·seu·ram

ቲቪው አይሰራም

I want to	... ma·yeut	... ማየት
watch ...	ə·feul·lə·gal·lō	እፈልጋለሁ
a film	film	ፊልም
the news	ze·na	ዜና
a soap opera	teu·keu·ta·tai film	ተከታታይ ፊልም
sport	sport	ስፖርት

RELIGION & HOLIDAYS

ሃይማኖ
ትና በዓላት

Make a sə·leut, 'vow', at an island monastery. Smell the a·beu·ba, 'flowers', over Meskel. Whatever your religion, you'll find Ethiopia's traditions and festivals a fascinating blend.

RELIGION
ሃይማኖት

Religion plays a major role in Ethiopian social and cultural life, which includes Christian, Muslim, Jewish and pagan traditions.

Talking about Religion
ስለ ሃይማኖት ማውራት

It's considered normal to inquire about someone's religion, but strange for people to have no religion.

What's your religion?

hai·ma·no·təh	ሃይማኖትህ ምንድን ነው-?
mən·dən nō? (m)	
hai·ma·no·təsh	ሃይማኖትሽ ምንድን ነው-?
mən·dən nō? (f)	
hai·ma·no·to	ሃይማኖትዎ ምንድን ነው-?
mən·dən nō? (pol)	

Catholic	ka·to·lik	ካቶሊክ
Christian	krəs·ti·yan	ክርስቲያን
Hindu	hin·du	ሂንዱ
Jewish	ai·hu·da·wi	አይሁዳዊ
Muslim	əs·lam	እስላም
Orthodox	or·to·doks	ኦርቶዶክስ
Protestant	pro·tes·tant	ፕሮቴስታንት

To avoid confusion with Amharic words with similar sounds, but different, offensive meanings, Buddhists are advised to use the term yeu əs·ya hai·ma·not, 'Eastern religion'. Shinto followers are advised to use the term yeu ja·pan hai·ma·not, 'Japanese religion'.

I'm not a strict follower.
   at·ba·ķi ai·deul·leu·hum   አጥባቂ አይደለሁም

I believe in God/Allah.
   beu əg·zya·ber/al·lah   በእግዚሃብሔር/አላህ
   am·nal·lō   አምናለሁ

I believe in destiny/fate.
   beu ə·dəl/a·ga·ţa·mi am·nal·lō   በ እድል/በእጋጋሚ አምናለሁ

I'm interested in astrology/
philosophy.
   (ko·keub ķo·ţeu·ran;   (ኮከብ ቆጠራን/ፍልስፍናን)
   fəl·sə·fə·nan) leu ma·weuķ   ለማወቅ ፍላጎት አለኝ
   fə·la·got al·leuny

At the Church & Monastery

ቤተ ክርስቲያንና ደብር

Dating back to the 4th century AD, the Ethiopian Orthodox religion has influenced everything from Ethiopian eating habits to everyday greetings. Many devoted followers visit churches several times a week, bowing, touching the walls and ground, and giving alms to the needy outside. The main church services are on Sunday mornings from 6 am.

If you're visiting a church, try to do as the locals do – if shoes are left outside, do the same. Women usually cover their heads in neu·ţeu·la, 'shawls'. Ask permission before entering monasteries.

Am I allowed to enter?
   meug·bat yi·cha·lal?   መግባት ይቻላል?

Can I pray here?
   əz·zi meu·şeu·lai yi·cha·lal?   እዚህ መፀለይ ይቻላል?

When does the next service begin?
   yeu·mi·ķeu·ţəl·lō ķə·da·se   የሚቀጥለው ቅዳሴ
   meu·che yi·jeu·mə·ral?   መቼ ይጀምራል?

This is my contribution to
(the monastery).
   yi·he leu (deub·ru) ər·da·ta nō   ይህ ለ (ደብሩ) እርዳታ ነው·

angel	meul'ak	መልአክ
Bible	meu·ṣa·haf ḳə·dus	መጽሐፍ ቅዱስ
chanting/songs	ze·ma	ዜማ
church	be·teu krəs·ti·yan	ቤተ ክርስቲያን
church leader	a·bun	አቡን
clergy	deub·teu·ra	ደብተራ
cross	meus·ḳeul	መስቀል
God	əg·zer	እግዜር
mass/service	ḳə·da·se	ቅዳሴ
monastery	deu·bər	ደብር
monastery head	ab·bat	አባት
monk	meu·neu·ku·se	መነኩሴ
nun	meu·neu·ku·se	መነኩሴ
prayer	ṣeu·lot	ጸሎት
prayer sticks	meu·ḳwa·mi·ya	መቋሚያ
priest	ḳess	ቄስ
sistrum (jangling rattles)	ṣeu·na·ṣəl	ጸናጽል
turban	təm·təm	ጥምጥም
Ark of the Covenant (including replicas)	ta·bot	ታቦት

At the Mosque   መስጊድ

Islam has a strong following in eastern and southern Ethiopia. It is said that during the time of the Prophet Mohammed, an Ethiopian named Bilal was the first muz·zin to call the faithful to prayer. Universal Muslim words like i·mam are used in Amharic, as are relevant words in local languages like Harari (Harar is one of the principle holy cities of Islam). Always ask permission before entering mosques.

giving alms	za·kat	ዛካት
Koran	ḳu·ran	ቁርአን
mosque	meus·gid	መስጊድ
obligatory prayer	sa·lat	ሳላት
profession of faith	sha·ha·da	ሻሃዳ

At the Synagogue   ምኵራብ

People often prefer to use be·teu əs·ra·el instead of feu·la·sha to refer to Ethiopia's unique Jewish community. Special Jewish celebrations include Rosh Hashanah (Jewish New Year).

| holy book | to·rah | ቶራ |
| priest | ka·hən | ካህን |

Pagan Worship   ጣኦት ማምለክ

The celestial deity *Wak* (waḳ) remains popular with groups in the south, especially in relation to farming and weather. Trees, springs, mountains and other objects of nature are considered to hold strong spiritual qualities. Local languages are used.

ancestor	ḳə·də·meu a·yat	ቅድመ አያት
paganism	ṭa'ot mam·leuk	ጣኦት ማምለክ
sacred place	yeu·teu·ḳeu·deu·seu bo·ta	የተቀደሰ ቦታ

SUPERSTITIONS   አምልኮ

Superstitions play a powerful role in Ethiopian life, crossing all religious boundaries. People read fortunes in coffee sediment and even animal entrails. It's said that if someone gives you bu·da (the evil eye), you'll suffer grave harm. Health is also believed to be affected by strange forces.

Where can I find protection from bu·da?
   yeu bu·da meud·ha·nit yeut   የቡዳ መድኃኒት የት
   yi·geu·nyal?   ይገኛል?
He/She is possessed by bu·da.
   bu·da beu·low/beu·lat   ቡዳ በላው/በላት

curse	ər·gə·man	እርግማን
guardian spirit	ad·bar	አድባር
the evil eye	bu·da	ቡዳ
protection from bu·da	yeu bu·da meud·ha·nit	የቡዳ መድኃኒት
spirit (benevolent or evil)	zar	ዛር
type of fortune teller	ko·keub ḳo·ṭa·ri	ኮከብ ቆጣሪ
witch doctor/sorcerer	ṭeun·ḳwai	ጠንቋይ

FESTIVALS & HOLIDAYS

በዓላትና የእረፍት ጊዜዎች

Dates listed here are for the Gregorian calendar; they may vary.

What time does the parade/
celebration start?
    seul·fu/beu'a·lu beu sənt seu'at
    yi·jeu·mə·ral?

ሰልፉ/በዓሉ በስንት ሰዓት
ይጀምራል?

What's the purpose of this occasion?
    yi·he a·meut be'al leu mən·dən
    nõ yeu·mi·keu·beu·rõ?

ይህ ዓመት በዓል
ለምንድነው የሚከበረው?

Can I watch?
    ma·yeut yi·cha·lal?

ማዋት ይቻላል?

bell	deu·weul	ደወል
ceremony	sə·neu sə·reu'at	ሥነ ሥርዓት
drum	keu·beu·ro	ከበሮ
fasting	şom	ጾም
festival/holiday	a·meut be'al	ዓመት በዓል
festival banquet	də·gəs	ድግስ
incense granules	ə·ṭan	ዕጣን
incense stick	neud	ነድ
Muslim pilgrimage	ha·ji	ሃጅ
parade	seu·ləf	ሰልፍ
(to go on a) pilgrimage	meu·sa·leum	መሳለም
tent (large)	dass	ዳስ

Secular Holidays

በሕዝብ የሚከበሩ ቀኖች

yeu seu·ra·teu·nyoch ḳeun
የሠራተኞች ቀን
1 May – International Labour Day

yeu ad·wa dəl meu·ta·seu·bi·ya
የአድዋ ድል መታሰቢያ
2 March – Victory of Adwa. Celebrating Menelik II's famous
defeat of Italian colonial forces at the Battle of Adwa in 1896,
thus maintaining Ethiopia's independence from European rule.

yeu ar·beu·nyoch meu·ta·seu·bi·ya
የአርበኞች መታሰቢያ
April or May – Patriots' Victory Day (Liberation Day). Ethiopia's ar·beu·nya (patriots) are honoured in the anniversary of
Italy's defeat in WWII.

Christian Festivals & Holy Days

የክርስቲያን በዓላትና የተቀደሱ ቀኖች

Bright processions, traditional costumes, and colourful dances are the hallmark of most Ethiopian Orthodox festivals, which include:

geun·na/lə·det   ገና/ልደት
6 or 7 January – Ethiopian Christmas. People attend all-night church services from Christmas eve onwards. Some communities play geun·na, a traditional sport (see page 186). This is a smaller celebration than fa·si·ka (Easter).

ṭəm·keut   ጥምቀት
19 January – Feast of Epiphany, celebrating Christ's Baptism. Three days of bright and colourful celebrations, including a procession where church *tabots* (see page 197) are taken to a body of water. Priests bless the water and pass the blessing to onlookers by sprinkling holy water on them. Dancing and singing follows. The final day is the feast of St Michael the Archangel.

fa·si·ka   ፋሲካ
April or May – Ethiopian Orthodox Easter Sunday. Family members gather to feast and celebrate, following overnight mass. Spicy meat dishes are eaten with gusto, ending the long Lent fast. See Food, page 144 for fasting terms.

eun·ku·ṭa·ṭash   እንቁጣጣሽ
11 September – Ethiopian New Year and feast of St John the Baptist. Families and friends gather together for a springtime celebration of renewed life and the beginning of a new year on the Ethiopian calendar.

meus·ḳeul   መስቀል
27 or 28 September – Celebrates the finding of Christ's cross by Empress Helena in the 4th century AD. People stack poles topped with yeu meus·ḳeul a·beu·ba (daisies) to form a pyramid around a cross known as deu·meu·ra. This is later fanned by chi·bo (torches of eucalyptus twigs). Dancing and feasting follow.

Although not public holidays, the following are popular with children and young adults: bu·he (12 July in the north-east, 21 August elsewhere), where children carry bread and torches in memory of young shepherds following Christ and the disciples up Mount Tabor. On fəl·seu·ta (24 August) young girls celebrate the Ascension of Mary.

Happy ...!	
ən·kwan leu ...	እንኳን ለ ... አደረሰህ!
a·deu·reu·seuh! (m)	
ən·kwan leu ...	እንኳን ለ ... አደረሰሽ!
a·deu·reu·seush! (f)	
ən·kwan leu ...	እንኳን ለ ... አደረሰዎት!
a·deu·reu·sot! (pol)	
Merry Christmas!	
ən·kwan leu geun·na	እንኳን ለገና አደረሰዎት!
a·deu·reu·sot!	

Saints' Days   የቅዳሳን ቀኖች

Saints remain popular throughout Ethiopia. Each church holds an annual ceremony for their specific saint, with feasting and celebrations in the local community. Families celebrate particular saints' days by inviting priests and visitors and giving alms. Though not national holidays, the following are popular occasions:

a·bu·neu man·feus kə·dus   አቡነ መንፈስ ቅዱስ
   mid-March – Pilgrims climb a rocky, extinct volcano on Mount Zqualla in Ethiopia's south to celebrate Abune Manfes Kedus, an Ethiopian saint

ma·ri·yam si·yon   ማርያም ጽዮን
   late November – Festival in Aksum at St Mariam of Zion church, in which the church's *tabot*, believed to be the original Ark of the Covenant, is carried out

kul·lə·bi   ቁልቢ
   late December – Feast of St Gabriel, the saint who protects homes. The feast includes a pilgrimage to the church in Kullibi in Eastern Ethiopia.

Several days of the month are named after saints and holy figures.
Farmers often use these instead of numeric dates.

lə·deu·ta	1st (Birth of Mary)	ልደታ
ba·ta	3rd (St Mary)	ባታ
ab·bo	5th (St Gebre Manfes Kedus)	አቦ
sə·las·se	7th (Trinity)	ስላሴ
mi·ka'el	12th (St Michael)	ሚካኤል
ki·da·neu mə·reut	16th (Covenant of Mercy)	ኪዳነ ምሕረት
gab·re'el	19th (St Gabriel)	ገብርኤል
ma·ri·yam	21st (St Mary)	ማርያም
gi·yor·gis	23rd (St George)	ጊዮርጊስ
teuk·leu hai·ma·not	24th (legendary Ethiopian saint)	ተክለ ሃይማኖት
meud·ha·ne a·leum	27th (Saviour of the World)	መድኃኔ አለም
beu'al weuld	29th (Festival of the Son)	በአል ወለድ

Muslim Festivals & Holy Days

የእስላም ዓመት በዓልና የተቀደሱ ቀኖች

Universal Muslim festivals and occasions are respected and
celebrated by Ethiopian Muslims. Don't forget that dates vary
from year to year.

Idd Al Fiṭr   ኢድ አልፈጥር
    November or December – End of month-long Ramadan
    fasting. Great feasting and celebrations, particularly in Harar and
    other Muslim centres; it usually lasts three days. Another
    important date during Ramadan is Lailat al Qadr, in which
    Muslims pray for Allah to grant them a good destiny.

Mau·lid   መውሊድ
    (May or April) Birth of the Prophet Mohammed

Idd Al Adha   ኢድ አል አድሃ
    (February or January) The culmination of the Hajj, the holy
    pilgrimage to Mecca (one of the five pillars of Islam)

WEDDINGS · ·ウርግ

You can use the general term 'Congratulations' at weddings, christenings and other social occasions.

> Congratulations!
> ən·kwan deus al·leuh/ · · እንኳን ደስ አለህ/
> al·leush! (m/f) · · አለሽ!

You'll probably come across a few Ethiopian weddings in your travels. In urban areas, many people choose their own partners and have ceremonies similar to Western weddings – with the added spice of joyful singing, dancing and ululations.

engagement (to get engaged)	meu·ta·cheut	መታጨት
honeymoon	yeu cha·gu·la gi·ze	የጫጉላ ጊዜ
wedding	seurg	·ウርግ
wedding cake	yeu seurg kek	የ·ウርግ ኬክ
wedding present	yeu seurg sə·ţo·ta	የ·ウርግ ስጦታ

MUSLIM PIGRIMAGE

A famous event on the Ethiopian Muslim calendar is the pilgrimage to the shrine of Sheikh Hussein, a 13th-century mystic prophet. Thousands of pilgrims travel for weeks or months to reach the sacred site near Goba in the south. Celebrations occur twice a year, on the anniversaries of the birth and death of the Prophet Mohammed.

RELIGION & HOLIDAYS

TOASTS & CONDOLENCES

የደስታና የሃዘን መግለጫ

Ethiopians are quick to offer congratulations and encouragement, but birthdays are only celebrated in childhood, and even then, usually only by city children.

Good luck!
 meul·kam ə·dəl!   መልካም ዕድል!
Hope it goes well!
 cheur yig·ṭeu·məh/   ቸር ይግጠምህ/
 yig·ṭeu·məsh! (m/f)   ይግጠምሽ!
Chin up/Be strong!
 ai·zoh/ai·zosh! (m/f)   አይዞህ/አይዞሽ!

Ethiopians go out of their way to express condolences to people suffering from illness or the loss of a loved one. At funerals, you will hear mu·sho (mournful chants) and leuḳ·so (wailing).

May God bring your health back.
 əg·zer yi·ma·rəh/   እግዜር ይማርህ/
 yi·ma·rəsh (m/f)   ይማርሽ
My deepest sympathy.
 neubs yi·mar   ነብስ ይማር
 (lit: may the soul be forgiven)

Most urban medical professionals speak fluent English. In more isolated areas, it's best to carry a first-aid kit.

I'm sick.
    a·mo·nyal　　　　　　　　　　　አሞኛል

My (male) friend is sick.
    gwa·deu·nya·yen a·meum·mō　　　ጓደኛዬን አመመው·

My (female) friend is sick.
    gwa·deu·nya·yen a·meum·mat　　ጓደኛዬን አመማት

He/She needs medical treatment.
    hə·kə·mə·na yas·feul·lə·geu·wal/　ሕክምና ያስፈልገዋል/
    yas·feul·lə·ga·tal　　　　　　　ያስፈልጋታል

I need medical treatment.
    hə·kə·mə·na yas·feu·lə·geu·nyal　ሕክምና ያስፈልገኛል

I need a doctor (immediately).
    ha·kim (bas·cheu·kwai)　　　　ሐኪም (ባስቸኳይ)
    ə·feul·lə·gal·lō　　　　　　　　እፈልጋለሁ·

I'm hurt/injured.
    teu·go·də·chal·lō　　　　　　　ተጎድቻለሁ

I've been bitten by a (dog).
    (wu·sha) neu·keu·seuny　　　　(ውሻ) ነከሰኝ

It's an emergency!
    as·cheu·kwai nō!　　　　　　　አስቸኳይ ነው·!

Where can I find a (good) ...?	(ṭə·ru) ... yeut yi·geu·nyal?	(ጥሩ) ... የት ይገኛል?
dentist	yeu ṭərs ha·kim	የጥርስ ሐኪም
doctor	ha·kim	ሐኪም
hospital	hos·pi·tal	ሆስፒታል
medical centre	yeu hə·kə·mə·na ṭa·bi·ya	የህክምና ጣቢያ
nurse	neurs	ነርስ
pharmacy	far·ma·si	ፋርማሲ·

I need ...	... ə·feul·lə·gal·lō	... እፈልጋለሁ·
My (male) friend needs ...	gwa·deu·nya·ye ... yas·feul·lə·geu·wal	ጓደኛዬ ... የስፈልገዋል
My (female) friend needs ...	gwa·deu·nya·ye ... yas·feul·lə·ga·tal	ጓደኛዬ ... የስፈልጋታል
an ambulance	am·bu·lans	አምቡላንስ
transport to the hospital	weu·deu hos·pi·tal meu·ki·na	ወደ ሆስፒታል መኪና
an examination/ a check-up	hə·kə·mə·na/ mər·meu·ra	ሕክምና/ ምርመራ
first aid	yeu meu·jeu·meu·ri·ya ər·da·ta	የመጀመሪያ እርዳታ
medicine/ tablets	meud·ha·nit/ kə·nin	መድሃኒት/ ክኒን
urgent treatment	as·cheu·kwai hə·kə·mə·na	አስቸኳይ ሕክምና

AT THE DOCTOR
ሐኪም ቤት

(Please) Help me.
(ə·ba·kon) yir·duny
(እባክዎን) ይርዱኝ

I have a pain here.
əz·zi ga ya·meu·nyal
እዚህ ጋ ያመኛል

That hurts!
ya·mal!
ያማል!

I'm feeling better.
teu·shə·lo·nyal
ተሽሎኛል

I'm feeling worse.
bə·so·bə·nyal
ብሶብኛል

I'm on medication for ...
leu ... meud·ha·nit
ə·yeu·weu·seud·ku nō
ለ ... መድሃኒት
እየወሰድኩ ነው·

Where's the toilet?
shənt be·tu yeut nō?
ሽንት ቤቱ የት ነው·?

HEALTH

THE DOCTOR MAY SAY ...

mən ho·nu?
ምን ሆኑ?
  What's the problem?

yeut lai ya·mə·hal/
የት ላይ ያምሃል/
ya·mə·shal? (m/f)
ያምሻል?
  Where does it hurt?

yeu weur a·beu·ba lai neush?
የወር አበባ ላይ ነሽ?
  Are you menstruating?

tə·ku·sat al·leuh/al·leush?
ትኩሳት አለህ/አለሽ?
  Do you have a temperature?

keu·jeu·meu·reuh/
ከጀመረህ/ከጀመረሽ
keu·jeu·meu·reush
ስንት ጊዜ ሆነ?
sənt gi·ze ho·neu? (m/f)
  How long have you been like this?

keuz·zi beu·fit yi·he chig·gər
ከዚህ በፊት ይህ ችግር
neub·beu·reu·bəh/
ነበረብህ/ነበረብሽ?
neub·beu·reu·bəsh? (m/f)
  Have you had this before?

meud·ha·nit tə·weus·dal·leuh/
መድሃኒት ትወስዳለህ/
tə·weus·jal·leush? (m/f)
ትወስጃለሽ?
  Are you on medication?

ta·cheu·sal·leuh? (m)
ታጨሳለህ?
ta·cheu·shal·leush? (f)
ታጨሻለሽ?
  Do you smoke?

meu·teut tə·teu·tal·leuh/
መጠጥ ትጠጣለህ/
tə·teu·chal·leush? (m/f)
ትጠጫለሽ?
  Do you drink?

drag tə·weus·dal·leuh/
ድራግ ትወስዳለህ/
tə·weus·jal·leush? (m/f)
ትወስጃለሽ?
  Do you take drugs?

yeu·mais·ma·mah/
የማይስማማህ/
yeu·mais·ma·mash
የማይስማማሽ
neu·geur al·leu? (m/f)
ነገር አለ?
  Are you allergic to anything?

ər·guz neush?
እርጉዝ ነሽ?
  Are you pregnant?

AILMENTS ሕመሞች

I'm ill.
 a·mo·nyal   አሞኛል
I've been vomiting.
 yas·meul·lə·seu·nyal   ያስመልሰኛል
I feel tired.
 deu·kə·mo·nyal   ይከሞኛል
I can't sleep.
 ən·kəlf əm·bi al·leuny   እንቅልፍ እምቢ አለኝ

I feel ...
 dizzy   ra·sen a·zo·reuny   ራሴን አዞረኝ
 shivery   yan·keu·teu·kə·teu·nyal   ያንቀጠቅጠኛል

Different verbs are used depending on what the ailment is.

I have ...	... al·leu·bəny	... አለብኝ
anaemia	deum ma·neus	ደም ማነስ
asthma	as·ma	አስማ
diabetes	sə·kwar beu·shə·ta	ስኳር በሽታ
high blood pressure	deum bə·zat	ደም ብዛት

I have (a) ...	... yi·zo·nyal	... ይዞኛል
cold	gun·fan	ጉንፋን
malaria	yeu weu·ba beu·shə·ta	የወባ በሽታ
dysentery	yeu teuk·mat beu·shə·ta	የተቅማጥ በሽታ
rabies	yeu wu·sha beu·shə·ta	የውሻ በሽታ
venereal disease	yeu a·ba·leu zeur beu·shə·ta	የአባለዘር በሽታ
skin disease	yeu ko·da beu·shə·ta	የቆዳ በሽታ

I have a ...	... ya·meu·nyal	... ያመኛል
backache	weu·geu·ben	ወገቤን
headache	ra·sen	ራሴን
sore throat	gu·ro·ro·yen	ጉሮሮዬን
stomachache	ho·den	ሆዴን
toothache	tər·sen	ጥርሴን

HEALTH

I have (a/an) ...

bite (insect)	teu·neu·deuf·ku	ተነደፍኩ
breathing	meu·teun·feus	መተንፈስ
problems	yas·cheu·gə·reu·nyal	ያስቸግረኛል
broken (leg)	(əg·re) teu·seub·rwal	(እግሬ) ተሰበሯል
burn (from fire)	ə·sat a·ḳa·ṭeu·leuny	እሳት አቃጠለኝ
constipation	hod dər·ḳeut al·leuny	ሆድ ድርቀት አለኝ
diarrhoea	yas·ḳeu·mə·ṭeu·nyal	ያስቀምጠኛል
fever	tə·ku·sat al·leuny	ትኩሳት አለኝ
fleas	ḳu·nə·cha beu·lany	ቁንጫ በላኝ
food poisoning	yeu mə·gəb	የምግብ መበከል
	meu·beu·keul nō	ነው· ያሳመመኝ
	ya·sa·meu·meuny	
heat exhaustion	bə·zu ṣeu·hai meu·tany	ብዙ ፀሐይ መታኝ
indigestion	ya·ḳə·reu·nyal	ያቅረኛል
itch	ya·sa·kə·keu·nyal	ያሳከከኛል
sunburn	bə·zu ṣeu·hai meu·tany	ብዙ ፀሃይ መታኝ
sunstroke	məch meu·tany	ምች መታኝ
wound	ḳo·sə·yal·lō	ቆስያለሁ·

I've been vaccinated.

| teu·keu·tə·bi·yal·lō | ተከትቤአለሁ· |

I have my own syringe.

| yeu·ra·se sə·rinj al·leuny | የራሴ ስሪንጅ አለኝ |

This is my usual medicine.

| bə·zu gi·ze yi·he·nən | ብዙ ጊዜ ይሄንን መድሃኒት |
| meud·ha·nit nō yeu·mə·weus·dō | ነው· የምወስደው· |

If you can't find something you need in the following list, try
using the English word for it.

accident	a·deu·ga	አደጋ
addiction	sus	ሱስ
bite (dog)	nə·kə·sha	ንክሻ
blood group	yeu deum ai·neut	የደም አይነት
blood pressure	yeu deum gə·fit	የደም ግፊት
blood test	yeu deum mər·meu·ra	የደም ምርመራ
contagious	teu·la·la·fi	ተላላፊ
emergency	as·cheu·kwai	አስቸኳይ
faeces/stools	ai·neu mə·dər	አይነ ምድር
inhaler	ai·yeur weu·deu wəst meu·sab	አየር ወደ ውስጥ መሳብ
to have an injection	meur·fe meu·weu·gat	መርፌ መወጋት
malnutrition	yeu mə·gəb ma·neus	የምግብ ማነስ
medicine	meud·ha·nit	መድሃኒት
patient	beu·shə·teu·nya	በሽተኛ
poison	meurz	መርዝ
pus	meu·gəl	መግል
splinter	chi·reut	ጭረት
syringe	sə·rinj	ስሪንጅ
urine	shənt	ሽንት
vitamin	vi·ta·min	ቪታሚን

HEALTH

SOUNDING OFF

Excuse me!	yi·kər·ta!	ይቅርታ!
Bless you!	yi·ma·rəh! (m)	ይማርህ!
(sneezing)	yi·ma·rəsh! (f)	ይማርሽ!
to sneeze	mas·neu·ţeus	ማስነጠስ
cough	sal	ሳል
hiccup	sə·kə·ta	ስቅታ
fart	feuss	ፈስ

PARTS OF THE BODY   የሰውነት ክፍሎች

| I have a pain in my ... | ... ya·meu·nyal | ... ያመኛል |
| I can't move my ... | ... man·keu·sa·keus al·chəl·ləm | ... ማንቀሳቀስ አልችልም |

HEALTH

ankle	kur·chəm·chə·mit	ቁርጭምጭሚት
appendix	tərf an·jeut	ትርፍ አንጀት
arm	kənd	ክንድ
back	weu·geub	ወገብ
bone	a·tənt	አጥንት
chest	deu·reut	ደረት
ears	jo·ro	ጆሮ
eyes	ain	አይን
face	fit	ፊት
finger	ţat	ጣት
foot	ə·gər	እግር
hand	əj	እጅ
head	rass	ራስ
heart	ləb	ልብ
kidney	ku·la·lit	ኩላሊት
knee	gul·beut	ጉልበት
leg	ə·gər	እግር
liver	gu·beut	ጉበት
lung	sam·ba	ሳምባ
mouth	aff	አፍ
muscle	ţun·cha	ጡንቻ
neck	an·geut	አንገት
nose	a·fən·cha	አፍንጫ
shoulder	tə·kə·sha	ትከሻ
skin	ko·da	ቆዳ
spine	yeu jeur·ba a·tənt	የጀርባ አጥንት
stomach	hod	ሆድ
teeth	tərs	ጥርስ
throat	gu·ro·ro	ጉሮሮ
tongue	mə·las	ምላስ
tonsils	ən·təl	እንጥል
vein	yeu deum sər	የደም ስር

HEALTH

WOMEN'S HEALTH
የሴቶች ጤና

Could I see a female doctor?
yeu set dok·teur ma·yeut ə·cha·lal·lō?
የሴት ዶክተር ማየት እችላለሁ?

I'm pregnant.
ər·guz neuny
እርጉዝ ነኝ

I think I'm pregnant.
ya·reu·geuz·ku yə·meu·sə·leu·nyal
ያረገዝኩ ይመስለኛል

I'm on the Pill.
yeu weu·lid meu·keu·la·keu·ya meud·ha·nit ə·yeu·weu·seud·ku nō
የወሊድ መከላከያ መድኃኒት እየወሰድኩ ነው

I haven't had my period for ... weeks.
yeu weur a·beu·ba·ye leu ... sa·mənt al·meu·țam
የወር አበባዬ ... ሳምንት አልመጣም

I'd like to use (contraceptive pills).
(yeu·șəns meu·keu·la·keu·ya meud·ha·nit) mō·seud ə·feul·lə·gal·lō
(የፅንስ መከላከያ መድኃኒት) መውሰድ እፈልጋለሁ

I'd like to have a pregnancy test.
yeu ər·gə·zə·na mər·meu·ra ə·feul·lə·gal·lō
የእርግዝና ምርመራ እፈልጋለሁ

abortion	șən·sən mas·weu·reud	ፅንስን ማስወረድ
cystitis	yeu shənt fi·nya beu·sha·ta	የሽንት ፊኛ በሽታ
diaphragm	di·yaf·ram	ዲያፍራም
female circumcision	yeu set gə·rə·zat	የሴት ግርዛት
menstruation	yeu weur a·beu·ba	የወር አበባ
to have a miscarriage	as·weu·reu·dat	አስወረዳት
period pain	beu·weur a·beu·ba gi·ze yeu·mi·seu·ma hə·meum	በወር አበባ ጊዜ የሚሰማ ሕመም
venereal disease	yeu a·ba·leu zeur beu·sha·ta	የአባለ ዘር በሽታ

SPECIAL HEALTH NEEDS ልዩ የጤና ፍላጎቶች

I have diabetes/epilepsy.
(sə·kwar beu·shə·ta; yeu·mi·ţəl (ስኳር በሽታ/የሚጥል
beu·shə·ta) al·leu·bəny በሽታ) አለብኝ

I'm anaemic.
deum ma·neus al·leu·bəny ደም ማነስ አለብኝ

I'm allergic to ...	... ais·ma·ma·nyəm	... አይስማማኝም
My (male) friend	gwa·deu·nya·ye ...	ጓደኛዬ ...
is allergic to ...	ais·ma·ma·wəm	አይስማማው\-ም
My (female) friend	gwa·deu·nya·ye ...	ጓደኛዬ ...
is allergic to ...	ais·ma·ma·təm	አይስማማትም
codeine	ko·din	ኮዲን
penicillin	pe·ni·si·lin	ፔኒሲሊን
pollen	bə·nany	ብናኝ
bees	nəb	ንብ

ምን ሆኑ?

ቁንጥጫ በላኝ አለብኝ

I have a skin allergy.
yeu ķo·da meu·ķo al·leu·bəny የቆዳ መቆ አለብኝ

I have high/low blood pressure.
deum bə·zat/ma·neus ደም ብዛት/ማነስ አለብኝ
al·leu·bəny

I have a weak heart.
lə·be deu·ka·ma nō ልቤ ደካማ ነው\.

I'm on a special diet.
beu ha·ķim yeu·ta·zeu·zeu በሐኪም የታዘዘ ምግብ
mə·gəb ə·weus·dal·lō እወስዳለሁ\.

HEALTH

HEALTH

AT THE CHEMIST   መድኃኒት ቤት

It's better to use English when referring to medicines, but you can use Amharic for purchasing general pharmaceutical items.

Where's a chemist?
   meud·ha·nit bet yeut nō?   መድኃኒት ቤት የት ነው?

I want medicine for ...
   leu ... meud·ha·nit ə·feul·lə·gal·lō   ለ ... መድኃኒት እፈልጋለሁ

How many times a day?
   beu keun sənt gi·ze?   በቀን ስንት ጊዜ?

Can I drive on this medication?
   yi·hen meud·ha·nit keu·weu·seud·ku   ይሄን መድኃኒት ከወሰድኩ
   bo·hal·la   በኋላ መንዳት እችላለሁ?
   meun·dat ə·chə·lal·lō?

antibiotics	an·ti·bai·yo·tik	አንቲ ባዮቲክ
antiseptic	an·ti·sep·tik	አንቲሴፕቲክ
aspirin	as·prin	አስፐሪን
bandage	fa·sha	ፋሻ
Band-Aid (plaster)	yeu ku·səl plas·teur	የቁስል ፕላስተር
condoms	kon·dom	ኮንዶም
contraceptive	yeu səns	የፆታስ
pill	meu·keu·la·keu·ya	መከላከያ
	meud·ha·nit	መድኃኒት
cough medicine	yeu sal meud·ha·nit	የሳል መድኃኒት
cream (ointment)	krem/kə·bat	ክሬም/ቅባት
gauze	shash	ሻሽ
laxatives	yeu·mi·yas·keu·məţ	የሚያስቀምጥ
	meud·ha·nit	መድኃኒት
painkillers	hə·meum	ህመም
	yeu·mi·yas·ta·gəs	የሚያስታግስ
	meud·ha·nit	መድኃኒት
sleeping pills	yeu·mi·yas·teu·nya	የሚያስተኛ
	kə·nin	ክኒን

See Toiletries on page 132 for related words.

ALTERNATIVE TREATMENTS

ሴላ የሕክምና አይነቶች

Traditional medicine is popular in Ethiopia. See also Superstition on page 194.

chiropractor	kai·ro·prak·tor	ካይሮፕራክተር
healer	yeu ba·həl	የባሀል መድሃኒተኛ
	meud·ha·ni·teu·nya	
herbs	kə·ṭeu·la kə·ṭeul	ቅጠላ ቅጠል
homeopathy	ho·mi·yo·pa·ti	ሆሚዮፓቲ
massage	meu·ta·sheut	መታሸት

AT THE DENTIST

የጥርስ ሐኪም

Where's a dentist?
  yeu ṭərs ha·kim
  yeut yi·geu·nyal?

የጥርስ ሐኪም የት ይገኛል?

I have a toothache.
  ṭər·sen ya·meu·nyal

ጥርሴን ያመኛል

I don't want it extracted.
  ən·di·neu·ḳeul al·feul·lə·gəm

እንዲነቀል አልፈልግም

I want an anaesthetic.
  ma·deun·zeu·zha meur·fe
  ə·feul·lə·gal·lō

ማደንዘዣ መርፌ
እፈልጋለሁ

I need a filling.
  ṭər·sen mas·mo·lat
  ə·feul·lə·gal·lō

ጥርሴን ማስሞላት
እፈልጋለሁ

My tooth is broken.
  ṭər·se te·seb·rwal

ጥርሴ ተሰብሯል

My gums hurt.
  də·den ya·meu·nyal

ድዴን ያመኛል

| Ouch! | wəy! | ው.ይ! |

HEALTH

AT THE OPTOMETRIST

የዓይን ሐኪም

Where's an optometrist?
  yeu ain ha·kim yeut yi·geu·nyal?

የዓይን ሐኪም የት ይገኛል?

I'd like my eyes checked.
  ai·nen meu·meur·meur
  ə·feul·lə·gal·lō

ዓይኔን መመርመር
እፈልጋለሁ

I'm long/short sighted.
  kərb/ruk ma·yeut
  yas·cheu·gə·reu·nyal

ቅርብ/ሩቅ ማየት
ያስቸግረኛል

Could you fix my glasses?
  meu·neu·şa·ren sə·ra·liny?

መነፅሬን ስራልኝ?

I need new (glasses/contact lenses).
  ad·dis (meu·neu·şər; kon·takt
  lens) ə·feul·lə·gal·lō

አዲስ (መነፅር/ኮንታክት
ሌንስ) እፈልጋለሁ

ልዩ ፍላጎቶች   **SPECIFIC NEEDS**

DISABLED TRAVELLERS

አካላቸው የተጎዳ መንገደኞች

What services do you have for disabled people?

> a·ka·la·chō leu teu·go·da
> sō·woch mən a·geul·glot
> al·la·chu?

አካላቸው ለተጎዳ ሰዎች
ምን አገልግሎት አላችሁ?

Is there wheelchair access?

> leu wil·cher meug·bi·ya
> meun·geud al·leu?

ለዊል ቸር መግቢያ
መንገድ አለ?

Speak more loudly, please.

> ə·ba·kon chok yi·beu·lu

እባክዎን ጮክ ይበሉ

Are guide dogs permitted?

> ai·neu sə·wə·rən yeu·mi·meu·ra
> wə·sha tə·feuk·dal·la·chu?

አይን ስውርን የሚመራ ውሻ
ትፈቅዳላችሁ?

Can you please assist?

> ə·ba·ka·chu ər·duny?

እባካችሁ እርዱኝ?

Braille library	yeu bə·ran·na be·teu meu·ṣə·haf	የብራና ቤት መጽሃፍ
disabled person	a·ka·lu yeu·teu·go·da sō	አካሉ የተጎዳ ሰው
guide dog	ai·neu sə·wə·rən yeu·mi·meu·ra wə·sha	አይን ስውርን የሚመራ ውሻ
walking stick	mər·kuz	ምርኩዝ
wheelchair	teush·keur·ka·ri weun·beur; wil·cher	ተሽከርካሪ ወንበር/ ዊል ቸር

TRAVELLING WITH THE FAMILY

ከቤተሰብ ጋር መጓዝ

You may like to specify a·lə·cha mə·gəb (food that's not too hot or spicy) for children at restaurants.

Are there facilities for babies?
  leu hə·ṣan lə·joch mən
  a·geul·glot al·la·chu?

ለህፃን ልጆች ምን
አገልግሎት አላችሁ?

Do you have a child-minding service?
  yeu meu·wa·leu hə·ṣa·nat
  a·geul·glot al·la·chu?

የመዋለ ህፃናት አገልግሎት
አላችሁ?

Where can I find a/an
(English-speaking) babysitter?
  (ən·gli·zə·nya yeu·mət·chəl)
  yeu lə·joch mog·zit yeut
  a·geu·nyal·lō?

(እንግሊዝኛ የምትችል)
የልጆች ሞግዚት
የት አገኛለሁ?

Do you have a cradle/cot?
  yeu hə·ṣan al·ga al·la·chu?

የሕፃን አልጋ አላችሁ?

Is there a family discount?
  leu be·teu·seub ḳə·nash al·leu?

ለቤተሰብ ቅናሽ አለ?

Do you charge extra for children?
  leu lə·joch teu·cheu·ma·ri
  kə·fə·ya al·leu?

ለልጆች ተጨማሪ
ክፍያ አለ?

Do you have food for children?
  leu lə·joch mə·gəb al·la·chu?

ለልጆች ምግብ አላችሁ?

Are there any places for
children to play?
  leu lə·joch meu·cha·weu·cha
  bo·ta al·leu?

ለልጆች መጫወቻ
ቦታ አለ?

Is it nearby?
  əz·zi a·ka·ba·bi nō?

እዚህ አካባቢ ነው?

babysitter	mog·zit	ሞግዚት
cradle/cot	yeu hə·ṣan al·ga	የሕፃን አልጋ
nursery	meu·wa·leu hə·ṣa·nat	መዋለ ህፃናት

LOOKING FOR A JOB ሥራ መፈለግ

Foreigners on tourist visas are generally not allowed to seek or accept work in Ethiopia. Apply to the appropriate consulates and ministries for work and residence permits.

Do I need a work permit?
yeu sə·ra feu·ḳad yas·feul·lə·gal?   የስራ ፈቃድ ያስፈልጋል?

I've had experience.
yeu sə·ra ləmd al·leuny   የስራ ልምድ አለኝ

casual	gi·ze'a·wi	ጊዜአዊ
employee	seu·ra·teu·nya	ሰራተኛ
employer	ḳeu·ṭa·ri	ቀጣሪ
full time	ḳwa·mi	ቋሚ
job	sə·ra	ስራ
job advertisement	yeu sə·ra	የስራ
	mas·ta·weu·ḳi·ya	ማስታወቂያ
traineeship	səl·ṭeu·na	ስልጠና
wage	deu·moz	ደሞዝ
voluntary	feu·ḳa·deu·nya	ፈቃደኛ

ON BUSINESS ንግድና ሥራ

See Social Issues, page 115, and In the Country, page 161, for additional words related to overseas aid and development.

We're attending a ...	yeu ... teu·sa·ta·fi·woch neun	የ ... ተሳታፊዎች ነን
conference	gu·ba'e	ጉባኤ
meeting	səb·seu·ba	ስብሰባ
trade fair	nəgd ba·zar	ንግድ ባዛር

I'm on a course.
    kors lai neuny   ኮርስ ላይ ነኝ
I have an appointment with ...
    keu ... gar keu·teu·ro al·leuny   ከ ... ጋር ቀጠሮ አለኝ
Here's my business card.
    kar·den lə·stah/lə·stash (m/f)   ካርዴን ልስጣህ/ልስጣሽ
I need an interpreter.
    as·teur·gwa·mi ə·feul·lə·gal·lō   አስተርጓሚ እፈልጋለሁ
I'd like to use a computer.
    kom·pyu·teur meu·teu·keum   ኮምፒዩተር መጠቀም
    ə·feul·lə·gal·lō   እፈልጋለሁ
I'd like to send a fax/an email.
    faks/i·mel meu·lak   ፋክስ/ኢሜል መላክ
    ə·feul·lə·gal·lō   እፈልጋለሁ

SPECIFIC NEEDS

እባክዎን ጮጭ ይበሉ

ከ ጓደኛዬ ጋር
ቀጠሮ አለኝ

aid organisation	ər·da·ta də·rə·jat	እርዳታ ድርጅት
aid worker	yeu ər·da·ta	የእርዳታ
	də·rə·jat seu·ra·teu·nya	ድርጅት ሠራተኛ
client	deun·beu·nya	ደንበኛ
colleague	yeu sə·ra	የስራ ባልደረባ
	bal·deu·reu·ba	
distributor	a·keu·fa·fai	አከፋፋይ
exhibition	eg·zi·bi·shən	ኤግዚቢሽን
investment	meu·wa·leu nwai	መዋለ ንዋይ
labour	yeu gul·beut wa·ga	የጉልበት ዋጋ
manager	sə·ra as·ki·yaj	ስራ አስኪያጅ
permit	feu·kad	ፈቃድ
profit	tərf	ትርፍ
proposal	ha·sab	ሃሳብ
report	ri·port	ሪፖርት
sample	na·mu·na	ናሙና

FILM, TV & JOURNALISM

ፊልም ቲቪና ጋዜጠኛነት

May we film (here)?
(əz·zi) film man·sat
yi·cha·lal?

(እዚህ) ፊልም ማንሳት
ይቻላል?

We have a permit.
feu·ḳad al·leun

ፈቃድ አለን

We'd like to come (next Wednesday).
(yeu·mi·meu·ṭow rob)
meum·ṭat
ən·feul·lə·gal·leun

(የሚመጣው ሮብ)
መምጣት
እንፈልጋለን

Please speak to our boss.
a·leu·ḳa·chen
ya·neu·ga·gə·ru

አለቃችን ያነጋግሩ

We're filming here.
əz·zi film ə·ya·neu·san nō

እዚህ ፊልም እያነሳን ነው

We're shooting a ...   ... ə·ya·neu·san nō   ... እያነሳን ነው
   film   film   ፊልም
   documentary   təm·hər·ta·wi film   ትምህርታዊ ፊልም
   TV program   yeu ti·vi pro·gram   የቲቪ ፕሮግራም

I'm writing about ...
sə·leu ... ə·yeu·ṣaf·ku nō

ስለ ... እየፃፍኩ ነው

I would like to speak to
you (tomorrow).
(neu·geu) la·neu·ga·gə·rot
ə·feul·lə·gal·lō

(ነገ) ላነጋግርዎት
እፈልጋለሁ

I'll bring a translator.
as·teur·gwa·mi a·meu·ṭal·lō

አስተርጓሚ አመጣለሁ

ADOPTION & TRACING ROOTS

ዘመዶቻችን መፈለግና ጉድፈፈቻ

(I think) My ancestors came from this area.

kəd·meu a·ya·to·che keuz·zi	ቅድመ አያቶች ከዚህ
a·ka·ba·bi yeu meu·ṭu	አካባቢ የመጡ
(yə·meus·leu·nyal)	(ይመስለኛል)

I'm looking for my relatives.

zeu·meu·do·chen	ዘመዶቼን እየፈለኩ ነው።
ə·yeu·feul·leu·ku nō	

Is there anyone here by the name of ...?

... yeu·mi·ba·lu sō əz·zi	... የሚባሉ ሰው እዚህ
a·ka·ba·bi yi·no·ral·lu?	አካባቢ ይኖራሉ?

adoption	gud·feu·cha	ጉድፈፈቻ
adopted children	yeu gud·feu·cha lə·joch	የጉድፈፈቻ ልጆች
adoption contract	yeu gud·feu·cha wul	የጉድፈፈቻ ውል
contract	wul	ውል
court	fərd bet	ፍርድ ቤት
date of birth	yeu tu·ləd ḳeun	የትውልድ ቀን
family	be·teu·seub	ቤተሰብ
lawyer	ṭeu·beu·ḳa	ጠበቃ
orphaned	a·sa·da·gi	አሳዳጊ
	yeu·le·lō ləj	የሌለው ልጅ
representative	teu·weu·kai	ተወካይ
witness	mə·sə·kər	ምስክር

TELLING THE TIME ሰዓቱን ማወቅ

Ethiopia is three hours ahead of GMT/UTC time.

The Ethiopian method of marking time is quite different to the way it's done in most Western countries. The Ethiopian clock starts when the sun comes up, so don't be surprised if you're asked to breakfast at 2 o'clock in the morning! To avoid confusion when checking the time, always ask:

Is that Ethiopian/foreign time?
beu ha·beu·sha/feu·reunj በሃበሻ/በፈረንጅ
a·ko·ṭa·ṭeur nō? አቆጣጠር ነው?

What time is it?
sənt seu'at nō? ስንት ሰዓት ነው?

It's ...	... nō	... ነው
(one) o'clock	(and) seu'at	(አንድ) ሰዓት
quarter past (one)	(and) seu'at keu·rub	(አንድ) ሰዓት ከሩብ
half past (one)	(and) seu'at teu·kul	(አንድ) ሰዓት ተኩል
(ten) past (one)	(and) seu'at keu (as·sər)	(አንድ) ሰዓት ከ (አስር)
quarter to (one)	leu (and) seu'at rub gu·dai	ለ (አንድ) ሰዓት ሩብ ጉዳይ
(five) minutes to (one)	leu (and) seu'at (a·məst) gu·dai	ለ (አንድ) ሰዓት (አምስት) ጉዳይ

The Amharic equivalent to 'am' and 'pm' is expressed through phrases like 'in the morning', 'in the evening' or 'at night'.

It's (three) o'clock ...	keu ... (sost) seu'at nō	ከ ... (ሶስት) ሰዓት ነው
in the morning	ṭeu·wa·tu	ጠዋቱ
in the evening	mə·shə·tu	ምሽቱ
at night	le·li·tu	ሌሊቱ

When/What time ...?	meu·che/beu sənt seu'at ...?	መቼ/በስንት ሰዓት ...?
does it start	yi·jeu·mə·ral	ይጀምራል
does it finish	yal·kal	ያልቃል
does it open	yi·keu·feu·tal	ይከፈታል
does it close	yiz·zeu·gal	ይዘጋል

DAYS OF THE WEEK የሳምንቱ ቀኖች

Monday	seu·nyo	ሰኞ
Tuesday	mak·seu·nyo	ማክሰኞ
Wednesday	rob	ሮብ
Thursday	ha·mus	ሃሙስ
Friday	arb	ዓርብ
Saturday	ḳə·da·me	ቅዳሜ
Sunday	ə·hud	እሁድ

ETHIOPIAN CALENDAR
የኢትዮጵያ ቀን መቁጠሪያ

The Ethiopian calendar is made up of 12 months of 30 days each and a 13th month of five days (six in a leap year). The Ethiopian New Year commences on 11 September by the Gregorian calendar. Although most calendars and public facilities in Ethiopia carry both Ethiopian and Gregorian dates, it's worth becoming acquainted with Ethiopian dates, as they're still in common use.

Months ወሮች

The Ethiopian months do not exactly correspond to the Gregorian calendar months. To refer to Western dates, the English word for the particular month will be understood.

September/October	meus·keu·reum	መስከረም
October/November	ṭə·ḳamt	ጥቅምት
November/December	hə·dar	ኅዳር
December/January	ta·hə·sas	ታህሳስ
January/February	ṭər	ጥር
February/March	yeu·ka·tit	የካቲት
March/April	meu·ga·bit	መጋቢት
April/May	mi·ya·zi·ya	ሚያዚያ
May/June	gən·bot	ግንቦት
June/July	seu·ne	ሰኔ
July/August	ham·le	ሐምሌ
August/September	neu·ha·se	ነሐሴ
September (five or six days)	pa·gu·me	ጳጉሜ

TIME & DATES

DATES   ቀኖች

What day is it (today)?
    (za·re) ķeu·nu mən·dən nō?   (ዛሬ) ቀኑ ምንድን ነው?
What is the date (today)?
    (za·re) ķeu·nu sənt nō?   (ዛሬ) ቀኑ ስንት ነው?
It's the 1st/20th of (March).
    (March) and/ha·ya nō   (ማርች) አንድ/ሃያ ነው
Is that the Ethiopian/Gregorian
calendar date?
    beu ha·beu·sha/feu·reunj   በሀበሻ/በፈረንጅ
    zeu·meun a·ķo·ţa·ţeur nō?   ዘመን አቆጣጠር ነው?

PRESENT   የአሁን ጊዜ

immediately	weu·di·yow·nu	ወዲያውኑ
now	a·hun	አሁን
this afternoon	za·re ķeu·seu'at	ዛሬ ከሰአት
this evening	za·re mə·shat	ዛሬ ምሽት
this month	beuz·zi weur	በዚህ ወር
this morning	za·re ţeu·wat	ዛሬ ጠዋት
this week	beuz·zi sam·mənt	በዚህ ሳምንት
this year	beuz·zi a·meut	በዚህ ዓመት
today	za·re	ዛሬ
tonight	za·re ma·ta	ዛሬ ማታ

PAST   ያለፈው ጊዜ

day before	ķeu tə·nan·tə·na	ከትናንትና
yesterday	weu·di·ya	ወዲያ
(three) days ago	ķeu (sost) ķeun beu·fit	ከ (ሶስት) ቀን በፊት
last night	tə·nan·tə·na ma·ta	ትናንትና ማታ
last week	ya·leu·fô sam·mənt	ያለፈው ሳምንት
last year	ya·leu·fô a·meut	ያለፈው ዓመት
yesterday	tə·nan·tə·na	ትናንትና
yesterday	tə·nan·tə·na	ትናንትና ከሰዓት
afternoon	ķeu·seu'at	
yesterday morning	tə·nan·tə·na ţeu·wat	ትናንትና ጠዋት

FUTURE

`የወደፊት

after (three) days	keu (sost) ķeun bo·hal·la	ከ (ሶስት) ቀን ቡኋላ
day after tomorrow	keu neu·geu weu·di·ya	ከነገ ወዲያ
next week	yeu·mi·meu·ṭow sam·mənt	የሚመጣው ሳምንት
next month	yeu·mi·meu·ṭow weur	የሚመጣው ወር
next year	yeu·mi·meu·ṭow a·meut	የሚመጣው ዓመት
tomorrow	neu·geu	ነገ
tomorrow afternoon	neu·geu keu·seu'at	ነገ ከሰዓት
tomorrow morning	neu·geu ṭeu·wat	ነገ ጠዋት
tomorrow night	neu·geu ma·ta	ነገ ማታ
within (three) days	beu (sost) ķeun wəsṭ	በ (ሶስት) ቀን ውስጥ

DURING THE DAY

በቀን ውስጥ

afternoon	keu·seu'at	ከሰዓት
evening	mə·shət	ምሽት
midnight	ə·ku·leu le·lit	እኩል ሌሊት
midday/noon	ə·ku·leu ķeun	እኩል ቀን
morning	ṭeu·wat	ጠዋት
night	ma·ta	ማታ
sunrise	yeu ṣeu·hai mō·ṭat	የፀሃይ መውጣት
sunset	yeu ṣeu·hai meug·bat	የፀሃይ መግባት

TIME & DATES

ቁጥሮች

Arabic numerals are commonly used to write numbers throughout Ethiopia.

CARDINAL NUMBERS

ተራ ቁጥሮች

1	and	አንድ
2	hu·leutt	ሁለት
3	sost	ሶስት
4	a·rat	አራት
5	a·məst	አምስት
6	sə·dəst	ስድስት
7	seu·bat	ሰባት
8	sə·mənt	ስምንት
9	zeu·ṭeuny	ዘጠኝ
10	as·sər	አስር
11	as·sra and	አስራ አንድ
12	as·sra hu·leutt	አስራ ሁለት
13	as·sra sost	አስራ ሶስት
14	as·sra a·rat	አስራ አራት
15	as·sra a·məst	አስራ አምስት
16	as·sra sə·dəst	አስራ ስድስት
17	as·sra seu·bat	አስራ ሰባት
18	as·sra sə·mənt	አስራ ስምንት
19	as·sra zeu·ṭeuny	አስራ ዘጠኝ
20	ha·ya	ሃያ
21	ha·ya and	ሃያ አንድ
22	ha·ya hu·leutt	ሃያ ሁለት
30	seu·las·sa	ሰላሳ
31	seu·las·sa and	ሰላሳ አንድ
40	ar·ba	አርባ
50	ham·sa	አምሳ
60	səl·sa	ስልሳ
70	seu·ba	ሰባ

80	seu·man·ya	ሰማንያ
90	zeu·ṭeu·na	ዘጠና
100	meu·to	መቶ
101	meu·to and	መቶ አንድ
200	hu·leutt meu·to	ሁለት መቶ
300	sost meu·to	ሶስት መቶ
400	a·rat meu·to	አራት መቶ
500	a·məst meu·to	አምስት መቶ
1000	and shi	አንድ ሺ
2000	hu·leutt shi	ሁለት ሺ
100,000	meu·to shi	መቶ ሺ
1,000,000	and mil·li·yon	አንድ ሚሊዮን

I want (three) ...
  (sost) ... ə·feul·lə·gal·lō   (ሶስት) ... እፈልጋለሁ
(One) tea.
  (and) shai   (አንድ) ሻይ
I only asked for (one).
  (and) bə·cha nō ya·zeuz·kut   (አንድ) ብቻ ነው· ያዘዝኩት

NUMBERS & AMOUNTS

ORDINAL NUMBERS   መደበኛ ቁጥሮች

1st	an·deu·nya	አንደኛ
2nd	hu·leu·teu·nya	ሁለተኛ
3rd	sos·teu·nya	ሶስተኛ
4th	a·ra·teu·nya	አራተኛ
5th	a·məs·teu·nya	አምስተኛ
6th	sə·dəs·teu·nya	ስድስተኛ
7th	seu·ba·teu·nya	ሰባተኛ
8th	sə·mən·teu·nya	ስምንተኛ
9th	zeu·ṭeu·neu·nya	ዘጠነኛ
10th	as·sə·reu·nya	አስረኛ

FRACTIONS ክፍልፋይ

1/4	and a·ra·teu·nya; rub	አንድ አራተኛ/ሩብ
1/2	gə·mash	ግማሽ
1/3	and sos·teu·nya	አንድ ሶስተኛ
3/4	sost a·ra·teu·nya	ሶስት አራተኛ
1 ½	and mu·lu and	አንድ ሙሉ
	hu·leut·teu·nya	አንድ ሁለተኛ

ETHIOPIC NUMBERS

Ethiopic numbers are not widely used in writing, largely due to the lack of 'zero'.

፩	፪	፫	፬	፭	፮	፯	፰	፱	፲
1	2	3	4	5	6	7	8	9	10

USEFUL WORDS ጠቃሚ ቃሎች

about	ya·həl	ያህል
amount	meu·ṭeun/bə·zat	መጠን/ብዛት
change	meuls	መልስ
coin	san·tim	ሳንቲም
count	meu·ku·ṭeur	መቁጠር
(a) dozen	deur·zeun	ደርዘን
enough	beu·ḳi	በቂ
Ethiopian birr	bərr	ብር
a few	tən·nish	ትንሽ
last	meu·cheu·reu·sha	መጨረሻ
less	yan·neu·seu	ያንስ
a lot/many	bə·zu	ብዙ
more	teu·cheu·ma·ri	ተጨማሪ
once	and gi·ze	አንድ ጊዜ
percent	meu·to·nya	መቶኛ
single	and	አንድ

size	lək	ልክ
some	an·dand	አንዳንድ
too little	beu·ṭam tən·nish	በጣም ትንሽ
too much	beu·ṭam bə·zu	በጣም ብዙ
total	ṭeuk·lal·la	ጠቅላላ
twice	hu·leutt gi·ze	ሁለት ጊዜ
weight	kəb·deut	ክብደት
the whole amount	beu·mu·lu	በሙሉ

Additional emergency medical phrases can be found in the Health chapter, page 201.

Danger!	a·deu·geu·nya!	አደገኛ!
Fire!	ə·sat!	እሳት!
Help!	ər·duny!	እርዱኝ!
It's an emergency!	as·cheu·kwai nō!	አስቸኳይ ነው!
Stop!	kum!	ቁም!
Thief!	le·ba!	ሌባ!
Catch him!	ya·zō!	ያዘው!
Watch out!	teu·teun·keuk!	ተጠንቀቅ!
Go away!/	teu·meul·leuss!	ተመለስ!
Go back!		

There's (a/an) ...	... al·leu	... አለ
There's been (a/an) ...	... neub·beur	... ነበር
(car) accident	(yeu meu·ki·na)	የ (መኪና)
	a·deu·ga	አደጋ
fighting	wə·gi·ya	ውጊያ
fire	yeu ə·sat ka·teu·lo	የእሳት ቃጠሎ
flood	yeu wu·ha mu·lat	የውሃ ሙላት
robbery	zər·fi·ya	ዝርፊያ
rockfall	na·da	ናዳ

Somebody help me, please.
ə·ba·ka·chu ər·duny
I'm lost.

እባካችሁ እርዱኝ

meun·geud teuf·to·bə·nyal

መንገድ ጠፍቶብኛል

Is there a telephone around here?
əz·zi a·ka·ba·bi səlk al·leu?

እዚህ አካባቢ ስልክ አለ?

I'd like to make a call.
səlk meu·deu·weul ə·feul·lə·gal·lō

ስልክ መደወል እፈልጋለሁ

It's urgent!
as·cheu·kwai nō!

አስቸኳይ ነው!

EMERGENCIES

POLICE   ፖሊስ

Call the police!
| po·lis ṭə·ra! (m) | ፖሊስ ጥሪ! |
| po·lis ṭə·ri! (f) | ፖሊስ ጥሪ! |

Where's the nearest police station?
yeu·mi·ḳeur·bō po·lis ṭa·bi·ya
yeut nō?

የሚቀርበው ፖሊስ ጣቢያ
የት ነው?

I've been ...
attacked	teu·meu·tow	ተመታሁ
hurt	teu·go·də·chal·lō	ተጎድቻለሁ
raped	teu·deu·feur·ku	ተደፈርኩ
robbed	teu·zeu·reuf·ku	ተዘረፍኩ

ሰላም ደህና ነህ?

ደህና ነኝ

They've stolen my watch/money.
seu·a·ten/geun·zeu·ben
seu·reu·ḳuny

ሰአቴን/ገንዘቤን
ሰረቀኝ

I've lost my bag/passport.
shan·ṭa·ye/pas·por·te
ṭeuf·to·bə·nyal

ሻንጣዬ/ፓስፖርቴ
ጠፍቶብኛል

I don't speak Amharic.
a·ma·rə·nya al·chəl·ləm

አማርኛ አልችልም

I don't understand.
al·geu·ba·nyəm

አልገባኝም

I'm sorry, I didn't realise I was
doing anything wrong.
yi·ḳər·ta a·la·weu·kum

ይቅርታ አላወኩም

I'm sorry/I apologise.
yi·ḳər·ta beu·ṭam az·nal·lō

ይቅርታ በጣም አዝናለሁ

I didn't do it.
ə·ne a·la·deu·reu·kum

እኔ አላደረኩም

What am I accused of?

beu mən·dən nō yeu·teu·keu·seus·kut?	በምንድነው· የተከሰስኩ·ት?

You'll be charged with ...	yi·keu·seu·sal·lu	... ይከሰሳሉ·
You're charged with ...	teu·keu·seu·wal	... ተከሰዋል

anti-government activity	şeu·reu meun·gəst beu·ho·nu teu·gə·ba·roch	ፀረ መንግስት በሆኑ ተግባሮች
assault	keu sō gar beu·meu·ţa·lat	ከሰው· ጋር በመጣላት
disturbing the peace	hu·keut beu meuf·ţeur	ሁ·ከት በ መፍጠር
illegal entry	hə·geu weuţ beu·ho·neu meun·geud a·geur wəşţ beu·meug·bat	ሕገ ወጥ በሆነ መንገድ አገር ውስጥ በመግባት
murder	beu neufs gə·də·ya weun·jeul	በነፍስ ግድያ ወንጀል
not having a visa	ya·leu vi·za beu·meu·zeu·wa·weur	ያለ ቪዛ በመዘዋወር
overstaying your visa	beu vi·za keu·teu·feu·keu·dō gi·ze beu·lai beu·meu·ko·yeut	በቪዛ ከተፈቀደው· ጊዜ በላይ በመቆየት
possession (of illegal substances)	beu həg yeu teu·keu·leu·keu·leu ə·sə beu·meu·yaz	በሕግ የተከለከለ እጽ በመያዝ
rape	sō·wən a·sə·geu·də·do beu meud·feur	ሰው·ን አስገድዶ በመድፈር
robbery/theft	beu zər·fi·ya	በዝርፊያ
traffic violation	yeu tra·fik həg beu·meu·ţas	የትራፊክ ሕግ በመጣስ
working without a permit	ya·leu sə·ra feu·ḳad beu meus·rat	ያለ ስራ ፈቃድ በመስራት

EMERGENCIES

I want to contact my embassy.
    em·ba·si·yen ma·neu·ga·geur   ኤምባሲዬን ማነጋገር
    ə·feul·lə·gal·lō   እፈልጋለሁ

I know my rights.
    meub·ten ow·kal·lō   መብቴን አዉቃለሁ

Can I make a phone call?
    səlk meu·deu·weul ə·chə·lal·lō?   ስልክ መደወል እችላለሁ?

I want a lawyer who speaks English.
    ən·gli·zə·nya yeu·mi·chəl   እንግሊዘኛ የሚችል ጠበቃ
    ţeu·beu·ka ə·feul·lə·gal·lō   እፈልጋለሁ

to be arrested	meu·ta·seur	መታሰር
cell	ma·reu·fi·ya bet	ማረፊያ ቤት
consulate	kon·sə·la	ቆንስላ
fine (payment)	meu·keu·cha	መቀጫ
guilty	ţə·fa·teu·nya	ጥፋተኛ
lawyer	ţeu·beu·ka	ጠበቃ
not guilty	keu weun·jeul neu·ṣa	ከወንጀል ነፃ
	meu·hon	መሆን
police officer	yeu po·lis bal·deu·reu·ba	የፖሊስ ባልደረባ
police station	po·lis ţa·bi·ya	ፖሊስ ጣቢያ
prison	ə·sər bet	እስር ቤት
prosecutor	a·ka·be həg	ዐቃቤ ሕግ
trial	fərd	ፍርድ

to be able/can   meu·chal   መቻል

> Can I take your photo?
> fo·to la·neu·sah ə·che·lal·lō? (m)   ፎቶ ላነሳህ እችላለሁ?
> fo·to la·neu·sash ə·che·lal·lō? (f)   ፎቶ ላነሳሽ እችላለሁ?
> fo·to la·neu·sa·chu ə·che·lal·lō? (pl)   ፎቶ ላነሳችሁ እችላለሁ?

above ...	keu ... lai	ከ ... ላይ
to accept	meu·keu·beul	መቀበል
accident	a·deu·ga	አደጋ
across ...	keu ... ma·do	ከ ... ማዶ
addiction	sus	ሱስ
address	ad·ra·sha	አድራሻ
to admit	ma·meun	ማመን
adult	awa·ki	አዋቂ
advice	mə·kər	ምክር
aeroplane	ai·ro·plan	አይሮፕላን
to be afraid of	meuf·rat	መፍራት
after	bo·hal·la	በኋላ
in the afternoon	keu·seu'at bo·hal·la	ከስዓት በኋላ
this afternoon	za·re keu·seu'at	ዛሬ ከስዓት
again	ən·deu·geu·na	እንደገና
age	əd·may	እድሜ
(three days) ago	keu (sost keun) beu·fit	ከ (ሶስት ቀን) በፊት
to agree	meus·ma·mat	መስማማት

> I don't agree.
> als·ma·mam   አልስማማም
>
> We've agreed!
> teus·mam·teu·nal!   ተስማምተናል!

agriculture	gə·brən·na	ግብርና
ahead	weu·deu·fit	ወደፊት
aid (organisation)	(ər·da·ta) də·rə·jət	(እርዳታ) ድርጅት
AIDS	edz	ኤድስ
air	ai·yeur	አየር
air-conditioner	yeu ai·yeur ma·keuz·keu·zha	የአየር ማተዝቀዣ
airmail	yeu ai·yeur meul'əkt	የአየር መልዕክት
airport	ai·ro·plan ma·reu·fi·ya	አይሮፕላን ማረፊያ
alarm clock	yeu·mi·deu·wəl seu'at	የሚደውል ሰዓት
all	hul·lu	ሁሉ

> I'm allergic to ...
> ... ais·ma·ma·nyəm   ... አይስማማኝም

to allow   meuf·keud   መፍቀድ

> It's allowed.
> teu·feuk·dwal   ተፈቅድዋል
>
> It's not allowed.
> al·teu·feu·keu·deum   አልተፈቀደም

A

D
I
C
T
I
O
N
A
R
Y

alone	bə·cha	ብቻ
already	as·keu·də·mo	እስቀድሞ
also	deg·mo • deu·mo	ደግሞ • ደሞ
altitude	keu·fə·ta	ከፍታ
always	hul·gi·ze	ሁልጊዜ
amputate	meu·ku·reut	መቁረጥ
ancient	yeu du·ro	የዱሮ
and	ə·na • -na	እና • -ና
angry	yeu·teu·na·deu·deu	የተናደደ
animals	ən·sə·sa	እንስሳ
animals (domestic)	yeu bet ən·sə·sa	የቤት እንስሳ
annual	a·meu·ta·wi	አመታዊ
ant	gun·dan	ጉንዳን
antibiotics	an·ti·bai·yo·tik	አንቲባዩቲክ
antiseptic	an·ti·sep·tik	አንቲሴፕቲክ
any	ma·nəm	ማንም
appointment	keu·teu·ro	ቀጠሮ
architecture	yeu hən·şa a·seu·rar	የሕንፃ አሰራር
to argue	meu·cheu·ka·cheuk	መጨቃጨቅ
arm	kənd	ክንድ
art	ki·neu tə·beub	ኪነ ጥበብ
art gallery	yeu sə·əl meu·zeu·ker	የስዕል መዘክር
artist	yeu ki·neu tə·beub sö	የኪነ ጥበብ ሰው
to ask	meu·teu·yeuk	መጠየቅ
aspirin	as·prin	አስፐሪን
asthma	as·ma	አስማ
aunt	a·kəst	አክስት

B

baby	hə·şan	ሕፃን
baby food	yeu hə·şan mə·gəb	የሕፃን ምግብ
babysitter	mog·zit	ሞግዚት
back (body)	jeur·ba	ጀርባ
backpack	shan·ta	ሻንጣ
bad	meut·fo	መጥፎ
bag	shan·ta	ሻንጣ
baggage	gwaz	ጓዝ
balcony	beu·reun·da	በረንዳ
ball	kwass	ኳስ
bandage	fa·sha	ፋሻ
bank	bank	ባንክ
bar	bun·na bet	ቡና ቤት
basket	kər·chat	ቅርጫት
bath	yeu geu·la meu·ta·teu·bi·ya	የገላ መታጠቢያ
bathing suit	yeu wa·na ləbs	የዋና ልብስ
battery	bat·ri	ባትሪ
to be	meu·hon	መሆን
beautiful	kon·jo	ቆንጆ

because	mək·ni·ya·tum	ምክኒያቱም
bed	al·ga	አልጋ
bedroom	meu·nyi·ta bet	መኝታ ቤት
before (time)	keu ... beu·fit	ከ ... በፊት
beggar	məs·kin • leu·many	ምስኪን • ለማኝ
to begin	meu·jeu·meur	መጀመር
below ...	keu ... beu·tach	ከ ... በታች
beside ...	keu ... gon	ከ ... ጎን
bet	wə·rə·rəd	ውርርድ
better	yeu·teu·shal·leu	የተሻለ
between	beu ... meu·ha·keul	በ ... መሃከል
Bible	meu·ṣə·haf ḳə·dus	መጽሐፍ ቅዱስ
bicycle	bəs·klet	ብስክሌት
big	təl·ləḳ	ትልቅ
bill	hi·sab	ሂሳብ
biography	yeu hi·wot ta·rik	የሕይወት ታሪክ
bird	weuf	ወፍ
bite (animal)	nə·kə·sha	ንክሻ
to be bitten (insect)	meu·neu·deuf	መነደፍ
blanket	bərd ləbs	ብርድ ልብስ
to bleed	meud·mat	መድማት
to bless	meu·ba·reuk	መባረክ
blood	deum	ደም
blood group	yeu deum ai·neut	የደም አይነት
blue	seu·ma·ya·wi	ሰማያዊ
boat	jeul·ba	ጀልባ
body	sō·neut	ሰውነት

| Bon appetit! | | |
| meul·kam mə·gəb! | | መልካም ምግብ! |

bone	a·ṭent	አጥንት
book	meu·ṣə·haf	መጽሐፍ
to book	beu·ḳəd·mi·ya	በቅድሚያ ቦታ
	bo·ta mas·meuz·geub	ማስመዝገብ
bookshop	meu·ṣə·haf bet	መጽሐፍ ቤት
border	dən·beur	ድንበር
boring	deu·ba·ri	ደባሪ
to borrow	meu·was	መዋስ
both	hu·leut·tu	ሁለቱ
bottle	ṭeur·mus	ጠርሙስ
bottle opener	yeu ṭeur·mus meuk·feu·cha	የጠርሙስ መክፈቻ
box	sa·ṭen	ሳጥን
boy	weund ləj	ወንድ ልጅ
brave	deuf·far • jeug·na	ደፋር • ጀግና
bread	dab·bo	ዳቦ
to break	meus·beur	መስበር
broken	yeu·teu·seu·beu·reu	የተሰበረ
breakfast	ḳurs	ቁርስ
breasts	ṭut	ጡት

to breathe	meu·teun·feus	መተንፈስ
bribe	gub·bo	ጉቦ
bridge	dəl·dəy	ድልድይ
to bring	mam·tat	ማምጣት
brother	weun·dəm	ወንድም
brown	bun·na ai·neut	ቡና አይነት
bruise	seun·beur	ስንበር
to build	meus·rat	መስራት
building	hən·sa	ሕንፃ
bus	ow·to·bəs	አው-ቶብስ
bus station	ow·to·bəs ṭa·bi·ya	አው-ቶብስ ጣቢያ
business	nəgd	ንግድ
business person	neu·ga·de	ነጋዴ
busy	sa·ra yeu·mi·beu·za·beut	ስራ የሚበዛበት
but	gən • neu·geur gən	ግን • ነገር ግን
to buy	meug·zat	መግዛት

I'd like to buy ...
... meug·zat ə·feul·lə·gal·lō ... መግዛት እፈልጋለሁ-

Where can I buy a ticket?
ti·ket yeut meug·zat ə·cha·lal·lō? ትኬት የት መግዛት እችላለሁ?

C

café	bun·na bet	ቡና ቤት
calendar	ḳeun meu·ḳu·teu·ri·ya	ቀን መቁጠሪያ
camera	ka·me·ra • fo·to man·sha	ካሜራ • ፎቶ ማንሻ
to camp	dən·kwan meut·keul	ድንኳን መትከል
camp site	dən·kwan meut·keu·ya bo·ta	ድንኳን መትከያ ቦታ
can (to be able)	meu·chal	መቻል

We can.
ən·cha·lal·leun እንችላለን

I can't.
al·chel·ləm አልችልም

can (tin)	ḳor·ḳo·ro	ቆርቆሮ
can opener	yeu ḳor·ḳo·ro meuk·feu·cha	የቆርቆሮ መክፈቻ
to cancel	meu·seu·reuz	መሰረዝ
candle	sha·ma	ሻማ
car	meu·ki·na	መኪና
to carry	meu·sheu·keum	መሸከም
castle	a·bə·ya·teu meun·gəst • gəmb	አብያተ መንግስት • ግምብ
cat	də·meut	ድመት
cave	wa·sha	ዋሻ
centimetre	sen·ti me·tər	ሴንቲ ሜትር
celebration	beu·'al	በዓል
chair	weun·beur	ወንበር
chance	a·ga·ṭa·mi	አጋጣሚ

D I C T I O N A R Y

change (coins)	zər·zər	ዝርዝር
to change	meu·keu·yeur	መቀየር
changing rooms	ləbs meu·keu·yeu·ri·ya ke·fe·loch	ልብስ መቀየሪያ ክፍሎች
charming	deus yeu·mil	ደስ የሚል
cheap	rə·kash	ርካሽ
cheat	a·tal·lai	አታላይ

Cheat!
weus·lat·ta! | | ወስላታ! |

to check (examine)	meu·meur·meur	መመርመር
checkpoint	ke·la	ኬላ
chemist	meud·ha·nit bet	መድኃኒት ቤት
chest	deu·reut	ደረት
chicken	do·ro	ዶሮ
child	ləj	ልጅ
children	lə·joch	ልጆች
chocolate	cheu·ko·let	ቸኮሌት
to choose	meu·mə·reut	መምረጥ
church	be·teu kə·rəs·ti·yan	ቤተ ክርስቲያን
cigarettes	si·ga·ra	ሲጋራ
cinema	si·ni·ma bet	ሲኒማ ቤት
circus	seur·keus	ሰርከስ
city	keu·teu·ma	ከተማ
city centre	meu·hal keu·teu·ma	መሃል ከተማ
clean	nə·şuh	ንጹህ
to climb	mō·tat	መውጣት
clock	yeu teu·reu·pe·za seu'at	የጠረጴዛ ሰዓት
to close	meuz·gat	መዝጋት
closed	teu·zeug·twal	ተዘግቷል
clothing	ləb·soch	ልብሶች
cloud	deu·meu·na	ደመና
cloudy	deu·meu·na·ma	ደመናማ
coat hanger	yeu kot meus·keu·ya	የኮት መስቀያ
coin	san·tim	ሳንቲም
coins	san·ti·moch	ሳንቲሞች
cold (adj)	ķeuz·ķaz·za	ቀዝቃዛ

It's cold.
ķeuz·ķaz·za nō | | ቀዝቃዛ ነው· |

I have a cold.
gun·fan yi·zo·nyal | | ጉንፋን ይዞኛል |

cold water	ķeuz·ķaz·za wu·ha	ቀዝቃዛ ውሃ
colour	keu·leur • ķeu·leum	ከለር • ቀለም
to come	meum·tat	መምጣት
comedy	yeu·mi·ya·səķ	የሚያስቅ
companion	gwa·deu·nya	ጓደኛ
compass	kom·pass	ኮምፓስ

to confirm (a booking)	ma·reu·ga·geuţ	ማረጋገጥ

Congratulations! ən·kwan deus al·leuh/ al·leush! (m/f)		እንኳን ደስ አለህ/ አለሽ!

constipation	hod dər·keuţ	ሆድ ድርቀት
consulate	kon·sə·la	ቆንስላ
contact lenses	kon·takt lens	ኮንታክት ሌንስ
contraception	yeu şans meu·keu·la·keu·ya meud·ha·nit	የወሲስ መከላከያ መድሃኒት
contract	wul	ው·ል
convent	yeu se·toch geu·dam	የሴቶች ጉዳም
to cook	mə·gəb meus·rat	ምግብ መስራት
cool (colloquial)	a·rif	አሪፍ
corner	ma'ə·zeun	ማዕዘን
corruption	mu·sə·na	ሙስና
cotton	ţəţ	ጥጥ
country	a·geur	አገር
countryside	geu·ţeur	ገጠር
cough	sal	ሳል
to count	meu·ķu·ţeur	መቁጠር
crafts	ţə·beub	ጥበብ
credit card	kre·dit kard	ክሬዲት ካርድ

Can I pay by credit card? beu kre·dit kard meuk·feul yi·cha·lal?		በክሬዲት ካርድ መክፈል ይቻላል?

cup (drink)	ku·ba·ya	ኩባያ
cupboard	ķum sa·ţən	ቁም ሳጥን
current affairs	yeu seu·mo·nu weu·re	የሰሞኑ ወሬ
customs	gəm·ruk	ግምሩክ
to cut	meu·ķu·reuţ	መቀረጥ
cycling	bəsk·let meu·ga·leub	ብስክሌት መጋለብ
cyclist	sai·kə·leu·nya	ሳይክለኛ

D

dad	a·ba·ye	አባዬ
daily	beu·yeu·ķeu·nu	በየቀኑ
dairy products	weu·ţeut neuk yeu mə·gəb wə·ţe·toch	ወተት ነክ የምግብ ውጤቶች
to dance	meu·da·neus • meu·cheuf·feur	መዳነስ • መጨፈር
dangerous	a·deu·geu·nya	አደገኛ
date (appointment)	ķeu·ţeu·ro	ቀጠሮ
date (time)	ķeun	ቀን
to date (someone)	meuķ·ţeur	መቅጠር
date of birth	yeu tu·ləd ķeun	የትውልድ ቀን
daughter	set ləj	ሴት ልጅ

236

dawn	nə·gat	ንጋት
day	ķeun	ቀን
dead	mut	ሙት
deaf	deun·ko·ro	ደንቆሮ
death	mot	ሞት
to decide	meu·weu·seun	መወሰን
deep	țəlķ	ጥልቅ
deforestation	yeu deun meu·meun·țeur	የደን መመንጠር

It's delayed
zeu·gəy·twal · · · · · · · · · · · · · · ዞግዪቷል

dentist	yeu țərs ha·kim	የጥርስ ሃኪም
to deny	meu·kad	መካድ
to depart (leave)	leu meu·hed meu·neu·sat	ለመሄድ መነሳት
desert	beu·reu·ha	በረሃ
destination	meu·dreu·sha	መድረሻ
detail	zər·zər	ዝርዝር
diabetic	sə·kwar beu·sha·ta ya·leu·beut	ስኳር በሽታ ያለበት
diarrhoea	ķə·zeun	ቅዝን
dictionary	meuz·geu·beu ķa·lat	መዝገበ ቃላት
to die	meu·mot	መሞት
different	le·la	ሌላ
difficult	as·cheu·ga·ri	አስቸጋሪ
dinner	ə·rat	እራት
dirty	ķo·sha·sha	ቆሻሻ
disabled	a·ka·leu sən·kul	አካለ ስንኩል
discount	ķə·nash	ቅናሽ
to discover	mag·nyeut • meuf·țeur	ማግኘት • መፍጠር
disease	beu·sha·ta	በሽታ
distributor (person)	a·keu·fa·fai	አከፋፋይ
to do	mad·reug	ማድረግ

What are you doing?
mən ta·deur·gal·leuh? (m) · · · · · · ምን ታደርጋለህ?
mən ta·deur·gi·yal·leush? (f) · · · · · ምን ታደርጊያለሽ?

I didn't do it.
ə·ne a·la·deu·reu·kum · · · · · · · · እኔ አላደረኩም

doctor	ha·kim	ሐኪም
dog	wu·sha	ውሻ
doll	a·shan·gu·lit	አሻንጉሊት
door	beur	በር
double	hu·leutt	ሁለት
double bed	and al·ga leu hu·leutt sō	አንድ አልጋ ለሁለት ሰው
to dream	həlm mal·leum	ሕልም ማለም
dress	ķeu·miss	ቀሚስ
drink	meu·țeuț	መጠጥ
to drink	meu·țeu·țat	መጠጣት

to drive	meun·dat	መንዳት
drivers licence	meun·ja feu·ḳad	መንጃ ፈቃድ
drug (medicine)	meud·ha·nit	መድኃኒት
drum	keu·beu·ro	ከበሮ
to be drunk	meus·keur	መስከር
to dry (clothes)	meud·reuḳ	መድረቅ

E

each	ə·yan·dan·du	እያንዳንዱ
ear(s)	jo·ro	ጆሮ
early	keu·deum bə·lo	ቀደም ብሎ
early (morning)	ma·leu·da	ማለዳ
earth (soil)	a·feur	አፈር
earthquake	yeu meu·ret meun·ḳeuṭ·ḳeuṭ	የመሬት መንቀጥቀጥ
east	məs·raḳ	ምስራቅ
easy	ḳeul·lal	ቀላል
to eat	meub·lat	መብላት
economy	e·ko·no·mi	ኢኮኖሚ
editor	a·zeu·gaj	አዘጋጅ
education	təm·hərt	ትምህርት
election	mar·cha	ምርጫ
electricity	e·le·trik	ኤሌትሪክ
embarrassment	a·sa·fa·ri	አሳፋሪ
embassy	em·bas·si	ኤምባሲ
emergency	as·cheu·kwai	አስቸኳይ
employer	keu·ṭa·ri	ቀጣሪ
empty	ba·do	ባዶ
end	meu·cheu·reu·sha	መጨረሻ
engagement	meu·ṭa·cheut	መጣጬት
engine	mo·teur	ሞተር
English	ən·gli·zə·nya	እንግሊዝኛ
to enjoy (oneself)	meu·deu·seut	መደሰት
enough	beu·ḳi	በቂ

| Enough! | | |
| beu·ḳa! | | በቃ! |

to enter	meug·bat	መግባት
envelope	en·veu·lop	ኤንቨሎፕ
environment (area)	a·ka·ba·bi	አካባቢ
epilepsy	yeu·mi·ṭəl beu·sha·ta	የሚጥል በሽታ
equality	ə·ku·lə·neut	እኩልነት
equipment	ə·ḳa	እቃ
evening	ma·shət	ምሽት
every day	beu·yeu·ḳeu·nu	በየቀኑ
example	mə·sa·le	ምሳሌ

| For example ... | | |
| leu mə·sa·le ... | | ለምሳሌ ... |

| to exchange | meu·leu·wa·weuţ | መለዋወጥ | **F** |
| exchange rate | yeu mə·nə·za·ri wa·ga | የምንዛሪ ዋጋ | |

| **Excuse me.** | | | |
| yi·kər·ta | | ይቅርታ | |

exit	meu·wa·çha	መውጫ
expensive	wədd	ውድ
express	feu·ţan	ፈጣን
eye	ain	አይን

F

face	fit	ፊት
factory	fab·ri·ka	ፋብሪካ
family	be·teu·seub	ቤተሰብ
famous	zə·neu·nya	ዝነኛ
fans (of a team)	deu·ga·fi	ደጋፊ
far	ruk	ሩቅ
farm	ər·sha	እርሻ
farmer	geu·beu·re	ገበሬ
fast (speed)	feu·ţan	ፈጣን
fat	weu·fram	ወፍራም
father	ab·bat	አባት
father-in-law	a·mat	አማት
fault (someone's)	ţə·fat	ጥፋት
fear	fər·hat	ፍርሃት
feelings	sə·met	ስሜት
fence	a·ţer	አጥር
festival	beu·al	በዓል
fever (temperature)	tə·ku·sat	ትኩሳት
few	tən·nish	ትንሽ
to have a fight	meu·ţa·lat	መጣላት
to fill	meu·mu·lat	መሙላት
film	film • si·ni·ma	ፊልም • ሲኒማ
to find	mag·nyeut	ማግኘት
finger	ţat	ጣት
to finish	meu·çheu·reus	መጨረስ
fire	ə'sat	እሳት
firewood	yeu ma·geu·do ən·cheut	የማገዶ እንጨት
first (name)	yeu meu·jeu·meu·ri·ya (səm)	የመጀመሪያ (ስም)
first-aid kit	yeu meu·jeu·meu·ri·ya	የመጀመሪያ
	ər·da·ta sa·ţən	እርዳታ ሳጥን
fish	a·sa	ዓሳ
flag	ban·di·ra	ባንዲራ
flashlight	yeu əj ba·tri	የእጅ ባትሪ
flea	ku·nə·cha	ቁንጪ
floor	weu·leul	ወለል
floor (storey)	fok	ፎቅ
flour	du·ket	ዱቄት

D I C T I O N A R Y

flower	a·beu·ba	አበባ
flower seller	a·beu·ba shach	አበባ ሻጭ
fly	zəmb	ዝምብ
to follow	meu·keu·teul	መከተል
food	mə·gəb	ምግብ
foot	ə·gər	እግር
football (soccer)	ə·gər kwass	እግር ኳስ
foreign	ba·ed	ባዕድ
foreigner	yeu wə·ch a·geur sö	የውጭ አገር ሰው
forest	cha·ka	ጫካ
forever	leu·zeu·la·leum	ለዘላለም
to forget	meur·sat	መርሳት

I forget.	
reu·sow	ረሳሁ

to forgive	yi·kər ma·leut	ይቅር ማለት
friend	gwa'deu·nya	ጓደኛ
full	mul·lu	ሙሉ
to have fun	meu·cha·wot	መጫወት
to make fun of/mock	ma·shof	ማሽፍ
funeral	keu·bər	ቀብር
future	weu·deu fit	ወደ ፊት

G

garage	ga·raj	ጋራዥ
garden	yat·kəlt bota	ያትክልት ቦታ
gate (entrance)	meug·bi·ya	መግቢያ
generally	ab·za·nya·wən gi·ze	አብዛኛው·ን ጊዜ
gift	sə·to·ta	ስጦታ
girl (child)	set ləj	ሴት ልጅ
to give	meus·teut	መስጠት

Could you give me ...?		
ə·ba·keh ... sə·teuny? (m)		እባክህ ... ስጠኝ?
ə·ba·kesh ... sə·chəny? (f)		እባክሽ ... ስጭኝ?

glass (drinking)	bər·che·ko	ብርጭቆ
glass (material)	meus·ta·wot	መስታወት
to go	meu·hed	መሄድ

Let's go.	
ən·hid	እንሂድ

We'd like to go to ...	
weu·deu ... meu·hed	ወደ ... መሄድ እንፈልጋለን
ən·feul·lə·gal·leun	

Go straight ahead.	
beu·keu·ṭe·ta hid/hij/hi·du (m/f/pl)	በቀጥታ ሂድ/ሂጅ/ሂዱ

God (Christian)	əg·zya·ber • əg·zer	እግዚሃብሄር • እግዜር
God (Muslim)	al·lah	አላህ

| good | tə·ru | ጥሩ |
| good hotel | tə·ru ho·tel | ጥሩ ሆቴል |

Good afternoon. ən·deu·mən walk/walsh (m/f)		እንደምን ዋልክ/ዋልሽ
Good evening/night. ən·deu·mən a·meu·sheuh/ a·meu·sheush (m/f)		እንደምን አመሽህ/አመሽሽ
Good health/Cheers! leu·te·na·chen!		ለጤናችን!
Good luck! meul·kam ə·dəl!		መልካም እድል!
Good morning. ən·deu·mən ad·deurk/ ad·deursh (m/f)		እንደምን አደርክ/ አደርሽ
Goodbye. deu·na hun/hu·nyi/ hu·nu (m/f/pl)		ደህና ሁን/ሁኚ/ሁኑ

government	meun·gəst	መንግስት
grandchild	yeu ləj ləj	የልጅ ልጅ
grandfather	weund a·yat	ወንድ አያት
grandmother	set a·yat	ሴት አያት
grass	sar	ሣር
great	təl·ləķ • ta·laķ	ትልቅ • ታላቅ

| Great!
beu·tam tə·ru! | | በጣም ጥሩ! |

green	a·reun·gwa·de	አረንጓዴ
to grow	ma·deug	ማደግ
to guess	meu·geu·meut	መገመት
guide (person)	meu·ri	መሪ
guide dog	meu·ri wə·sha	መሪ ውሻ
guitar	gi·tar	ጊታር

H

hair	şeu·gur	ፀጉር
half	gə·mash	ግማሽ
hand	əj	እጅ
handbag	yeu əj por·sa	የእጅ ጆርሳ
handicrafts	yeu əj sə·ra·woch	የእጅ ስራዎች
handsome	meul·keu meul·kam	መልከ መልካም
happy	deu·sə·teu·nya	ደስተኛ

| Happy birthday!
meul·kam lə·deut! | | መልካም ልደት! |

| hard (substance) | teun·ka·ra | ጠንካራ |

| hard (difficult) | keu·bad | ከባድ |
| to harass | mas·çheu·neuķ | ማስጨነቅ |

Do you have ...?		
... al·leuh? (m)		... አለህ?
... al·leush? (f)		... አለሽ?
... al·la·chu? (pl)		... አላችሁ-?
I have ...		
... al·leuny		... አለኝ
I don't have ...		
... yeul·leu·nyem		... የለኝም

he	əs·su	እሱ
head	rass	ራስ
health	țe·na	ጤና
to hear	meus·mat	መስማት
heat	mu·keut	ሙ-ቀት
heavy	keu·bad	ከባድ

Hello.		
țe·na yis·țəl·ləny		ጤና ይስጥልኝ
Hello. (answering telephone)		
al·lo		አሉ-

helmet	hel·met	ሄልሜት
help (n)	ər·da·ta	እርዳታ
here	əz·zi	እዚህ
high school	hu·leut·teu·nya deu·reu·ja	ሁለተኛ ደረጃ
	țəm·hərt bet	ትምህርት ቤት
hiking	yeu·gər gu·zo	የግር ጉዞ
hill	ko·reub·ta	ኮረብታ
to hire	meu·keu·ra·yeut	መከራየት
HIV	ech ai vi	ኤች አይ ቪ
holiday(s) (vacation)	yeu ə·reuft gi·ze	የዕረፍት ጊዜ
holiday(s)	beu·al • beu·a·loch	በዓል • በዓሉ-ች
honey	mar	ማር
honeymoon	yeu cha·gu·la gi·ze	የጫጉላ ጊዜ
horrible	ya·mi·ya·seu·ķeķ	የሚያስፈቅ
horse	feu·reus	ፈረስ
horse racing	ye feu·reus gəl·bi·ya	የፈረስ ግልቢያ
	wə·də·dər	ወድድር
hospital	hos·pi·tal	ሆስፒታል
hot	muķ	ሙ-ቅ

| I'm hot | | |
| mo·ķeuny | | ሞቀኝ |

| house | bet | ቤት |
| housework | yeu bet sə·ra | የቤት ስራ |

how	ən·det	እንዴት

How?
ən·det?   እንዴት?

How much is it?
sənt nō?   ስንት ነው-?

How do I get to ...?
weu·deu ... ən·det ə·he·dal·lō?   ወደ ... እንዴት እሄዳስሁ-?

How do you say ...?
... ən·det nō yeu·mi·bal·lō?   ... እንዴት ነው የሚባለው-?

human rights	yeu sō·woch neu·şa·neut	የሰዎች ነፃነት
hundred (one)	meu·to (and)	መቶ (አንድ)
to be hungry	meur·rab	መራብ
husband	bal	ባል

I

ice	beu·reu·do	በረዶ

I'm ill.
a·mo·nyal   አሞኛል

immigration	i·mi·gə·re·shin	ኢምግሬሽን
important	as·feu·la·gi	አስፈላጊ

It's important.
as·feu·la·gi nō   አስፈላጊ ነው-

It's not important.
as·feu·la·gi ai·deul·leum   አስፈላጊ አይደለም

in front of	fit leu fit	ፊት ለፊት
industry	in·dus·tri	ኢንዳስትሪ
inequality	meu·beu·la·leuţ	መበላለጥ
to give an injection	meur·fe mō·gat	መርፌ. መው-ጋት
injury	gu·dat	ጉዳት
insect	beu·reur·ro	በረሮ
inside	wəşţ	ውስጥ
insurance	was·te·na	ዋስትና
interesting	yeu·mi·yas·deu·seţ	የሚያስደስት
international	a·leum a·ķeuf	ዓለም አቀፍ
interview	ķa·leu meu·ţeu·yiķ	ቃለ መጠይቅ
island	deu·set	ደሴት
itch	ə·keuk	እከክ
itinerary	yeu gu·zo pro·gram	የጉዞ ፕሮግራም

J

jealous	ķeu·na·teu·nya	ቀናተኛ
jewellery	ge·ţa geţ	ጌጣ ጌጥ
job	sə·ra	ስራ

joke	ķeuld	ቀልድ
to joke	meu·ķeu·leud	መቀለድ
journalist	ga·ze·ţeu·nya	ጋዜጠኛ
journey	gu·zo	ጉዞ
juice	chə·ma·ķi	ጭማቂ
to jump	meuz·leul	መዝለል
jumper (sweater)	shu·rab	ሹራብ
justice	fə·ţəh	ፍትህ

K

key	meuķ·feu·cha • ķulf	መክፈቻ • ቁልፍ
to kill	meug·deul	መግደል
kilometre	ki·lo me·tər	ኪሎ ሜትር
kind	deug	ደግ
kindergarten	meu·wa·leu hə·ṣa·nat	መዋለ ሕፃናት
king	nə·gus	ንጉስ
to kiss	meu·sam	መሳም
kitchen	weuţ bet	ወጥ ቤት
knife	bi·la·wa	ቢላዋ
to know	ma·weuķ	ማወቅ

I know.		
ow·ķal·lō	አዉ·ቃለሁ·	
I don't know.		
a·la·wə·ķəm	አላዉ·ቅም	

L

lake	haiķ	ሃይቅ
land	meu·ret	መሬት
last	meu·cheu·reu·sha	መጨረሻ
last month	ya·leu·fō weur	ያለፈዉ ወር
last night	te·nan·te·na ma·ta	ትናንትና ማታ
last week	ya·leu·fō sam·mənt	ያለፈዉ ሳምንት
last year	ya·leu·fō a·meut	ያለፈዉ ዓመት

| It's late. | | |
| reu·feu·deu | ረፈደ | |

to laugh	meu·saķ	መሳቅ
launderette	lown·deu·ri	ላዉ·ንደሪ
law	həg	ሕግ
lazy	seu·neuf	ስነፍ
to learn	meu·mar	መማር
leather	ķo·da	ቆዳ
left (not right)	gə·ra	ግራ
leg	ə·gər	እግር
legal	hə·ga·wi	ሕጋዊ
lens	lens	ሌንስ

244

less	ya·neu·seu	ያነሰ
letter	deub·dab·be	ደብዳቤ
liar	wu·sheu·tam	ውሸታም
library	be·teu meu·ṣə·haf	ቤት መጻሕፍ
to lie	meu·wa·sheut	መዋሸት
life	hi·wot	ሕይወት
light (weight)	ḳeul·lal	ቀላል
light (sun/lamp)	bər·han	ብርሃን
light bulb	am·pul	አምፑል
lighter	lai·teur • ma·ḳeu·ṭa·ṭeu·ya	ላይተር • ማቀጣጠያ
to like	meuw·deud	መውደድ
line	meus·meur	መስመር
lips	keun·feur	ከንፈር
to listen	ma·da·meuṭ	ማዳመጥ
little (small)	tən·nish	ትንሽ
a little (amount)	tən·nish	ትንሽ
to live (reside)	meu·nor	መኖር

Long live ...!
... leu·zeu·la·leum yi·nur! ... ለዘላለም ይኑር!

local	a·ka·ba·bi	አካባቢ
location	sə·fə·ra	ስፍራ
to lock	meu·ḳo·leuf	መቆለፍ
long	reu·jim	ረጅም
long distance	reu·jim rə·ḳeut	ረጅም ርቀት
to look	ma·yeut	ማየት
to look for	meu·feul·leug	መፈልግ
to lose	ma·ṭat	ማጣት
lost property	yeu·ṭeu·fa ə·ḳa	የጠፋ ዕቃ
to love	maf·keur	ማፍቀር
lover	fəḳ·reu·nya	ፍቅረኛ
low (position)	zə·ḳə·teu·nya	ዝቅተኛ
luck	ə·dal	እድል
lucky	ə·də·leu·nya	እድለኛ
lunch	mə·sa	ምሳ
lunchtime	yeu mə·sa seu'at	የምሳ ሰዓት

M

made (of)	yeu·teu·seu·row	የተሰራው
magazine	meu·ṣə·het	መጽሔት
mail	pos·ta	ፖስታ
mailbox	yeu pos·ta sa·ṭən	የፖስታ ሳጥን
to make	meus·rat	መስራት
make-up (cosmetics)	meu·kwa·kwa·ya	መኳኳያ
man	sō	ሰው
manager	sə·ra as·ki·yaj	ስራ አስኪያጅ
many	bə·zu	ብዙ

| map | kar·ta | ካርታ |

| Can you show me on the map? kar·tow lai ya·sa·yu·nyal? | | ካርታው ላይ ያሳዩኛል? |

marijuana	ma·ri·wa·na	ማሪዋና
market	geu·bi·ya	ገቢያ
marriage	ga·bə·cha	ጋብቻ
to marry	mag·bat	ማግባት
mass (church)	kə·da·se	ቅዳሴ
massage	meu·ta·sheut	መታሸት
mat	mən·taf	ምንጣፍ
match(es)	kə·brit	ክብሪት

| It doesn't matter. gəd yeul·leum | | ግድ የለም |

maybe	mə·nal·bat	ምናልባት
medicine	meud·ha·nit	መድኃኒት
to meet	meu·geu·na·nyeut	መገናኘት
men	sõ·woch	ሰዎች
menstruation	yeu weur a·beu·ba	የወር አበባ
menu	yeu weur mə·gəb zər·zər • me·nu	የምግብ ዝርዝር • ሜኑ
message	meul'əkt	መልእክት
metal	bə·reut	ብረት
metre	me·tər	ሜትር
midnight	ə·ku·leu le·lit	እኩለ ሌሊት
milk	weu·teut	ወተት
mind	a'mə·ro	አእምሮ
minute	deu·ki·ka	ደቂቃ

| Just a minute, and gi·ze | | አንድ ጊዜ |

| mirror | meus·ta·weut | መስታወት |
| to miss | meu·na·feuk | መናፈቅ |

| I miss you. ə·na·fə·kə·hal·lõ (m) ə·na·fə·kə·shal·lõ (f) | | እናፍቅሃለሁ- እናፍቅሻለሁ- |

mistake	sə·hə·teut	ስህተት
to mix	meu·deu·ba·leuk	መደባለቅ
monastery	deu·bər	ደብር
money	geun·zeub	ገንዘብ
monk	meu·neu·ku·se	መነኩሴ
month	weur	ወር
in this month	beuz·zi weur	በዚህ ወር
monument	ha·wəlt	ሐውልት
moon	cheu·reu·ka	ጨረቃ
more (adj)	yi·beult	ይበልጥ
morning	teu·wat	ጠዋት
mosque	meus·gid	መስጊድ

mosquito net	yeu bim·bi meu·reub	የቢምቢ መረብ
mother	ən·nat	እናት
mother-in-law	a·mat	አማት
motorcycle	mo·teur sai·kəl	ሞተር ሳይክል
mountain	teu·ra·ra	ተራራ
mouth	aff	አፍ
mud	cha·ka	ጭቃ
mum	ə·ma·ye	እማዬ
muscle	ṭun·cha	ጡንቻ
museum	be·teu meu·zeu·kər	ቤተ መዘክር
music	mu·zi·ka	ሙዚቃ
musician	mu·zi·keu·nya	ሙዚቀኛ
Muslim	əs·lam	እስላም

N

name	səm	ስም
national park	bə·he·ra·wi park	ብሔራዊ ፓርክ
nationality (citizen)	ze·gə·neut	ዜግነት
nature	teu·feu·ṭro	ተፈጥሮ
near	a·ṭeu·geub	አጠገብ
necessary	as·feu·la·gi	አስፈላጊ
necklace	ha·bəl • yan·geut geṭ	ሐብል • ያንገት ጌጥ
needle and thread	meur·fe·na kər	መርፌና ክር
to need	meu·feul·leug	መፈለግ
net	meu·reub	መረብ
never	beu·cha·rash	በጭራሽ
new	ad·dis	አዲስ
news	ze·na	ዜና
newspaper	ga·ze·ṭa	ጋዜጣ
New Year	ad·dis a·meut	አዲስ ዓመት
next (adv)	keu·ṭe·lō	ቀጥሎ
next month	yeu·mi·meu·ṭow weur	የሚመጣው ወር
next to ...	keu ... a·ṭeu·geub	ከ ... አጠገብ
next week	yeu·mi·meu·ṭow sam·mənt	የሚመጣው ሳምንት
next year	yeu·mi·meu·ṭow a·meut	የሚመጣው ዓመት
nice	ṭe·ru	ጥሩ
night	ma·ta	ማታ
no (it's not there)	yeul·leum	የለም
no (it isn't)	ai·deul·leum	አይደለም
noisy	cha·cha·ta	ጫጫታ
none	ma·nəm	ማንም
north	seu·men	ሰሜን
nose	a·fən·cha	አፍንጫ
notebook	deub·teur	ደብተር
nothing	mə·nəm	ምንም
not yet	geu·na nō	ገና ኸው·
now	a·hun	አሁን
nuclear bomb	yeu nyu·ke·ler bom	የኒዉክለር ቦምብ

nuclear energy	yeu nyu·kə·ler hail	የኒውክሊር ሃይል
nun	meu·neu·ku·sit	መነኩሲት
nurse	neurs	ነርስ

O

obvious	gəls	ግልፅ
ocean	wuḳ·ya·nos	ውቅያኖስ
office	bi·ro	ቢሮ
often	bə·za gi·ze	ብዙ ጊዜ
oil (cooking)	zayt	ዘይት
oil (crude)	yal·teu·ṭa·ra·zayt	ያልተጣራ ዘይት
OK	ə·shi	እሽ
on	lai	ላይ
old	a·ro·ge	አሮጌ
on time	beu seu'at	በሰዓት
one-way (ticket)	meu·he·ja bə·cha (ti·ket)	መሄጃ ብቻ (ቲኬት)
only	bə·cha	ብቻ
open	kəft	ክፍት

It's open.		
kəft nō	ክፍት ነው·	

to open	meuk·feut	መክፈት
operator	o·pa·re·teur	ኦፕሬተር
opinion	ha·sab	ሐሳብ
opposite (prep)	teu·ka·ra·ni	ተቃራኒ
opposite (prep)	fit leu fit	ፊት ለፊት
or	waym	ወይም
oral (medicine)	yeu·mi·waṭ	የሚዋጥ
to order	ma·zeuz	ማዘዝ
ordinary	teu·ra	ተራ
to organise	ma·zeu·ga·jeut	ማዘጋጀት
organisation	ma·hə·beur	ማኅበር
original	wan·na	ዋና
original (adj)	yeu meu·jeu·meu·ri·ya	የመጀመሪያ
orphan	a·sa·da·gi yeu·le·lō ləj	አሳዳጊ የሌለው ልጅ
other	le·la	ሌላ
outside	wəch	ውጭ
over ...	beu ... lai	በ ... ላይ
owner	ba·leu·bet	ባለቤት

P

packet	pa·ko	ፓኮ
padlock	meu·ḳo·leu·fi·ya gan	መቆለፊያ ጋን
pagan	a·reu·ma·wi	አረማዊ
page	geuṣ	ገፅ
pain	wu·gat	ውጋት

painkillers	hə·meum yeu·mi·yas·ta·gəs	ሕመም የሚያስታግስ
	meud·ha·nit	መድሃኒት
to paint	meu·keu·bat	መቀባት
painter (art)	seu·a·li	ሰዓሊ
painting (art)	sə·el	ስዕል
palace	be·teu meun·gəst	ቤተ መንግስት
pan	meut·beu·sha	መጥበሻ
paper	weu·reu·keut	ወረቀት
parcel	tə·kəll	ጥቅል
parents	weu·la·joch	ወላጆች
park	meu·na·feu·sha bo·ta	መናፈሻ ቦታ
to park	ma·kom	ማቆም
party (fiesta)	gəb·zha	ግብዣ
passenger	meun·geu·deu·nya	መንገደኛ
passport	pass·port	ፓስፖርት
past	ya·leu·feu	ያለፈ
path	yeu·gər meun·geud	የግር መንገድ
patient (adj)	tə·gəs·teu·nya	ትዕግስተኛ
to pay	meuk·feul	መክፈል
payment	kə·fə·ya	ክፍያ
peace	seu·lam	ሰላም
peak (mountain)	chaf	ጫፍ
pen (ballpoint)	əs·krip·to	እስክሪፕቶ
pencil	ər·sass	እርሳስ
penknife	seun·ti	ስንጢ
pensioner	tu·reu·teu·nya	ጡረተኛ
people	sō·woch	ሰዎች
per cent	keu·meu·to	ከመቶ
performance	cheu·wa·ta	ጨዋታ
permanent	kwa·mi	ቋሚ
permission	feu·kad	ፈቃድ
person	sō	ሰው
personality	ba·hə·ri	ባህሪ
to perspire/sweat	ma·lab	ማላብ
petrol	ben·zin	ቤንዚን
pharmacy	far·ma·si • meud·ha·nit bet	ፋርማሲ • መድሃኒት ቤት
phone book	yeu səlk mow·cha	የስልክ ማውጫ
photo	fo·to	ፎቶ

May I take a photo?
fo·to man·sat yi·cha·lal?   ፎቶ ማንሳት ይቻላል?

to pick up	man·sat	ማንሳት
piece (bread)	ku·rash	ቁራሽ
pig	a·sa·ma	አሳማ
pillow	te·rass	ትራስ
place	bo·ta	ቦታ
place of birth	yeu·tu·ləd bo·ta	የተወልድ ቦታ
plain	leut ya·leu meu·ret	ለጥ ያለ መሬት
planet	a·leum	ዓለም

plant	teu·kel	ተከለ
to plant	meut·keul	መትከል
plate	sa·hen	ሳህን
plateau	am·ba	አምባ
platform	meud·reuk	መድረክ
play (theatre)	cheu·wa·ta • dra·ma	ጨዋታ • ድራማ
to play (a game)	meu·cha·wot	መጫወት
to play music	mu·zi·ka meu·cha·wot	ሙዚቃ መጫወት
to play cards	kar·ta meu·cha·wot	ካርታ መጫወት
plug (bath)	meud·feu·nya	መድፈኛ
to point	ma·meul·keut	ማመልከት
police	po·lis	ፖሊስ
politics	po·leu·ti·ka	ፖለቲካ
politician	po·leu·ti·keu·nya	ፖለቲከኛ
pollen	be·nany	ብናኝ
poor	deu·ha	ደሃ
popular	hezb yeu·mi·weu·dö	ሕዝብ የሚወደው·
possibly	me·nal·bat	ምናልባት

It's (not) possible.		
li·hon (ai·chel·lem)		ሊሆን (አይችልም)

postcard	post kard	ፖስት ካርድ
postage	tem·ber	ቴምብር
post office	pos·ta bet	ፖስታ ቤት
pottery	sheuk·la	ሽክላ
poverty	da·ha·neut	ድህነት
power	hail	ኃይል
power cut	yeu e·le·trik meu·kwa·reut	የኤሌትሪክ መቋረጥ
prayer	seu·lot	ፀሎት
prayer book	yeu seu·lot meu·se·haf	የፀሎት መጽሐፍ
to prefer	meu·me·reut	መምረጥ
to prepare	ma·zeu·ga·jeut	ማዘጋጀት
presenter (TV etc)	a·ke·ra·bi	አቅራቢ
president	prez·dant	ፕሬዝዳንት
pretty	kon·jo • wub	ቆንጆ • ውብ
price	wa·ga	ዋጋ
pride	ku·rat	ኩራት
priest	kess	ቄስ
prime minister	teuk·lai mi·nis·ter	ጠቅላይ ሚኒስትር
prison	e·ser bet	እስር ቤት
prisoner	es·reu·nya	እስረኛ
private	yeu·gel	የግል
promise	kal ki·dan	ቃል ኪዳን
proposal	ha·sab	ሐሳብ
prostitute	set a·da·ri	ሴት አዳሪ
to protect	meu·keu·la·keul	መከላከል
protest	teu·kow·mo	ተቃወሞ
to pull	meu·sab	መሳብ
to punish	meuk·tat	መቅጣት

pure	nə·suh	ንጹ·ህ
to push	meug·fat	መግፋት
to put	mas·keu·meut	ማስቀመጥ

Q

qualifications	chə·lo·ta	ችሎ·ታ
quality	ai·neut	አይነት
quarter	rub	ሩብ
queen	nə·gəst	ንግስት
question	tə·ya·ke	ጥያቄ
to question	meu·teu·yeuk	መጠየቅ
queue	teu·ra • seulf	ተራ • ሰልፍ
quick	keul·ta·fa	ቀልጣፋ
quiet	şeuţ ya·leu	ፀጥ ያለ
to quit	meul·keuk	መልቀቅ

R

race (sport)	wə·də·dər	ውድድር
racism	zeu·reu·nya·neut	ዘረኝነት
railway	yeu ha·did meun·geud	የሃዲድ መንገድ
railway station	ba·bur ţa·bi·ya	ባቡር ጣቢያ
rain	zə·nab	ዝናብ

| It's raining. | | |
| ə·yeu·zeu·neu·beu nō | | እየዘነበ ነው· |

rape	yeu weu·sib də·fə·reut	የወሲብ ድፍረት
rare	bərk	ብርቅ
rat	aiyţ	አይጥ
raw	ţə·re	ጥሬ
razor	yeu şim mə·laçh	የሲም ምላጭ
razor blades	mə·laçh	ምላጭ
to read	man·beub	ማንበብ
ready	zə·gə·ju	ዝግጁ
reason	mək·ni·yat	ምክንያት
receipt	deu·reu·seuny	ደረሰኝ
to receive	meu·keu·beul	መቀበል
recently	seu·mo·nun	ሰሞኑን
red	kai	ቀይ
Red Cross	kai meus·keul	ቀይ መስቀል
refrigerator	fri·ji • ma·keuz·keu·zha	ፍሪጅ • ማቀዝቀዣ
refugee	sa·deu·teu·nya	ስደተኛ
refund (money)	teu·meu·lash geun·zeub	ተመላሽ ገንዘብ
to refuse	əm·bi ma·leut	እምቢ ማለት
registered mail	ya·deu·ra deub·dab·be	ያደራ ደብዳቤ
to regret	meu·ko·cheut	መቆጨት
relationship (love)	yeu fə·kər	የፍቅር ግንኙነት
	gə·nu·nya·neut	

relatives	zeu·meu·doch	ዘመዶች
religion	hai·ma·not	ሃይማኖት
to remember	mas·ta·weus	ማስታወስ
to rent	meu·keu·ra·yeut	መከራየት
to repair	meu·teu·geun	መጠገን
to repeat	meud·geum	መድገም
reservation	beu ḳed·mi·ya bo·ta	በቅድሚያ ቦታ
	mas·meuz·geub	ማስመዝገብ
respect	ak·be·rot	አክብሮት
rest (relaxation)	e·reuft	እረፍት
to rest	ma·reuf	ማረፍ
restaurant	me·geb bet	ምግብ ቤት
to retire	ṭu·reu·ta mō·ṭat	ጡረታ መውጣት
to return	meu·meul·leus	መመለስ
rice	ruz	ሩዝ
rich (wealthy)	hab·tam	ሃብታም
to ride (a horse)	meu·ga·leub	መጋለብ
right (correct)	te·ḳe·ḳel	ትክክል

> You're right.
> te·ḳe·ḳel neuh/neush (m/f)   ትክክል ነህ/ነሽ

right (not left)	ḳeuny	ቀኝ
ring (on finger)	ḳeu·leu·beut	ቀለበት
ring (of phone)	deu·weul	ደወል

> I'll ring you.
> e·deu·we·lal·lō   እደውላለሁ

river	weunz	ወንዝ
road (main)	(wan·na) meun·geud	(ዋና) መንገድ
road map	yeu meun·geud kar·ta	የመንገድ ካርታ
to rob	meuz·reuf	መዝረፍ
rock	kwa·ṭeny	ቋጥኝ
romance	fe·ḳer	ፍቅር
room	ke·fel	ክፍል
room number	yeu ke·fel ḳu·ṭer	የክፍል ቁጥር
rope	geu·meud	ገመድ
round (adj)	keb	ክብ
rubbish	wu·da·ḳi/ḳo·sha·sha	ዉዳቂ/ቆሻሻ
rug	yeu·ger men·ṭaf	የገር ምንጣፍ
ruins	fe·rash	ፍራሽ
rules	he·goch	ሕጎች
to run	meu·roṭ	መሮጥ

S

to be sad	ma·zeun	ማዘን
saint	ḳe·dus	ቅዱስ
salary	deu·moz	ደሞዝ
salt	çhō	ጨው

U

too (as well) (use as suffix attached to subject)	-m	-ም

(She) too.
(əs·swa)m — እሷም

toothbrush	yeu tərs bu·rəsh	የጥርስ ቡርሽ
torch	yeu əj ba·tri	የእጅ ባትሪ
to touch	meun·kat	መንካት
tourist information office	yeu tu·rist bi·ro	የቱሪስት ቢሮ
towel	fo·ta	ፎጣ
track (path)	yeu·gər meun·geud	የእግር መንገድ
traffic	tra·fik	ትራፊክ
traffic lights	yeu tra·fik meub·rat	የትራፊክ መብራት
train	ba·bur	ባቡር
train station	ba·bur ta·bi·ya	ባቡር ጣቢያ
to translate	meu·teur·gom	መተርጐም
to travel	meu·gwaz	መጓዝ
tree	ba·hər zaf	ባሕር ዛፍ
trousers	su·ri	ሱሪ

It's true.
əw·neut nō — እውነት ነው።

to trust	ma·meun	ማመን
truth	haḳ	ሐቅ
to try	meu·mo·keur	መሞከር

Turn left.
weu·deu gra ta·teuf/
ta·teu·fi (m/f) — ወደ ግራ ታጠፍ/ታጠፊ

Turn right.
weu·deu ḳeuny ta·teuf/
ta·teu·fi (m/f) — ወደ ቀኝ ታጠፍ/ታጠፊ

TV	ti·vi	ቲቪ
twice	hu·leutt gi·ze	ሁለት ጊዜ
typical	ai·neu·teu·nya	አይነተኛ
tyre	gom·ma	ጎማ

U

umbrella	jan·tə·la	ጃንጥላ

Do you understand?
geub·bah? (m) — ገባህ?
geub·bash? (f) — ገባሽ?

I understand.
geu·bany — ገባኝ

I don't understand.
al·geu·ba·nyəm — አልገባኝም

unemployed	sə·ra feut	ስራ ፈት
unemployment	sə·ra a·tə·neut	ስራ አጥነት
union	ma·ha·beur	ማህበር
university	yu·ni·vers·ti	ዩኒቨርስቲ
unsafe	a·deu·geu·nya	አደገኛ
until (June)	əs·keu (jun·eu) də·reus	እስከ (ጁን) ድረስ
uphill	a·keu·beut	አቀበት
urgent	as·cheu·kwai	አስቸኳይ
useful	teu·ka·mi	ጠቃሚ

V

vaccination	kə·tə·bat	ክትባት
valuable	keuf ya·leu wa·ga yal·lō	ከፍ ያለ ዋጋ ያለው
vegetable	at·kəlt	አትክልት
vegetarian	at·kəlt bə·cha yeu·mi·beu·la	አትክልት ብቻ የሚበላ

> **I'm vegetarian.**
> sə·ga al·beu·lam   ስጋ አልበላም

very	beu·tam	በጣም
village	meun·deur	መንደር
virus	vai·reus	ቫይረስ
visa	vi·za	ቪዛ
to visit	meu·go·bə·nyeut	መጎብኘት
voice	dəms	ድምፅ
to vote	yeu mər·cha dəms meus·teut	የምርጫ ድምፅ መስጠት

W

> **Wait!**
> koy!/ko·yi! (m/f)   ቆይ!/ቆዪ!

waiter	a·sa·la·fi	አሳላፊ
waiting room	ma·reu·fi·ya kə·fəl	ማረፊያ ክፍል
to walk	beu·gər meu·hed	በግር መሄድ
wall	gəd·gəd·da	ግድግዳ
to want	meu·feul·leug	መፈለግ
war	tor·neut	ጦርነት
to wash (something)	ma·teub	ማጠብ
to wash (oneself)	geu·la meu·ta·teub	ገላ መታጠብ
watch (wrist)	yeu əj seu·at	የእጅ ሰዓት
to watch	meu·meul·keut	መመልከት
water	wu·ha	ውሃ
water bottle	yeu wu·ha teur·mus	የውሃ ጠርሙስ
waterfall	fwa·fwa·te	ፏፏቴ
way	meun·geud	መንገድ

> **Which way?**
> beu·yeut beu·kul?   በየት በኩል?

we	ə·nya	እኛ

to wear	meul·beus	መልበስ
wedding	seurg	ሠርግ
week	sam·mənt	ሳምንት
this week	beuz·zi sam·mənt	በዚህ ሳምንት
weekend	kə·da·me na əhud	ቅዳሜና እሁድ
to weigh	meu·meu·zeun	መመዘን
weight	kəb·deut	ክብደት
welcome	ən·kwan deu·na meu·tu	እንኳን ደህና መጡ
well	yeu wu·ha gud·gwad	የውሃ ጉድጓድ
west	mə'ə·rab	ምዕራብ
wet	ər·təb	እርጥብ
what	mən	ምን

What's he saying?
mən·dən nə yeu·mil·lô? ምንድነው- የሚለው-?

What time is it?
sənt seu'at nə? ስንት ሰዓት ነው-?

| when | meu·che | መቼ |

When does it leave?
meu·che yi·neu·sal? መቼ ይነሳል?

| where | yeut | የት |

Where's the bank?
ban·ku yeut nə? ባንኩ የት ነው-?

| white | neuch | ነጭ |
| who | man | ማን |

Who is it?
man nə? ማን ነው-?

Who are they?
ə·neu·man na·chô? እነማን ናቸው-?

whole (n)	mu·lu	ሙሉ
why	leu·mən	ለምን
wide	seuf·fi	ሰፊ
wife	mist	ሚስት
to win	ma·sheu·neuf	ማሸነፍ
wind	neu·fass	ነፋስ
window	meus·kot	መስኮት
wire	shi·bo	ሽቦ
to wish	meu·meu·nyeut	መመኘት
with	keu ... gar	ከ ... ጋር
with my friend	keu gwa·deu·nya·ye gar	ከጓደኛዬ ጋር
within	beu ... wəst	በ ... ውስጥ
within (an hour)	beu (and seu'at) wəst	በ (አንድ ሰዓት) ውስጥ

I'll return within (one year).
beu (and a·meut) wəst በ (አንድ አመት)
ə·meul·leu·sal·lô ውስጥ እመለሳለሁ-

without	ya·leu	ያለ
woman	set	ሴት
women	se·toch	ሴቶች
wood	ən·cheut	እንጨት
word	kal	ቃል
to work	meus·rat	መስራት
world	a·leum	ዓለም
World Cup	yeu a·leum wan·cha	የአለም ዋንጫ
to worry	mas·seub	ማሰብ
worship	mam·leuk	ማምለክ
worth	tə·kəm	ጥቅም
wound	ku·səl	ቁስል
to write	meu·saf	መጻፍ
writer	seu·ha·fi	ጸሐፊ
wrong	sə·hə·teut	ስህተት

Y

year	a·meut	ዓመት
this year	beuz·zi a·meut	በዚህ ዓመት
yes	ow	አዎ
yesterday	tə·nan·tə·na	ትናንትና
yet	geu·na	ገና
you (m/f)	an·teu • an·chi	አንተ • አንቺ
you (pol)	ər·swo	እርስዎ
young	weu·tat	ወጣት

Z

| zebra | yeu me·da a·hə·ya | የሜዳ አህያ |

INDEX

INDEX

I
N
D
E
X

Year 92

model: ACuRa $ 3,500

206) 335-7330

Phrasebooks

Lonely Planet phrasebooks are packed with essential words and phrases to help travellers communicate with the locals. With colour tabs for quick reference, an extensive vocabulary and use of script, these handy pocket-sized language guides cover day-to-day travel situations.

- handy pocket-sized books
- easy to understand Pronunciation chapter
- clear & comprehensive Grammar chapter
- romanisation alongside script to allow ease of pronunciation
- script throughout so users can point to phrases for every situation
- full of cultural information and tips for the traveller

'... vital for a real DIY spirit and attitude in language learning'
– *Backpacker*

'the phrasebooks have good cultural backgrounders and offer solid advice for challenging situations in remote locations'
– *San Francisco Examiner*

Australian *(Australian English, Aboriginal & Torres Strait languages)* • Baltic *(Estonian, Latvian, Lithuanian)* • Bengali • Brazilian • British *(English, dialects, Scottish Gaelic, Welsh)* • Burmese • Cantonese • Central Asia *(Kazakh, Kyrgyz, Pashto, Tajik, Tashkorghani, Turkmen, Uyghur, Uzbek & others)* • Central Europe *(Czech, German, Hungarian, Polish, Slovak, Slovene)* • Costa Rica Spanish • Czech • Eastern Europe *(Albanian, Bulgarian, Croatian, Czech, Hungarian, Macedonian, Polish, Romanian, Serbian, Slovak, Slovene)* • East Timor *(Tetun, Portuguese)* • Egyptian Arabic • Ethiopian *(Amharic)* • Europe *(Basque, Catalan, Dutch, French, German, Greek, Irish, Italian, Maltese, Portuguese, Scottish Gaelic, Spanish, Turkish, Welsh)* • Farsi *(Persian)* • Fijian • French • German • Greek • Hebrew • Hill Tribes *(Lahu, Akha, Lisu, Mong, Mien & others)* • Hindi & Urdu • Indonesian • Italian • Japanese • Korean • Lao • Latin American Spanish • Malay • Mandarin • Mongolian • Moroccan Arabic • Nepali • Pidgin • Pilipino *(Tagalog)* • Polish • Portuguese • Quechua • Russian • Scandinavian *(Danish, Faroese, Finnish, Icelandic, Norwegian, Swedish)* • South-East Asia *(Burmese, Indonesian, Khmer, Lao, Malay, Pilipino (Tagalog), Thai, Vietnamese)* • South Pacific *(Fijian, Hawaiian, Kanak languages, Maori, Niuean, Rapanui, Rarotongan Maori, Samoan, Tahitian, Tongan & others)* • Spanish *(Castilian, also includes Catalan, Galician & Basque)* • Sinhala • Swahili • Thai • Tibetan • Turkish • Ukrainian • USA *(US English, vernacular, Native American, Hawaiian)* • Vietnamese

Also available; Journeys travel literature, illustrated pictorials, calendars, diaries, Lonely Planet maps and videos. For more information on these series and for the complete range of Lonely Planet products and services, visit our website at **www.lonelyplanet.com**.